The Immigrant Heritage of America

Cecyle S. Neidle, *Editor*

THE
GERMAN-AMERICANS

By LA VERN J. RIPPLEY
St. Olaf College

TWAYNE PUBLISHERS

A DIVISION OF G. K. HALL & CO., BOSTON

Library of Congress Cataloging in Publication Data

Rippley, LaVern J.
  The German-Americans.

  (The Immigrant heritage of America)
  Bibliography: p. 259 - 63.
  Includes index.
  1. German Americans — History. I. Title.
E184.G3R48   973'.04'31   75-26917
ISBN 0-8057-8405-5

For my son, John Francis
and
For my daughter, Larissa Jean

Contents

About the Author

La Vern J. Rippley's German ancestors immigrated from Donaueschingen, Baden in 1863. Arriving with the surname *Rieple*, they settled in Waumandee (Buffalo Co.), Wisconsin where the author was born in 1935. After receiving his M.A. at Kent State and before earning his Ph.D. at Ohio State University, Rippley spent a year in Munich as a Fulbright Fellow. He taught two years in high school and three years at Ohio Wesleyan before accepting the chairmanship of the German Department at St. Olaf College in 1967 for a seven year stint. He is presently a professor of German at St. Olaf.

Rippley has authored, or translated and edited, four books. The first was *The Columbus Germans* (Ohio: Männerchor, 1968), followed by *Of German Ways* (Minneapolis: Dillon, 1970), *Excursion Through America* by Nicolaus Mohr (Chicago: R. R. Donnelley, 1973), and with Armand Bauer, *Russian-German Settlements in the United States* by Richard Sallet (Fargo: Institute For Regional Studies, 1974).

During the past dozen years, Rippley has visited the German-speaking countries fifteen times and in 1974 spent a sabbatical in Austria. He is the author of over sixty book reviews and fifty-odd articles, several of which are cited in this book. He enjoys lecturing on a variety of topics to school and community audiences.

Foreword

Professor Rippley has made an important contribution to American history. Working largely from original and widely scattered sources, he has brought together material which might otherwise have been lost over the passing years.

The very success of the German immigrant in the United States — his tendency quickly to become part of American life as an individual, rather than as part of an ethnic group — has made it difficult to follow his tracks. Since the first escapees from oppressive rulers in the German princely states came to America before the Revolutionary War, German immigrants became enamored of the New World and became involved in the American scene around them. Genealogy was not their consuming passion; they became absorbed in their new communities. The story of the Germans in America and their distinctive contribution to our national development is an important component of the story of America.

We are becoming increasingly appreciative of the value of diversity in our national life. Each of the native strains that has come to our shores has made its contributions and left its mark. For all of us, life in America is a more thrilling experience because of this confluence of cultures.

We must not forget that when the United States was a developing country, it was on the receiving end of foreign aid. The most valuable foreign aid we received were the shiploads of immigrants who came to our shores, educated in European schools, trained in European concepts of religion, family life and civic order. The German immigrants were a valuable asset to this country from the day they arrived. They made immediate contributions to agriculture, commerce and industry. Some of them had achieved eminence in their own fields before they came to this hemisphere, and they brought with them the advanced technology and scholarship of the laboratories and universities of Europe. The dependence of American medicine and science on German roots is widely appreciated, but a similar situation prevails in many other fields — artistic, religious, manufacturing and commercial — as Dr. Rippley points out.

Students of American history are properly accustomed to associating the early British immigration with the search for freedom. This search was also true of the German immigrants. The Germans brought a liberal tradition to these shores and widely supported the Revolution. In 1848, when reactionary rulers in Berlin and Vienna suppressed attempts of liberals to implement constitutional reforms, thousands fled to America to escape arrest, and the United States was enriched by a remarkable group of men and women. They were violently opposed to slavery and to corrupt city political machines. And when they found freedom here, they encouraged their relatives in Germany to follow their examples. An 1847 letter from New York, distributed widely in Frankfurt, said, "Look across the Ocean. See the greatness, the flowering of our Republic. Try to govern yourselves. Don't let supercilious scholars throw dust in your eyes."

Professor Rippley describes the routes of the arrivals in the late 1900's, who were drawn to America by new western railroads eager to find farmers to populate their rights of way. He tells many fascinating tales of the development of new fields of science and engineering — most notably nuclear physics — by groups who transplanted German training to these shores. His surveys are inclusive and his interests are catholic. He chronicles saints and scoundrels. His history embraces all the German-speaking immigrants, regardless of their area of origin, their religion, or the time of their arrival.

The German philosopher Johann Gottlieb Fichte, during the Napoleonic wars which forced many Germans to leave their homeland, wrote: "If nothing else, our best traditions might outlive us on fresh soil . . . and the better side of a German culture might survive the perils of the present."

Time has proved the truth of this prediction, and Dr. Rippley tells the fascinating story of how it all happened.

HENRY S. REUSS
Member of Congress
Fifth District, Wisconsin

Acknowledgments

No author ever writes a book without the help of others. I owe debts of gratitude to my German-American father, Louis G. Rippley (formerly Rieple) who gave me my heritage and my interest in it; the late Professor Dieter Cunz of Ohio State University, who inspired me to study the German element in the United States; Dr. Robert E. Ward, editor of *German-American Studies*, for reading the manuscript and making suggestions for improvement; Klaus Wust, editor of the *Report: A Journal of German-American History*, for reading the manuscript; Dr. Kenneth Bjork, professor emeritus of history at St. Olaf College and editor of the Norwegian-American Historical Association, for reading the manuscript; the Honorable Henry S. Reuss, United States Congressman from the Wisconsin Fifth District, for his kindness in writing a foreword; Sidney A. Rand, President of St. Olaf College, for financial assistance with the typing; Marian Tursich for compiling the index; and the staff of Rolvaag Memorial Library, for generous help in procuring research materials. Finally, I am especially grateful to Dr. Cecyle S. Neidle, editor of Twayne's Immigrant Heritage of America Series, for her thorough care in editing, pruning, and improving my manuscript.

Although the book is dedicated to my two young children, I owe thanks to my librarian wife, Barbara Jean, for her patient support and for compiling my bibliography. In spite of the assistance of others, any errors of fact or conception that may be discovered are mine alone.

LA VERN J. RIPPLEY

Northfield, Minnesota

CHAPTER 1

German History

IF AN IMAGINARY GIANT STOOD ON A PEAK OF THE ALPS MIDWAY between the Rhine bend at Basle and the Königsee near Salzburg, Germany would look like a staircase descending to the North Sea. From this vantage point, the Alpine range functions as an east-west barrier between northern and southern Europe. Germany abuts this natural border on its southern edge. To the north, the tiers or steps run to the east and west until they vanish in foreign countries.

Czechoslovakia juts into Germany from the east. When the new nation of Czechoslovakia was called into existence by the Versailles treaty in 1919, these former districts of the Hapsburg Empire, the "lands of the Czechs and Slovaks," possessed natural boundaries, at least as far as Germany was concerned. Known formerly as Bohemia, the Czech part of Czechoslovakia, though set off on the west and north by high mountain ranges, was historically, economically, and culturally integrated into the Holy Roman Empire of the German Nation. Paradoxically, the German-Czech border, throughout most of history, did not function as a boundary to set Germany apart from Bohemia.

Except for the Czech borders and the southern Alpine line, then, Germany's borders have always been open. Nor were they demarcated by rivers. In the north, the Danish-German border has fluctuated periodically and the North Sea coast itself has shifted and changed dramatically over the centuries. When the German Empire was created from the merging of smaller states in 1870, it bordered ten different countries, more than any other nation in Europe except Russia. Even today, with smaller territory than that of New England, Germany borders nine countries.

This means that Germany was immersed in central Europe and her history developed accordingly. Curtained off from the south by the Alps, Germans have quixotically longed to visit Italy from the

15

age of the Hohenstaufens in 1200 to the present. Open to visitors and influences on the remaining three sides, Germany absorbed countless types and retained innumerable differences so that German political unity has always been elusive. A vintner on the Moselle never had much in common with a Silesian peasant, not to mention the antipathy between the Bavarians and the Hamburgers. Today, ravaged by war, Germany has been divided unnaturally from north to south by an ideological mountain range far higher than the Alps which the Germans have always crossed so readily. Citizens of a partitioned nation, the Germans are still children of a common ethnic heritage, one which included more than its share of division, splintering, and discord.

The dawn of Germany's history occurred in the shadow of the Roman Empire. Cities stretching along the northern Rhine to the Main and southeastward along the Danube to the Hungarian border have names derived from the Latin. Examples are Cologne (Colonia Aggrippinensis), Koblenz (Confluentes), Mainz (Moguntiacum), Augsburg (Augusta Videlicorum), Regensburg (Castra Regina), Passau (Castra Batava), Linz, Austria (Lentia), and Vienna (Vindabona).

Although the Teutons subdued the Roman Empire by 500 A.D., it was the latter that culturally absorbed the former. During the migration of nations that occurred prior to the Teutonic triumph, Angles, Jutes, and large contingents of Saxons departed the continent to take up residence in England, where they formed the basis of Anglo-Saxonism and its culture. In the heart of German territory, the various tribes were for several centuries unmindful of the linguistic and cultural bonds they shared with one another. Eventually Charlemagne welded them into the Carolingian Empire, but this Frankish nation soon fractured into the local duchies of Bavaria, Swabia, Franconia, Saxony, Thuringia, and others. Fourteen centuries later, descendants of the Anglo-Saxons and of the Bavarians, Swabians, and others on the continent would emigrate again and reconvene on the North American continent. In the United States during the nineteenth century, there were as many immigrants from Germany as from England — which is not to say that either group was conscious of its common heritage in the distant past of the early Middle Ages.

The first missionary to the Germans was an Irish monk called Bonifatius, who founded a monastery in the center of Germany at Fulda. In due time, all of Germany became Christian though it continued to rub elbows with heathens to the east for several hundred years. One menace to German Christianity, until it was converted about 1000 A.D., was the Hungarian tribe to the southeast. Another was the Slavic culture east of the Elbe River. Conversion of this territory was vested with the bishop of Magdeburg whose task it was to extend the cross and the scepter eastward in the first *Drang nach Osten*, about 1100 A.D.

Systematic control over the Prussians waited for the Teutonic Knights, an organization that consisted of half monks, half crusading soldiers. Known as the Knights of the Order, the crusaders were founded by the son of Frederick Barbarossa for the protection of the Holy Land. The knights, who wore a white mantle overlaid with a black cross, bequeathed this black-white color scheme to the Prussian flag. They were invited to establish their order in Prussia by Conrad, the Duke of Masovia in Poland. In 1225 the grand master of the order, Hermann von Salza, waged a war on behalf of the Pope against the heathen Prussians. In return for the favor, Conrad of Masovia guaranteed to the order all the land it had wrested from the Prussians. Ruled by a religious order-state which had been granted autonomy by imperial and papal decree, the lands of the Teutonic Knights were not politically assimilated into Germany until the foundation of the German Empire in 1871.[1]

The Teutonic Order constituted the beginning of Prussia which became and remained the primary German state until 1948, at which time the seat of power was moved out of Königsberg and Berlin to Bonn on the Rhine. For 800 years, leadership within German-speaking Europe was polarized between two centers, both lying far to the east: Prussia and Austria.[2] At roughly the same time when the Teutonic Knights secured Prussia from Slavic control for the North Germans, the Hapsburg family was emerging as successor to the Hohenstaufens and as leader of the South Germans. With few interruptions, Prussia and Austria have been struggling for control of the Pan-German area until our time. As a result, there has always been a Prussia (and only briefly a Germany), and an Austria, both of which were integrated in the Holy Roman Empire. The political situation created a confusing national identity problem for those who spoke the German language.

Further splitting the German "personality" was the break away from Hapsburg control by sections of the Swabian and Alemani tribes which formed the independent Swiss Confederation in 1499. Swiss independence was the conclusion of a movement that began

in 1291 with the defensive alliance formed by the imperial cantons
of Uri, Schwyz, and Unterwalden to resist Hapsburg authority and
imperial taxes. At first totally German-speaking, Switzerland grew
territorally and linguistically so that today it is 74 percent German-
speaking with French, Italian, and Romansh comprising the
minority languages spoken in the confederation.

The last Holy Roman Emperor to be crowned by the Pope was the
Hapsburger, Charles V (emperor from 1519 - 1558), who brought
Spain into the German nation and, by that act, also the Spanish
colonies in America. Thus, Florida as well as large stretches of land
from Louisiana to California once belonged technically to the German Empire of the Hapsburgs. Spanish missionaries interested in
converting the American Indians often did so in the name of the
Holy Roman Emperor of the German Nation, Charles V.

Of greater consequence for the colonization of the United States
with German immigrants was a domestic problem faced by Emperor
Charles V, the Protestant Reformation. Struggling successfully for
centuries against an external religious threat to the empire, namely
the Turks, the Hapsburgs failed to perceive and cope with the internal problem of religious dissent which erupted disastrously for the
German people.

At Wittenberg Martin Luther began a reform movement which
eventually evoked the intervention of Charles V, the Hapsburg
emperor. Determined to give the monk a hearing, Charles V in
April, 1521, listened at Worms when Luther took his position with
"Here I stand." Charles still held to the illusion that there was one
world, one empire, and one church. But neither the church nor the
empire any longer constituted a monolithic unity. The church had
become a regional force consisting of princes, bishops, and territorial
barons. They had received grants and privileges from the popes in
the form of concordats, designed by the Holy See to keep the
emperor weaker than the pope. By engendering strong anti-Rome
feelings, Luther won the support of German peasants, knights of the
German empire, and local German burghers. The Reformation in
Germany turned into a political as well as a religious phenomenon.
The motivation for joining the Lutheran movement was seldom
purely religious and usually political and economic. The reasons for
the early German emigration were also religious, as when the
separatists came to Pennsylvania in the 1680s, but they were
political and social as well.

Significantly, the Teutonic Order accepted Lutheranism, and

with the order went all of Prussia, thus determining the future religious texture of that German ruling state. As for Charles V and the Austrian Hapsburgers, they were too beset by problems with the Turks on the one side and an alliance of France with the papacy on the other, to resolve the religious cleavage. The peace concluded at Augsburg in 1555 granted the right of *cuius regio, eius religio,* "whoever owns the region, determines the religion." This arrangement solidified the territorial control of religion in the hands of the man in power. To religious dissenters was conceded only the right to emigrate. At first, most remained within Europe, but later many came to the United States.

The next major spur to German emigration was the Thirty Years' War which raged on and off from 1618 - 1648. Emanating from the religiously troubled Bohemian section of the Holy Roman Empire, the conflict soon enveloped the whole of Germany. The Catholic Hapsburgers reacted by demanding the reconversion of German abbeys and monasteries but all came to naught when King Gustavus Adolphus of Sweden, a convinced Lutheran, came to the aid of his coreligionists. Eventually he clashed with the imperial army and lost his life at Lutzen in 1632. France joined the fray against the Hapsburgs, partly because the Spanish were supplying money and soldiers to Emperor Ferdinand II of Austria and partly because the Spanish were stationed in Alsace and the Palatinate — too close to the French borders for comfort. When the war was concluded by the Peace of Westphalia in 1648, the Holy Roman Empire of the German Nation had become a paper formality.

The German peasants and middle classes were the real losers in the war. Of the twenty-one million people estimated living in Germany when the Thirty Years' War broke out, only thirteen million remained in 1648. Provincial populations were decimated. In the Palatinate, from whence the main body of early German immigrants came to the United States, only 50,000 survived from a prewar population of over one million. The state of Baden lost more than half of its buildings, forcing people to emigrate in search of shelter. Economically, it took centuries for the country to recover. One statistic indicates that the number of family dwellings in Germany prior to the war was not equaled until 1848, a full 200 years after hostilities had ceased.[3] According to the treaty of 1648, Brandenburg gained the most territory, whereas France secured Metz, Verdun, and Alsace. France and Sweden came to dominate German affairs.

The conversion of the electors of Brandenburg and the Knights of the Teutonic Order to Lutheranism had far-reaching effects. In Prussia, which was known as the Holy Roman Empire's "sand pit," the seeds of absolutism had struck deep roots. The Hohenzollern family acquired Brandenburg and Prussia. The Hohenzollern Elector, Frederick William, who reigned from 1650 - 1688, vastly increased the total Prussian territory. From 1712 - 1786, Frederick II, better known as Frederick the Great, ruled the country as an enlightened despot. Königsberg in East Prussia remained the coronation city for all Prussian kings, although in later years they ruled from Berlin. The two German kaisers who exercised authority over a unified Germany from 1871 - 1918 came, like Frederick the Great, from the Hohenzollern line.

During Frederick the Great's reign, Prussia struggled with Austria for control of all German-speaking territory. In the struggle known as the Seven Years' War (1756 - 1763), England sided with Prussia by supplying money and troops. Across the Atlantic in the United States, England fought the French and Indian War to divest France of her possessions east of the Mississippi. Also during Frederick's reign, Catherine the Great, a German princess, ascended the throne of Russia and began importing German farmers to develop the South Russian farmlands. German farmers also emigrated westward to Pennsylvania, but many more chose the overland routes to Russia. During the nineteenth century, that situation reversed itself and America got the largest share of German farmers as well as many descendants of those who had originally settled in Russia.

Soon after the American Revolution, Napoleon swept the continent of Europe. During that process liberalism was born in Germany, but when Napoleon reverted in the popular German mind from liberator to dictator, the new liberalism disappeared and eluded the grasp of the German populace. Throughout the nineteenth century, the economically powerful German middle class failed to support those who called for a democratic form of government in Germany. The strength of German liberalism was further diluted by the emigration of the lower classes and the political activists to the United States.

Among the political activists was Karl Marx (1818 - 1883), the son of a Prussian lawyer and a resident of Trier. Of Jewish ancestry, Karl's father embraced the Christian faith with the result that Karl, too, was a baptized Protestant. Marx sought to organize the proletariat, wrote about the exploitation of labor by capitalists, and explained it in *Das Kapital*. Expelled from Germany for his role in the revolutions of 1848, Marx moved to England, where he became a reporter for Horace Greeley's *New York Tribune*. Marx's efforts to counteract the industrialism of Germany had a counterproductive effect on the chances for a democratic government in Germany. Communist uprisings stirred up fear in the German bourgeoisie who came to prefer an authoritarian government to proletarian radicalism. In the years following the 1848 revolutions, therefore, German emigration to the United States grew to stunning proportions. In the years after Marx, the bourgeoisie in the Fatherland came to venerate the military more and more. Security for property owners was associated with the imperial apparatus established by Otto von Bismarck at Versailles in January, 1871, after the Franco-Prussian War. After this, Germany quickly became a world power, both militarily and economically. Industrialization and urbanization progressed at an unprecedented pace. In 1870 there were only eight cities with 100,000 people in all of Germany whereas by 1913 there were forty-eight whose populations reached beyond the one hundred thousand mark.

The German army and navy acquired prestige at home and generated fear abroad. In large measure, the economic and technological prowess of the German nation outgrew its political skill. As a result, England, France, and ultimately the United States grew suspicious of Germany, and alliances were formed to shield against the German threat. When Hitler took over Germany in 1933 there were new reasons for Germans to emigrate to America, but the one hundred thousand who arrived during the Nazi period were only a small segment in comparison to the nineteenth-century immigration from Germany. The century from 1850 to 1950 witnessed the rise of Germany from an insignificant collection of duchies to a world power. The United States, during this same century, became the home of the third largest number of German-speaking people in the world. As a result of two world wars and other forces, this third largest contingent of German peoples in the world has been assimilated. This historical phenomenon is the subject of the succeeding pages.

CHAPTER 2

Early German Immigration
to the United States

By the word "early" German immigration to the United States is meant the period from the discovery of America to the opening of the revolutionary war in 1776. For the most part, there was no immigration from the German-speaking states to America prior to the arrival of the first English settlers. However, there are historians who believe that a German called Tyrker, whose name appears in the Icelandic Sagas, may have accompanied Leif Ericson to the New World. Tyrker is credited with discovering grapes in North America and therefore also with naming the new land Vineland.[1]

It is worth noting that when Columbus discovered the New World, he did so primarily for Ferdinand and Isabella of Spain, but also in the name of the Hapsburg emperors who ruled Germany as a part of the Holy Roman Empire. It is well known that the German cartographers of Columbus' time were responsible for developing the globes and maps which showed the world as round, thus contributing in a small way to Columbus' discovery. Moreover, it was a German cosmographer, Martin Waldseemüller, who first suggested the name for the New World, "America."[2]

From the first year of its discovery, the German people were informed through publications about the New World, and they took a lively interest in its exploration. During late 1938 and early 1939, the New York Public Library held an exhibition of its early German works which related to America.[3] Sebastian Brant's *Narrenschiff* (*Ship of Fools*), published in 1494, was the first German book which made references to the discovery. Amerigo Vespucci's narrative recounting his four voyages to the New World between 1497 and 1504 enjoyed the success of at least fourteen editions in Germany by the year 1509. Several pamphlets and small volumes about Mexico appeared during the 1520s, and in 1557 a book was published by Hans Staden, *Warhaftige Historia und beschreibung einer Landt-*

22

*schafft der Wilden, Nacketen, Grimmigen Menschfresser /
Leuthen, in der Newenweldt America gelegen* . . . *(True History
and Description of a Land of Wild, Naked, Fierce Cannibals / People in the New World, America* . . .), which was subsequently
translated into many languages. The book was enormously popular.
So was Sebastian Franck's *Weltbuch (World Book)*. The latter when
first published in 1534 included but twenty-six pages on the New
World. The 1567 edition contained two volumes, one on the newly
found lands in which America figured prominently. Franck has been
accorded the same wide-ranging popularity as was enjoyed by his
contemporary Hans Sachs, both Nürnbergers. Of similar popularity
was the publication of Theodor de Bry's *Great Voyages*, at Frankfurt
in 1590 and 1634, which contained excellent engravings of Florida,
Virginia, and other areas. Thus, ample information about the new
continent kept seeping into the minds of potential German
emigrants at the time when the future American colonies were attracting their first settlers.

There is no record of German immigration to America during the
period of Spanish exploration of the Americas but a number of Germans were present in the colony of Jamestown, Virginia, after its establishment in 1607. In a short time, German craftsmen, vintners,
and tobacco farmers had settled in Virginia. Few as the foreigners
were, a question of their legal status arose, which was ultimately
resolved by the Naturalization Act of 1671. This provided for aliens
to gain the rights of natural-born subjects and led to a better Act of
Naturalization in 1680, which provided for "all possible encouragement . . . to persons of different nations to transport themselves
hither with their families and stocks, to settle, plant or reside. . . ."[4]
Liberalization and definition of the legal status of foreigners in
Virginia led to an increase in the immigration of Germans to the
New World.

A confusion in names gave rise to the myth that most, if not all,
German immigrants during colonial times were Palatines, that is,
immigrants from the German state known as the *Pfalz*. It is true that
Germans from southwestern Germany, including the Palatinate,
were proportionately more numerous during the 1700 - 1750 period.
However, the states of Baden, Würtemberg, and, somewhat later,
those of Hesse, Bavaria, Nassau, and the bishoprics of Cologne,
Osnabarück, Münster, and Mainz also contributed large numbers of
German emigrants to the American colonies.[5]

Both Hollanders and Germans in early America came to be known as "Dutch," a linguistic slip that occurred because the word "Dutch" so closely resembles a German's designation for himself, *Deutsch*. The confusion is justified on other grounds: early Germanic migration to the United States came from the Low Countries. Moreover, there never has been a clear language border between the northern region of Germany, which is referred to geographically and linguistically as Low German, and that country which, in the Germanic family of languages, is called Dutch. During this early period, furthermore, the political boundaries of the northern, low German states were fluid. Thus, when England was perhaps at war or just maintaining cool relations with its maritime competitor, Holland, it was expedient for American immigrants from the Low Countries to "switch nationality" temporarily from Dutch to German. Suffice it to say that there were many Germans in the Tidewater area of Virginia prior to 1700 though no precise information about their numbers and influence can be assessed.[6]

There were also many Germans in Maryland. For example, Augustin Herrman in 1661 obtained land from Lord Baltimore for the founding of a town to which he hoped to attract German immigrants. Herrman was not especially successful, but his name lives on because he was the first citizen naturalized in Maryland under the state's 1666 law, and because the small town of Port Herrman was named after him. George Hack of Cologne was another early German settler whose name survived in Maryland since his arrival about 1650, and it persists in the place-name of Hack's Point in Cecil County, Maryland.[7] Other early German settlers preferred the Hudson Valley in New York state, or, better yet, Pennsylvania. It should also be noted that it is difficult to trace early German settlers in the colonies because the bearers of certain early names, such as Geist, claimed Swedish nationality. No doubt the nationality of such persons was indeed Swedish, because large sections of Northern Germany were ceded to Sweden under the provisions of the Treaty of Westphalia in 1648. Other English-sounding names like Greening and Rayman, on further investigation, turn out to be German in origin.

In the Dutch colony of New Amsterdam, which was changed to New York under subsequent British control, the Dutch and Germans intermingled readily in early times. The second governor of the colony, Jacob Leisler, was a German who had been born in Frankfurt am Main. There were other prominent German settlers, but none of them left a distinctly German trail behind him.

Of more significance and permanence was the founding in 1683 of Germantown, Pennsylvania, which lives on today as a subdivision of Philadelphia. Germantown is important for two reasons. First, it was the first solidly German colony in America, and second, it was a colony of religious dissenters. As a refuge for the religiously oppressed, Germantown became a mecca for countless later immigrants who came to America to find religious freedom.[8] Actually, William Penn himself made trips to Germany in 1671 and 1677, spreading the gospel of his Quaker faith, although vanguard information about his Society of Friends had reached the continent somewhat earlier. The first group of German immigrants to accept Penn's invitation were Mennonites who arrived on the ship *Concord* and were shepherded by the young lawyer, Francis Daniel Pastorius, who had previously traveled extensively in America. Composed of one group of emigrants from Frankfurt and another from the city of Krefeld, the Mennonites bought some 43,000 acres of land six miles north of what was then the incipient city of Philadelphia.[9]

Incorporated as a town in 1689, Germantown retained its distinctly German character for over two centuries. German in this context means German traditions and practices as well as an appreciation for religious and political freedom. Looking upon democracy as a civic responsibility, the city fathers levied fines of three pounds for refusal to accept election to a public office. In another display of New World freedom the inhabitants of Germantown in 1688 made formal protests against Negro slavery.[10] Without the economic benefit of slave labor, the Pennsylvania Germans developed business, industry, fairs, farms, and factories of their own, becoming in many respects models for subsequent immigrants, German as well as others.

Of special importance for future Germans in America were the Pietists and similar groups of mystics, whose early arrival in Germantown made Pennsylvania known throughout Germany as a refuge for religious nonconformists. One name worthy of mention is Johann Kelpius who founded a semimonastic order on Wissahickon Creek and whose successors established the Ephrata Cloisters in Lancaster County.[11] They were bolstered by an influx of Swiss Mennonites and the Schwarzenau Brethren, so-called Dunkers (from the German *eintunken*, "to immerse"). Far outnumbering these enthusiasts were the Lutherans under the leadership of Heinrich Melchior Mühlenberg, one of the great fathers of the Lutherans in the United States. Less influential, but of great significance nevertheless, was Graf von Zinzendorf, from the estate in Saxony called Herrnhut. Zinzendorf was the man who revitalized an existing settlement on the Lehigh River, calling it Bethlehem. Ever since it has been the home of the United Brethren, or Moravians. This pietistic religious sect traces its origins to the Bohemian martyr John Huss (1372 - 1415) who lived in Prague, Czechoslovakia. Zinzendorf arrived in Pennsylvania in 1741 and spent all of 1742 in America, most of it in Pennsylvania. An official in the Saxon court at Dresden, Zinzendorf first became involved with the Pietists by sheltering fleeing Moravians on his estate in 1722, calling it Herrnhut (the Lord's Watch). In 1727 he dedicated himself to full-time work for the Lord which led to his banishment from Saxony in 1736. As an ordained Lutheran minister since 1734 and a bishop in the Moravian Church since 1737, Zinzendorf came to America as a broadly equipped religious emissary.[12]

Zinzendorf arrived in Pennsylvania under the name, von Thürnstein. Almost immediately he posed a threat to Mühlenberg's leadership of the Lutheran Church in America. Eventually Mühlenberg reasserted his control, and while the Moravians still considered themselves members of the Lutheran Church, they became more and more separate. Zinzendorf, unable to capture the Lutheran diaspora, dedicated himself to reviving the scattered and fading Moravian Church. In his short stay, he made Bethlehem, Pennsylvania, and Salem, North Carolina, the future brain centers of the United Brethren.[13]

Zinzendorf left another legacy in America, his missionary work among the Indians.[14] It represented a major life-long goal for the count, and by the time of his death at Herrnhut in May, 1760, Moravian missionaries were actively engaged in teaching and converting the Indians of North America. The most famous Indian missionary colonies of the Moravian Church were those of Gnadenhütten and Schönbrunn in northeastern Ohio, which were annihilated in 1781 by the Wyandot Indians at the instigation of the British. In recent years the pioneer buildings have been restored and opened as a museum.

In the first half of the eighteenth century, German immigration swelled considerably along the inland frontier located back of the Atlantic seaboard and east of the Appalachian mountains. The South as well, particularly Georgia, harbored many Germans. One especially interesting group was made up of Austrian Salzburgers — German Protestants who were exiled in 1731 by decree of the Catholic Archbishop. More than 30,000 were banished, many of whom were welcomed in Protestant countries, notably, Prussia, but others journeyed to Georgia with the blessings of the English government.[15] The first Salzburgers to reach America were organized for the exodus at Berchtesgaden by Baron von Reck. Arriving in Rotterdam in 1733 they were joined by two pastors, John M. Boltzius and Israel Christian Gronau, whose diaries furnish a wealth of insight into the minds of these Salzburgers.[16] Formerly in charge of the Lutheran orphanage in Halle, Pastor Boltzius was of the same religious affiliation as Count Zinzendorf.

In 1734, the Salzburgers received permission from General Oglethorpe to select lands twenty-five miles north of Savannah, along the right bank of the Savannah River. They named the settlement Ebenezer. Two years later, in 1736, another shipload of Germans headed for Georgia, this time accompanied by John Wesley, the founder of Methodism, and his brother Charles. After returning to England, John Wesley recalled fondly his meetings with leaders of the Moravian Church in America. Thus we see that a tenuous bond developed between the German Moravians and German Methodists in America. Wesley was enthusiastic about his encounter with the German immigrants; but he concluded later that his efforts to convert the American Indians to his faith had been misguided. His intimate experience with Indians led him to respect their way of life, which resulted in a conversion of himself rather than a conversion of the natives.[17]

In moral outlook as well as life-style, the Georgian Salzburgers had much in common with their German countrymen in Pennsylvania. Both opposed slavery and promoted brotherly love. Like so many other religious sects in America, however, they had their share of doctrinal altercations. In fact, the great pioneer Lutheran leader, Mühlenberg, once visited the Salzburgers in 1774 - 75 and among other things arbitrated a theological dispute. At the time of his visit, the Ebenezer colony had reached its peak of about 500 members.[18]

What is characteristic of the very early German immigrants to America is that they settled in separate colonies, each with his own specific brand of religious commitment. They kept in touch with each other and their views paralleled each other sufficiently to encourage a flow of visitors between them. The writings which they left behind furnish interesting commentaries on the whole of American life. For instance, when Baron von Reck was en route back to Germany from Georgia he traveled by way of Pennsylvania. While in Georgia he tells of visiting with slaves: "A master forces them [Negroes] to work for him all week without giving them anything to eat. He then permits them to work on Sunday for wages, and they must earn enough then so that they can eat the rest of the week. A master will never punish even the greatest misdeed with death because that would make him lose a slave. The Negroes know this, of course, and for that reason are easily given to knavish tricks." He also noted that "people here have a superabundance of horses; one hardly ever sees anybody walk, be it man, woman, or child."[19]

There were other areas on the Atlantic Coast where Germans settled in the eighteenth century. Waldoboro in Maine was one, another was in northwestern Massachusetts where place names like Adasdorf, Bernardsdorf, Leyden and others date from colonial times. New Jersey had its German population as did the Carolinas. In New York, they were to be found mostly along the Hudson River and in the Mohawk Valley. In general, they settled behind the edge of the ocean along a line running southwest from Albany, behind Lancaster, Pennsylvania, west of the Shenandoah Valley in Virginia, south to Charlotte, North Carolina, and southwest to the Georgia border.

Some characteristics of the Germans in the United States before the revolutionary war can be summarized. First, they sought out land which was highly suitable for farming. Second, they cultivated the limestone regions from the northeast to the southwest, which were said to be the most fertile lands in colonial America. Whether they acquired these lands because they had superior knowledge with regard to the geological features that made the best farms, or whether their choice of homesteads resulted from haphazard or otherwise historically explainable causes is a moot question.[20] Third, the German element established important granaries for the colonies which served as a breadbasket for the revolutionary war forces. Eastern Pennsylvania, the Shenandoah and Mohawk Valleys, as well as the western halves of North and South Carolina constituted areas of successful farming by German immigrants. Finally, the Germans made a valuable contribution to the budding Republic by settling in the Pittsburgh area after the British conquered Fort Duquesne from the French. A few years later, German farmers near Pittsburgh delivered supplies to American revolutionary war soldiers on roads built by the British.[21]

On this fringe of white civilization, the conflict with resentful Indians was continuous and dangerous. Due perhaps to the pacifist Amish, Quakers, and Mennonites among them, the Germans seem to have had less troubles with the Indians than did settlers of other nationalities.[22] In part, the Indians warred to stop the confiscation of their lands by the Europeans. In part, they went to war with the whites because of political instigation. The French enlisted them in the French and Indian War. In retaliation for the involvment of both the Indians and the Germans with the French in the struggle for Fort Duquesne, the British destroyed the Moravian Indian missions at Gnadenhütten.[23] Subsequently the Germans willingly served in British-led regiments. Later, the Indians joined the British in the final battle for Fort Duquesne.[24] Later, the Americans recruited the Indians to fight against the English and their German mercenaries.

As the revolutionary war approached and with it the birth of the American nation, the German element in the future United States was of considerable size. It amounted to about one tenth of the total population. In a state like Pennsylvania, however, there were some 110,000 Germans, estimated at about one third of the state's population. The next largest bloc was in New York State where about 25,-000 Germans lived. Taken together, the colonies harbored a population of about 225,000 Germans at the outbreak of the revolutionary war.[25]

Emigration from Germany to America prior to the revolutionary war was decidedly from the Rhine region and movement out of the country was by way of the Rhine. This region included the territory west of the Palatinate as well as that east of the Rhine, especially Baden-Württemberg. Adequate ports of embarkation were not yet constructed in Germany and therefore it was necessary to sail down the Rhine into Holland where departure was effected largely from Rotterdam.[26]

During the colonial period, German immigration consisted of group movements. The eighteenth century was the age when whole communities migrated — often banded together by a new religious creed that was not tolerated in the mother country. The nineteenth century, by contrast, was the period when individuals (and individual families) emigrated in search of economic improvement rather than freedom to pursue their separatist religions.[27]

Other generalities about early immigration from Germany are that the Germans tended to intermarry with the Anglo-Saxon population more readily on the frontier than on the coastal strip, where the English aristocracy remained aloof from the peasant population.[28] Farms for the German settler meant the family farm. Few Germans engaged in cash crop tobacco farming, preferring grains

and animal husbandry instead.[29] Also, Germans are credited with in-
venting the Conestoga wagon, presumably because they covered
their market wagons with linen cloth and hitched them behind a
breed of horses called the Conestogas which were common in the
Lancaster-Reading region of Pennsylvania.[30]

German farms were large. In the area around Frederick, Maryland, they averaged 370 acres. The farmers were frugal, built large
barns, kept extensive gardens, and hired as little help as possible.
They tried to keep a farm in the same family for generations and
were given to superstition, a tendency which gave rise to the continuing tradition of hex signs on barns in the Pennsylvania German
area.

For several reasons, the colonial Germans were not interested in
politics. In the first place, they spoke a foreign language, and
English was the official language of colonial governments. Secondly,
their tradition was not to participate in government at all. Thirdly,
unlike the English, Irish, and Scotch immigrants, they were not
automatically citizens as British subjects were. This meant that the
Germans were a group separated by language and by their mores
from the English-speaking majority in America. Living apart and
often in German-speaking communities, the Germans sometimes
aroused suspicion and prejudice in colonial American legislatures.
Due to these feelings of animosity, certain Germans were not especially sympathetic to the urge of colonial America to break away
from England. English tea laws, for example, did not arouse the
Germans, because they did not drink tea. Going their separate ways,
groups such as the Moravians in North Carolina refused an order
issued by the rebellious colonial government that they revoke their
oaths of allegiance to the English crown. In the end, their stub-
bornness almost cost them their lands.

However, there were substantial numbers of Germans who were
active in the revolutionary war. The reason, it appears, was not so
much because the war promised them independence from England,
but because it provided the German-speaking western frontiersmen
with an opportunity to redress grievances against the English-
speaking oligarchy along the Atlantic seaboard. Mostly, the Germans in colonial America were scattered and thinly represented in
the total population with the result that they had little political
clout. Furthermore, the Germans in America had virtually nothing
in common but a language. Geographically they came as Palatines,
Salzburgers, Württembergers, and Hanoverians. Religiously, they

were Mennonites, Dunkers, Lutherans, Calvinists, and a few Catholics. Politically, they worried only about their local and private affairs.[31]

Schools among the Germans in the colonies were in the hands of the churches and this meant mostly either Lutheran or Reformed. Heinrich Mühlenberg provided for the three R's by way of Lutheran church schools. Michael Schlatter did the same for the Reformed Church. The Book, *Schulordnung* (School rules), was written in 1750 by the Mennonite schoolteacher, Christopher Dock, and printed by Christopher Sauer of Philadelphia, the same man who founded the Germantown Academy in 1761.

Before concluding about the prerevolutionary war period, a final word should be said about the redemption system. Shipping companies often transported European emigrants to America without directly charging the passengers. Occasionally, a local ruler in a German principality also resorted to selling his "sons" to a shipper or a foreign government for what little they would bring on the auction block. "Redemptioning" was, therefore, the process by which agents loaded ships with ablebodied men and proceeded to anchor in an American port where the newcomers were sold to the highest bidder. Since the shipping company had born the costs of transportation without charging the passenger, potential employers in America reimbursed the shipper when paying the going price for an emigrant who in turn worked for as many years as were necessary to redeem the costs of passage.[32] In a land where the sale of black slaves was taken for granted, we should not be surprised to learn that the redemption of Germans was scarcely frowned upon by anyone. American laws binding the contracts of redemption continued in effect until 1819 when the U. S. Congress passed a law, not abolishing redemption, but limiting the weight of passengers permitted on ships docking at U. S. ports to two for every five tons of the ship's weight. This action effectively outlawed shipment in steerage, which brought with it an end to the system of redemption because the law ruled out the possibility of huge profits.[33]

CHAPTER 3

The Germans In
The Revolutionary War
and Beyond

LARGE NUMBERS OF GERMANS IN COLONIAL AMERICA LIVED IN THE agricultural valleys located on the frontier inland from the Atlantic ocean. This means they engaged in skirmishes with the Indians and were accustomed to military operations of a guerrilla nature. Since many had come to America to escape economic and physical oppression by unscrupulous German princes, it was logical that the majority was antimonarchal in sentiment and on the side of the American Revolution. Not least, perhaps, the Germans who left Europe were outsiders of one kind or another, be it of a religious or social nature. As outsiders, they were individualists who ran against the established Anglo-American current. After arriving in America, it appears, their spirit of individualism grew sharper through a life of isolation on the frontier.

Understandably, the Germans were not sympathetic to British rule. When Benjamin Franklin, appearing before Parliament in Great Britain, was asked to what extent the Germans in America were dissatisfied with the Stamp Act, he reaffirmed Parliament's suspicions: "Yes, even more [than the native population] and they are justified, because in many cases they must pay double for their stamp-paper and parchments."[1]

At the outbreak of the revolutionary war, the Germans formed the largest single nationality in America next to the British. As an ethnic group with roots in continental Europe, they felt far less loyal to the British crown than did the British subjects. Since the Germans were instinctively unfriendly toward the Tories who favored continuing the union with Great Britain, they were easy converts to the American cause of freedom. Initially the Germans refrained from taking part in colonial politics, but when they did become involved, they naturally gravitated to the Democratic party. Like all colonial Democrats, the Germans were not owners of estates, had never received gifts from the British crown, and therefore were scarcely attuned to the *status-quo* politics of the British eastern seaboard establishment.

Consequently, when the revolutionary war began, several German regiments were raised with ease, the first in Pennsylvania and Maryland. Later thousands of Germans served both in their own regiments, where German was spoken, and subsequently in other units, which included men of various national origins. Along with the Irish, the Germans proved to be among the toughest troops in the line wherever gritty engagements with the British regulars occurred.

Recruiting a German-American unit frequently turned out to be a church-related enterprise. Fundamentally differing attitudes lay behind this action. Aristrocratic Englishmen in the colonies often theorized about individual freedom and the right to bear arms, but the Germans in America felt ill at ease with British philosophical thought. More often than not, the colonial Germans were religious fundamentalists and they rejected liberal English ideas, which they felt were outgrowths of rationalism. The church, to them, was a protective curtain which was supposed to keep them isolated from "dangerous" theories. On the practical level, the Germans found it offensive when they were forced to pay church taxes to the English crown along with Episcopal church members. However, in spite of paying church taxes, the Germans, because they were religious dissenters, did not enjoy equal rights with members of the official Episcopal church. This created an explosive anti-English attitude among the church-conscious Germans. Therefore, German-American clergymen almost unanimously declared themselves in support of the revolution.[2]

Religious antagonism coupled with a latent inferiority complex toward the English made it easy for pastors to preach "the gospel" of enlistment. For example, the German Lutheran and Reformed churches of Philadelphia jointly circularized a forty-page pamphlet through their church branches in New York and South Carolina. It reported that the Pennsylvania Germans were forming militia companies and it begged coreligionists to follow suit.[3] Germans in these churches also formed armed guards called "Associators" who aided in founding a revolutionary army. Pastor Helmuth of the Lutheran Church at Lancaster, Pennsylvania, wrote in 1775 that the whole country was ready for war, that every man was armed, and that the enthusiasm was indescribable. Even the Quakers and Mennonites whose creed forbade them to bear arms, in large numbers renounced their dogma in order to join the fight for independence.[4]

Probably the most spectacular if not the best-known German-American religious leader in the War of Independence was Johann Peter Mühlenberg, the eldest son of Heinrich Melchior, the patriarch of German Lutheranism in the United States. Known simply as Peter, young Mühlenberg studied at Halle before being expelled for bad conduct, after which he served for a time in Europe with a regiment of German dragoons. Later he returned to America to study theology and was ordained in the Evangelical Lutheran Church in 1768. Thereupon he became an assistant rector to churches at New Germantown and Bedminster, New Jersey.[5]

Peter was bred to be a leader. His mother was the daughter of Conrad Weiser, the distinguished Indian agent of Pennsylvania who in 1750 had served the government of Virginia in its dealings with the Iroquois. Thus it was fitting and consistent with family tradition for Peter Mühlenberg to have accepted the call in 1772 to serve the German inhabitants in the area of Woodstock, Virginia. In 1774, he presided over a meeting of citizens of Dunmore, Virginia, which was called "to consider the best mode to be fallen upon to secure their liberties and properties." They resolved and pledged "that we will most heartily and unanimously concur with our suffering brethren of Boston, and every other part of North America, who are the immediate victims of tyranny."[6]

Mühlenberg participated in meetings and conventions of one kind or another until the task fell to him to mobilize the German inhabitants of western Virginia. When Virginia created six new regiments, the state ordained that one of them be called a German regiment and "be made up of German and other officers and soldiers (with) Peeter Mulenberg [sic], Colonel."[7] From his Woodstock pulpit in January, 1776, Mühlenberg eloquently proclaimed: "That in the language of holy writ, there was a time for all things, a time to preach, and a time to pray, but those times had passed away; that there was a time to fight, and that time had now come!"[8] Disclosing military garb beneath his ministerial robes, he descended the pulpit and ordered drums to beat at the church door for recruits. When more than three hundred men signed up, Peter decided never to put on clerical robes again. The rest of Mühlenberg's biography is the story of his feats of bravery and victory as a general in the revolutionary army.

Another German hero in the War of Independence was Nicolaus Herckheimer or Herkimer, who earlier had gained the limelight for his efforts during the French and Indian War as a leader of the German settlers in the Mohawk Valley. For his staunch career as brigadier general in the revolutionary army and for the sacrifice of his own life in the process, the state of New York named the city of Herkimer for him and erected a monument there in his honor. George Washington himself complimented Herkimer for his leadership during the early period of the revolutionary war.[9]

The American Revolution was of great interest to the Europeans, and consequently many immigrants joined in the American war effort. Some were adventurers. Others were more distinguished foreigners who came officially or unofficially to bring aid from their home governments to the American cause. Undoubtedly the most prominent and the most capable individual in this category was Frederick William Augustus Henry Ferdinand, Baron von Steuben.

Born at Magdeburg, Prussia, Steuben followed family tradition in becoming a soldier. He fought in the War of the Austrian Succession and the Seven Years' War in Europe (the French and Indian War in America). Legend has it that Steuben gave up a high-ranking position in the Prussian army for the great American cause, asking only that the king of Prussia transfer his high annual salary to his nephew.[10] However, there is ample reason to believe that Steuben promoted himself in rank and honors while crossing the Atlantic.

Steuben was probably penniless and therefore came to seek his fortune in the New World. Material in the Prussian archives indicates that he never rose higher than the rank of captain in the Prussian army and that Frederick the Great dropped him from the army after the Seven Years' War.[11] His private letters to friends in Germany in which he relates the many adventuresome exploits he had participated in while in America suggest that Steuben was an excellent storyteller. Yet, the myth of his being a lieutenant general in the service of the king of Prussia may not be due as much to Steuben as to Benjamin Franklin. After Steuben met him in Paris, Franklin wrote letters introducing Steuben to Washington and the Continental Congress. Perhaps Franklin was aware of the facts but realized the deeper implications, namely, that he had to "sell the Baron" to the Americans to get the benefit of his services. If so, Franklin proved himself to be a good judge of character. Using as precedent the promotion of other foreigners like De Kalb, Lafayette, and others to high rank, the Congress on January 12, 1778, passed a resolution accepting Steuben's enlistment for service with the introductory comment, "Whereas the Baron Steuben, a lieutenant general in foreign service, has . . . offered his services . . .".[12]

The following month Steuben was on his way to join Washington at Valley Forge, accompanied by his translator, Pierre Duponceau and a small retinue. Shortly thereafter, Steuben was appointed inspector general of the Continental army and given the task of developing discipline among American soldiers. Steuben grew to legendary stature. By day he drilled the troops and practiced maneuvers; by night he wrote the first manual of field operating procedures for the American army — in French — which his interpreter translated into English. On the cold muddy slopes of Valley Forge, an American army gradually took shape as a result of Steuben's unfamiliar but highly successful Prussian tactics. Of equal importance, Steuben's book of regulations, commonly known as the "Blue Book," provided a much needed new approach, one which was likewise unfamiliar to the British enemy officers.

Washington seems to have relied heavily on Steuben as an advisor and as a deputy to put the Virginian regiments in shape. At Yorktown, Steuben proved to be the only member of Washington's staff who knew the art of military siege. Some have even said that Steuben's influence was so considerable that the American forces for a time "seemed in danger of becoming an overseas branch of the Prussian Army."[13]

Obviously Steuben's many feats in the war effort, though not always appreciated, were considerable. Unlike Lafayette and other foreign warriors in the American Revolution, Steuben was slow to receive much credit for his accomplishments. But by the time he died in 1794, he had been made an honorary citizen of New York City and of Albany, and Congress had bestowed on him a reasonable pension. New York State gave him 16,000 acres of land in Oneida County. Since then his name has lent prestige to German societies all over America, not to mention the many places on the map of the United States, such as Steubenville, Ohio.[14] Likewise, Steuben Day is still the crowning event in the German-American community of New York City as illustrated by the elaborate festivities and parade which is held annually. The New York press, especially the German-language newspaper, *New York Sonntagsblatt Staats-Zeitung und Herold*, each September dedicates many pages and columns to descriptions of events and plans on this occasion.

In 1776, Washington disbanded his old headquarters company, or "bodyguard" because it was reported to contain Tories. In its place, Washington acquired an all-German-speaking unit. Called the Independent Troop of Horse, the new bodyguard consisted entirely of German-Americans recruited in Berks and Lancaster Counties, Pennsylvania. It contained fourteen officers and fifty-three men under the command of Major Van Heer, who had been a cavalry officer in the army of Frederick the Great. The German bodyguard came into the service of Washington in 1778 and stood by him until it was disbanded at the end of the war.[15]

While it should be emphasized that no effort is being made here to present a list of those Germans who played major roles in the revolutionary war effort, there is one other person who must receive cursory treatment. He was Johannes Kalb, the son of a Franconian peasant who, like Steuben, came to America with a self-chosen title, Baron Johann de Kalb.[16] Though born at Huettendorf near Bayreuth in 1721, Kalb never distinguished himself in his homeland. Instead, he turned up one day in a regiment of the French army in 1743. For his service to the French in the Seven Years' War, Kalb was granted the nobility title of De Kalb. Kalb came to the colonies with Lafayette and Washington quickly made him a major general. After service in New Jersey and Maryland, General Kalb was sent with his Maryland division to aid General Gates in warding off the British forces in the Carolinas. Here General Kalb met his fate in hand-to-hand battle with the armies of Cornwallis at Camden. After the American General Gates turned and fled, Kalb with his Marylanders tried desperatley to save the day. Wounded eleven times, he was finally carried from the field and expired three days later on August 19, 1780, at Camden, South Carolina.

Finally, in a brief discussion of the Germans in the revolutionary war, mention must be made of the Hessians. A Hessian, strictly speaking was someone from the state of Hesse, but popularly the term "Hessian" was applied to all the German soldiers who involuntarily served under the British flag in the revolutionary war. The Hessians were brought to America in the age-old role of mercenaries — in this case, as foreign soldiers fighting for the British crown.

Throughout history, certain nations have hired members of other countries to fight their wars. While this practice was declining in the eighteenth century, the "big-spender" princes of Germany were eager to avail themselves of any means to secure a better balance of payments. Such countries as Holland and Russia had refused to accept tempting offers to "hire" out soldiers to Great Britain. King George III, himself a Hanoverian sovereign, also protested, however weakly, against the use of Hanoverian troops in a mercenary capacity. Frederick the Great strictly forbade any of his subjects to serve in the English army, and he went so far as to refuse permission to other princes who wanted to ship their soldiers through his territories to America in the service of England.[17] The system of recruiting German mercenaries and "selling" them abroad was so commonplace, however, that a manual existed on how it might be best accomplished.[18]

Many historians agree that the Hessians were not particularly good or reliable fighters. Since the Americans knew this almost immediately, the Continental Congress approved a plan to lure the Hessians away from serving the British. When a large contingent of Hessians was captured at Trenton, New Jersey, Washington furnished them an opportunity to visit the Pennsylvania German areas, whereupon a number of them volunteered for service in the American army. Nevertheless, Washington declined advice to form an all Hessian American regiment, for he believed that their loyalty was as questionable to America as to the British.

It is reliably estimated that at the close of the revolutionary war some 12,000 of the original 30,000 Hessians sent to North America chose to remain. No records indicate that they were in any way distinct from their countrymen who had emigrated to America on their own initiative.[19] We know also that during the revolutionary war thousands of Germans served among the French troops under Rochambeau. The Royal Allemand de Deux Ponts was in fact not a French but a German regiment serving the colonies between 1780 - 1783 under the command of Prince Christian of Zweibrücken-Birkenfeld. In addition, there were divisions of Alsatians, Lotharingians, and others. Some were perhaps mercenaries, others were German nationals who served America officially under the French flag.

Several comments about the influence of the American Revolution on German immigration to the United States can be made. In the first place, the War of Independence caught the fancy of important German writers like Goethe, Schiller, Kant, Klopstock, and Lessing. America accquired a reputation that was synonymous with freedom of life and politics, and which was almost idyllic in nature. So deep-rooted was this European faith in America that it persists with some modification to this day. In the second place, Frederick the Great became friendly toward the budding United States of America. On principle, Frederick was ambivalent toward the independent colonies because he was bound by treaty to England. Besides, if he had favored the colonies openly, the British province of Hanover might have joined forces with England. As the War of Independence progressed, France, in March 1778, recognized the new United States. Frederick did not follow suit immediately. However, he did help by opening Prussian ports to American vessels and by permitting the purchase of military supplies in Prussia by the colonies. In 1779, he aided the American cause by refusing to serve as a mediator to end the war.[20] Shortly before his death in 1786, Frederick the Great did recognize the United States. This was important because Prussian-American friendship strengthened the fledgling nation for the storms to come. Moreover, with Prussia in a position of leadership among the German states, the American affiliation with Prussia promised the benefit of immigrants and trade well into the nineteenth century.[21]

In the years immediately following the war, and continuing into the early decades of the nineteenth century, not even German travelers, much less German immigrants, came to America. Gradually, however, letters from established German immigrants and from Hessian soldiers who had remained in America paved the way for curiosity seekers and adventurers from Germany. In time, German scholars also became fascinated by America and by the strategic significance of the military expeditions during the revolutionary war. Through their writings, they revealed the attractions of the United States to the potential German settler.[22] Significantly, in the writings of travelers and historians, the newly established republic acquired the new image of an independent country and ceased being thought of as a territorial extension of England.

As a result of the contribution by German immigrants to the revolutionary war, state governments realized just how much they owed to this ethnic group of Americans. A new spirit of mutual respect evolved, exemplified by such action as having laws and government proceedings routinely translated into German.[23] In other words, through the necessities of war, the Germans in America became valued citizens. The Revolution was not only fought by the Americans against the English; it was also fought as a conflict between the German-settled frontier and the English-dominated Atlantic seaboard. Due to their performance in the war, the German farmers on the frontiers were no longer ignored. As conditions in America improved, the German immigrants took a more active interest in public affairs and self-government. They also wrote descriptive letters back to Germany inviting new immigrants to join them.

From the end of the revolutionary war to 1820, it is generally assumed that German immigration to the United States was slight. This is difficult to confirm because the United States Censuses kept no figures on nativity before 1820. Studies of later waves of immigration indicate, however, that whenever there was political turmoil or economic recession in the home country, people tended to forget about emigration until the storm had passed. It was after the soldiers came home and the economy recovered that new waves of emigration formed.

The years 1789 - 1815, then, represent a period when German emigration to America undoubtedly ebbed to the zero mark. The French Revolution and the Napoleonic Wars had essentially cut Europe off from the rest of the world. Perhaps this condition was beneficial for the United States because it provided an opportunity for the new Republic to build up an economic base and to solidify its political independence with a more or less stable population. In Europe and especially in Germany, the Napoleonic period was characterized by continuous political reorganization and realignment. Restlessness and instability permeated every tax office, every church, and every local town hall. Authority fluctuated and shifted on all sides. Social positions collapsed. What little property and fortunes people had accumulated frequently vanished with the result that laws, loyalties, and liabilities were swiftly reoriented.

After the defeat of Napoleon, however, the blockade was lifted and a demobilized Germany not only discovered that it had an oversupply of labor, but that it was simultaneously inundated with factory-made English goods which brought disaster to the German family industries, particularly weaving. Likewise, the supply and demand for food became radically unbalanced. States like the Rhineland, the Palatinate, Baden and Württemberg had dense populations and lands highly unsuitable for agriculture. Due to an ancient law of inheritances in southwestern Germany, agricultural lands had to be divided equally among living children so that by

1800, many farms had become too tiny for a family's subsistence. It was this land policy that compelled the people to engage in home manufacture which, in turn, allowed a continuation of the shrinking land system. Making clocks, tools, and weaving at home was fine, except that it made the people so employed abnormally vulnerable to social and economic changes. When peace returned to Europe after the defeat of Napoleon, there came an end to the continental system of restrictive trade. Foreign products flooded onto the continent wreaking disaster on Germany's home industry.[24]

On the American side of the Atlantic, the War of 1812 was another factor, however minor, in deterring immigration from Germany. Thereafter, the United States enjoyed economic prosperity. Fertile land became available at a low price; western lands in the new states of Kentucky, Tennessee, and Ohio were opened up and secured for settlers. Transportation companies, land speculators, and officials of the new states were eager for immigrants to fill the population vacuum. And it was principally to Germany (as well as Ireland) that they turned their attention.

The Napoleonic era was cruel to Germany in a backhanded sort of way. During the wars on the Continent, England experienced an economic boom as did Germany. The populations of England and of Germany soared during wartime prosperity. However, even before Napoleon the increase had been rising above tolerable limits, alarming writers like Robert Malthus. By 1790, disaster might have struck in Germany as well as in England except for a peculiar agricultural discovery that saved the day: the potato. No crop grown previously was known to produce as much food per acre as the potato. The potato temporarily bought time when wheat supplies could no longer be produced in adequate quantities on Europe's exhausted soil. In Germany, the potato and the war boom together ushered in a temporary and a false sense of security. Just how false would be proved by the potato famines of the 1840s as we shall see in Chapter 6.

In a way, France was better off because Napoleon's campaigns annihilated army after army so that throughout the remainder of her history, France never had to worry about overpopulation.[25] Great Britain found an escape valve for her overpopulation in her colonial empire. In the decelarating economy of the post-Napoleonic era in Germany, however, there was a surplus of people who were eagerly received by the sparsely populated United States of America.

It should also be noted that in 1803 Napoleon sold the vast territory of the Louisiana Purchase to the United States, immensely increasing America's capacity to accommodate immigrants. To be sure, the acquired land was not immediately needed. European immigrants as well as the newly independent Americans had plenty of available acreage in which to settle. In the early days of the new Republic, a pattern of westward movement was initiated when people gravitated away from the eastern seaboard. When westward expansion was developing, in the early 1800s, the Germans comprised a large precentage of the population in the Mohawk Valley in the north, at the headwaters of the Ohio River in the middle, and at the Cumberland Gap in the south. As migration toward the West progressed, the Germans were automatically represented by large numbers on the lands adjacent to these three zones.

Some scholars theorize that settlement in the early part of the nineteenth century involved three classes of people. First came the trapper or trader. This man was not typically a German. Next came the restless opportunist — the hunter, cattle grazer, or road builder. Nor was this man of German descent. Finally there were those who were attracted to farming as a way of life on the frontier. Several authors find that the Germans with their large families were strongly represented in this settler class.[26]

As the nineteenth century began, German settlements were established northwest of the Cumberland Gap in what is known as the Blue Grass region. Names of cities like Frankfort, Flemingsburg, and Harrodsburg, Kentucky testify to the influx of Germans. A similar pattern can be traced in northeastern Ohio. North of the forty-first parallel and westward 120 miles from the Pennsylvania border lay the Western Reserve, which was settled primarily by Yankees. Immediately to the south of the Reserve, however, a Pennsylvania German belt of farmers developed early in the nineteenth century. Several place-names in this region indicate an early German population — Berlin, Dresden, Frankfort, Potsdam, Freeburg, and others. Likewise, the biblical names, Bethlehem, Salem, and Nazareth derive from Pennsylvania German Moravians and Amish settlers in the area.

Germans arrived in considerable numbers also in the Scioto River Valley of southern Ohio, especially Ross County. Most did not come directly from Germany but from Virginia and Maryland.[27] The strongly German character of Cincinnati also dates from this time. In subsequent years, but still in the first quarter of the century,

Pennsylvania Germans together with some new immigrants moved into western Ohio, forming a line of settlements from Cincinnati in the south to Toledo in the north.

In conclusion, it can be stated that in 1830 the Germans in the United States extended westward from New York, New Jersey, and Pennsylvania in the north and from Maryland and Virginia in the south, forming roughly a triangle with one corner in Ohio, another corner in New York and a third corner in Virginia. Mostly, the Germans in this triangle had reached the United States before or immediately after the revolutionary war. Few arrived during and immediately after the Napoleonic Wars in Europe. Only after 1830 did emigration from Germany to the United States accelerate, so much so in fact, that for the next fifty years, Germany would supply more immigrants to the United States than any other country.

CHAPTER 4

The Germans in Pre-Civil War America

WHEN GERMAN IMMIGRATION TO THE UNITED STATES QUICKENED after 1830, its mainstream flowed into the regions around the Great Lakes and along the Ohio River. It also streamed up the Mississippi to its confluence with the Missouri. German immigrants poured into this area initially because of a book published by Gottfried Duden. Duden had investigated the wonders of the New World, lived on a farm in Missouri for three years, and returned to Germany in 1829 to write of his experiences, first in periodicals, then in a volume of his collected reminiscences.[1]

In the report, Duden wrote glowingly of life on his middle western farm. At a time of discontent among the German masses, he directed hopes to America, stressing its pastoral beauties. In short, he made the youthful United States into a utopia for the oppressed and the downtrodden. Disenchanted German settlers later referred to Duden as *der Lügenhund*, ("lying dog"), but by then it was too late to escape the hardships of pioneer life in America. Controversial though he may have become thirty years after his publications appeared, there is no question that he was trusted in the 1830s when thousands of Germans departed for the "Promised Land."

All the major cities that attracted the Germans at this time were in the North — Chicago, Detroit, Milwaukee, Cincinnati, and St. Louis. As a rule, the Germans who arrived in the nineteenth century avoided the South. In the late eighteenth century large numbers of Germans had settled south of New Orleans and northward from the city along the Mississippi in a region once known as the German Coast. Some of them came directly from Germany, others from way stations in Maryland, Pennsylvania, or New York. Although German traditions once flourished in these colonies, they all but disappeared by the outbreak of the Civil War.[2]

44

Due mainly to the climate and a lack of familiarity with the economics of plantation farming the Germans did not settle south of a line formed by the southern borders of Ohio, Indiana, Illinois, and Missouri.[3] However, small colonies developed in a few southern port cities — Norfolk, Wilmington, Charleston, Savannah, Jacksonville, Pensacola, and Mobile. Apparently these German settlements resulted from trade between the southern states and Germany, notably commerce involving tobacco and cotton. In addition, there were small German islands in western South Carolina, Memphis, Nashville, Knoxville, and Chattanooga.[4]

The distribution of the Germans in the United States in the pre - Civil War period, then, was concentrated in a belt two hundred miles wide, stretching across the northern tier of states from New York and Maryland to the Mississippi River. Maps for each decade from 1850 - 1930 show concentrations of Germans in only four areas outside this belt, namely, New Orleans, the rural area around San Antonio and Austin, Texas, the vicinity of San Francisco, and in the St. Louis region of Missouri.[5]

The Germans played a role in the development of New Orleans, but by 1860, the total number as well as the percentage of Germans in the city had declined significantly.

The situation in Texas was radically different. Germans began immigrating to Texas in the 1820s when the territory was still part of Mexico. Baron von Bastrop founded a German settlement on the Colorado River near Austin as early as 1823, and gave his name to Bastrop County.[6] Heavy German immigration began after 1831 when Friedrich Ernst of Oldenburg received a grant of land from the Mexican Government in northwestern Austin County. Delighted with his land, Ernst wrote enthusiastically to a friend, and the letter was published in an Oldenburg newspaper and in a book on Texas. The result was a sizable influx of Germans to Texas from the northern Low German regions of Oldenburg, Westphalia, and Holstein. That the Ernst letter was printed was accidental; that it bore fruit can be ascribed to a society founded by wealthy Germans for promoting overseas colonization. Officially called the "Verein zum Schutze deutscher Einwanderer in Texas," it was often referred to as the "Mainzer Adelsverein," the "Adelsverein," or simply the "Verein."[7]

Organizers of the society had two objectives: land investments that would increase in time and a safe outlet for countrymen who wanted to emigrate. Managed first by Prince Carl von Solms-Braunfels and later by Baron von Meusebach, the society operated under the following conditions. Each emigrant paid $120 if single or $240 if married and agreed to cultivate fifteen acres and live on the tract for three years. The society promised to furnish the emigrant transportation, a quarter section of free land, and a house free. The society would also supply the basic farming tools and make improvements needed in the settlement, such as hospitals, schools, churches, and canals. Shipment was by way of Galveston and Indianola.

Between 1844 and 1846 the society transported 7,380 Germans to Texas, but one year later in 1847 it went bankrupt. Bad management, poor soil, hostile Comanches, and unclear titles to the property contributed to the collapse. Lands which were to be allocated to settlers were on the Fisher-Miller Grant in west-central Texas. New Braunfels and Fredericksburg are examples of towns along the route leading from the Gulf of Mexico to the grant area.

Distressing as the collapse of the "Adelsverein" was, it did not spell the end of German immigration to Texas. As happened in the German belt of the North, the Texas Germans wrote letters to their friends and relatives in Germany. As a result, fellow countrymen chose to join their predecessors, thereby adding to the number of Germans in Texas so substantially that a German community has survived to this day. Estimates of the German population in Texas prior to the Civil War range downward from 30,000. As a percentage of the total Texas population, the Germans accounted for 20 percent in the peak years between 1846 and 1850. The heaviest concentrations of German-born in 1850 were located along a line from Galveston northwestward to Austin, New Braunfels, and Fredericksburg.[8] It was in this chain of settlements that President Lyndon B. Johnson grew to manhood. In September, 1908, the German-language paper, *Fredericksburg Wochenblatt*, announced his birth on August 27. Much later, the president entertained Chancellors Konrad Adenauer and Ludwig Erhard in his native Fredericksburg.[9]

Galveston, an island city fifty miles southeast of Houston, was an important seaport before the Civil War. Like New Orleans, it attracted Germans to its lucrative enterprises. In 1857, a New Orleans editor wrote that every steamer leaving New Orleans for Galveston was "crowded with Germans of some wealth who are going to Texas to select a future home."[10] During the mid-1850s, the German fraction of the population of Galveston hovered between one third and one half, a percentage that left its mark on the city's architecture, parks, music, and intellectual life. Skilled Germans dominated the building trades, crafts, and milling industry. After the Civil War the Galveston port declined and with it the German colony.

The third area outside the high density German belt was San Francisco. Thanks to a favorable climate and high potential for trade, the area appealed to white settlers at an early time. German interest in the region, however, dates from 1838 when John A. Sutter penetrated the hinterlands of San Francisco. Sutter was born in the German Duchy of Baden but trained in a German-speaking Swiss military academy. After various business exploits in the far Northwest, he moved inland to the area of Sacramento and founded the settlement of New Helvetia, named in honor of Switzerland. Since California belonged to Mexico at that time, Sutter held Mexican citizenship and served for a time as governor of this northern Mexican territory.

Sutter's success in cattle raising and wheat growing enabled him to build an estate which employed some three hundred whites and an "army" of peaceful Indians. On this land in 1847, he built a saw-mill on the present site of Coloma and called it Sutter's Mill. In January, 1848, his overseer at the mill, James Marshall, startled Sutter by finding gold in the creek bed. Failing to secure guarantees from the Mexican government to keep the discovery a secret, Sutter bowed to the inevitable, for the rush was on, straight across his land and crops. Sutter's crops were trampled, his livestock slaughtered, and the prosperous Sutter was plunged into poverty. After California was admitted to the Union, Sutter appealed his case for damages to the United States Congress, but he never regained either his property or recompense.[11]

Due to the gold rush, people all over the world heard the news and thousands hastened to California. The Germans, however, were not lured to the goldfields in significant numbers. Rather, they were attracted to the commercial center of San Francisco as well as to the agricultural lands in the Sacramento Valley and Stockton. Wheat was needed to feed the burgeoning population and what was left over could easily be exported. Several Germans established the first wine growing enterprises in California at this time, especially in the Napa Valley. In 1858, Charles Krug started his viniculture and in the same year, the Germans, Grundlach and Dresel founded their Rhine Farm.

Frontier California experienced rapid population growth. The

1850 census reported some 92,000 people of whom 3,100 were German-born. By 1860 the population had risen to 380,000 with a corresponding rise of the German-born to 20,900 and, in both instances, the cities of Sacramento and San Francisco had by far the largest concentrations of Germans.

In spite of substantial numbers of Germans in Texas and California, the heartland of German-American settlement remained in the northern tier of states east of the Mississippi. That large numbers of Germans chose Texas and California can be ascribed to extraordinary promotion.

In California there were projects similar to those in Texas, for instance, that of George Hansen and his Los Angeles Vineyard Society, which initiated a colony near Los Angeles in 1857.[12] Just as a nobleman and a company planned the Texas colonies, so, too, Baron Christian Charles Josias Bunsen, a friend of King Frederick William IV of Prussia, invented the scheme to populate California with his countrymen.

In 1842, the Mexican government concocted an offer to sell California to the Prussian government.[13] Although the offer never came to fruition, it did gain publicity for the territory which, thus, became a target of emigration. Moreover, California enthusiasts published pamphlets in German describing Sutter's holdings and analyzing the prospects for California as a future trade center. One such pamphlet was *Obercalifornien*, published by Heinrich Kuenzel in 1848; another was Schmoelder's *Neuer praktischer Wegweiser*, published in three parts in 1849, of which 120 pages were dedicated to California. There is reason to believe that the editors of *Emigrants' Guide to California* lifted generous portions from Schmoelder's publication.[14]

When gold brought California before the public in Europe and America, additional travel guides and books were published in German. Titles such as Osswald's *Californien und seine Verhältnisse* (California and Its Prospects), *Californiens Gegenwart und Zukunft* (California's Present and Future), *Briefe eines Deutschen aus Californien* (Letters of a German from California), *Authentische Nachrichten über Californien* (Authentic Reports about California), and many others called attention to the utopian state of California and provided settlers with practical information about it.[15]

The fourth region of heavy German settlement in the 1830s was in what is today Warren County, Missouri. Tantalized by the skillful pen of Gottried Duden, thousands of Germans from Westphalia and Hanover headed for Missouri to find Duden's utopic dreamland. Soon they were followed by counts, barons, scholars, preachers, and gentlemen. They were all men of means, but they were unaccustomed to working as farmers and laborers. Because so many had been educated at the classical German Gymnasium, where Latin and Greek were everyday fare, they acquired the epithet in America of "Latin Farmers" living in the "Latin Settlement." They were cultivated men, but impractical and unsuited for life on the frontier.

On the heels of the Latin farmers, a sizable immigration came to Missouri, mostly under the auspices of the *Giessener Gesellschaft*. This society developed plans to concentrate Germans in a territory which could eventually be admitted to the Union as a German state. During the decades that followed, three states came under consideration for such ambitious dreams — Missouri, Texas, and Wisconsin.[16] Led by two idealists, Paul Follenius and Friedrich Münch, the Giessen society proclaimed its intentions: "We must not go from here without realizing a national idea or at least making the beginnings toward its realization; the foundation of a new and free Germany in the great North American Republic shall be laid by us." After leaving Bremen in 1834, the members of the colony sailed via New Orleans to Arkansas, then northward to the confluence of the Missouri with the Mississippi. While Follenius and Münch were unsuccessful in establishing an independent *Germania* (German state) on the American continent, Münch got elected to the Missouri legislature. His influence attracted the attention of German immigrants, in particular, the Lutherans from Saxony, who made St. Louis into a bastion of German Lutheranism in the United States.

Having described where the Germans were located prior to the Civil War, let us describe what kind of people they were. The term "Forty-eighter" is the most important one, for it characterizes a distinctive class of German-Americans. Forty-eighters were participants in the revolutions which swept Europe in 1848, occasioning the largest amount of bloodshed in the cities of Vienna, Berlin, and in the southwest German state of Baden. Those political refugees who fled from the upheaval or were expelled by their repressive governments for participating in the revolutions came to be known in America as Forty-eighters, even though few of them arrived prior to 1850.[17]

The year 1848 was filled with turmoil in the German-speaking countries. In May, an assembly of elected German representatives gathered in the *Paulskirche* at Frankfurt, where they organized a provisional democratic government for Germany. In Berlin and Vienna, however, reactionary rulers quickly suppressed every attempt of liberals to implement constitutional reform. Lacking an army to deal with the disorder that developed in the streets, the high-minded liberals failed to secure popular backing. In chambers and salons, sophisticated debate continued and strong-headed intellectuals spoke brilliantly, but in a matter of days, their initiatives were drowned in blood. As a consequence, thousands of them fled to avoid arrest, while others decided on principle to continue their lives outside Germany in order to demonstrate their dissatisfaction with the reactionary policies.

Although our focus is on the influence exerted by the Germans on America, we might mention that there is evidence to support the view that the revolutions of 1848 were exported from America to Germany. At the preliminary meetings of the Frankfurt Parliament, Friedrich Hecker, later a political refugee in America, proposed an article demanding abolition of the hereditary monarchy and the formation of a confederation along the model of the United States. At the meeting, the proposal was rejected by fellow liberals as too radical. But it reflected accurately statements issuing from America and appearing on lithographed sheets in the Frankfurt area. One contained the motto: "Deutsche, werdet praktisch / Und ihr werdet frei" ("Germans, be practical and you will become free"). It was dated at New York, May 25, 1847, and signed L. M. The text concluded with a plea, "Look across the ocean, see the greatness, the flowering of our Republic! Try to govern yourselves! . . . Don't let supercilious scholars throw dust in your eyes."[18]

A second appeal was titled "Zuruf eines Deutschen aus Amerika" (Appeal of a German from America), dated March 25, 1848, and signed by C. Richter, Brewer. In part the text read: "In publishing this appeal it is my intention to encourage the Germans in the United States to do all in their power to stir up a glimmering spark in Germany, so that through the establishment of freedom the honor of the Germans will be saved and the well-being of our German brethren restored."[19] The publication was circulated widely in the Frankfurt area. Appeals such as these were heeded, democracy was heralded, but the results proved disastrous. Countless arrests and speedy departures for the United States ensued.

In the eyes of these political refugees from Germany, the United States was not only a constitutional democracy but had a romantic appeal as well. The freedom that existed in the United States at the time may have been tarnished by slavery; nevertheless it exercised an irresistible lure on the German Forty-eighters. Once established in America, these idealists wasted no time before they began criticizing anything and everything — such as organized religion — which, in their opinion, placed restrictions on freedom.

In spite of their numerical insignificance, the Forty-eighters wielded great influence. Estimates put their total variously between 4,000 and 10,000 — an extremely small number in comparison to the 1,186,000 Germans who came to the United States between 1820 and 1860.[20]

Typically, the Forty-eighter was an uprooted intellectual who underwent bitter disillusionments in the United States. At first, many joined the established German farmers in the Midwest, but they soon found the rigors of frontier life and the naiveté of their simpler countrymen hard to bear. They knew the classics and read Latin and Greek, but that did not compensate for their lack of muscle with which to break the prairie soil. Soon native Americans referred to these Germans by the same name devised for Duden's followers, the "Latin Farmers."[21]

Although unsuccessful at farming, the Latin farmers contributed much to the cultural life of many small towns in the Midwest. City libraries, reading societies, discussion groups and debating clubs sprang up within an atmosphere of hardship and crudeness characteristic of the frontier. Frequently the first German-language theater productions in the United States were staged by Forty-eighters.[22] Some of this cultural activity in small-town America was possible for the Forty-eighters but impossible for earlier German immigrants because the Forty-eighters had the means, whereas earlier newcomers were often destitute. Nevertheless, the Forty-eighters deserve this credit, and one might add, were quick to claim it.

Vociferous, strong-headed, often liberal to the point of being radical, the Forty-eighters were refugees from an unsuccessful revolution. As liberals, they were militant critics of America's many religious sects, organized churches, and the established clergy. Intolerant of these institutions, the Forty-eighters proclaimed their interest in new ideas and were proud to be known as freethinkers. In politics they were violently opposed to slavery and to what they con-

sidered corruption in city governments. They opposed fundamentalist religious groups who tried to enact state and local laws for Sunday closing and fought tirelessly against the prohibition of
alchoholic beverages.

These outspoken extremists drew fire from many sides — from the
native Americans as well as from their more conservative German
countrymen who had emigrated to the United States prior to 1848.
Intellectually intolerant, the Forty-eighters were gifted and wealthy
enough to make their opinions felt. Often they founded newspapers
and scholarly societies, gave lectures, and wrote books to propagate
their convictions.

The task of determining just how much influence the German
Forty-eighters had on civic affairs in the United States is still in
progress.[23] In Wisconsin, for example, one would expect to find that
the Germans were deeply involved in politics. Yet, while many
Forty-eighters were active, the state never sent a German-born
senator to Washington, and, except for Carl Schurz, no German
from Wisconsin ever gained national prominence during the
nineteenth century. Only one Forty-eighter, Edward Salomon,
became governor, and he was elected as lieutenant-governor,
succeeding to the governorship only upon the death of Governor
Harvey in 1862. It must be assumed, therefore, that Salomon was
not governor because of voter support, though once in office, he performed with distinction. In 1869, Salomon moved to New York,
where he became a leader of that city's German-American community. The nationally acclaimed German city of Milwaukee was
unable to elect a German-born mayor until 1884, and the Wisconsin
legislature never had more than a few German-born members. No
Forty-eighter ever attained the reputation of being either the
spokesman or the representative of the German voters of Wisconsin.[24]

In politics, the Forty-eighters differed sharply from earlier German immigrants. Vociferously antislavery, the Forty-eighters supported the Republican party from the day of its birth in Wisconsin in
1854. The older Germans — sometimes called the "Grays," whereas
the Forty-eighters were known as the "Greens" — cared little about
slavery. The established Grays found their ideas of liberty and
equality in the Jeffersonian doctrines of the Democratic party. But
the Democrats were identified with slavery, and therefore the
Greens opposed them. Paradoxically, neither group of Germans

wanted anything to do with slavery. The Grays were, of course, less vocal in opposition to it. Whether pro- or antislavery, the Democratic party always signified to the Grays the party of the common man, including the foreign-born. In short, it represented the poor against the rich. In the eyes of the Grays, the Republican party arose out of the old Whig party, the haven of Nativists, Know-Nothings, and wealthy capitalists. To them, the Republicans also represented a puritanical view of the Sabbath, prohibition of liquor, and special favors for the powerful. Perhaps the split between the numerically small Greens and the more numerous Grays explains why the Forty-eighters were not often successful in politics.

The agnosticism, anticlericalism, and intellectualism of the Greens further alienated the older German immigrants, many of whom had come to America to find religious tolerance. The Forty-eighters also irritated the Grays by setting up schools which competed with the established German parochial schools.[25] Their social clubs, too, tended to supplant the conservative church circles and inevitably, German musical organizations, theaters, reading societies, and gymnastic groups weakened the authority of the church in the older German communities. Fundamentalist church leaders, therefore, instinctively resented the Forty-eighters for these activities.

As if rubbing salt in the wounds, the Green Forty-eighters went further. They flaunted their tastes in the faces of their Gray countrymen, by calling them barbarians, without art, music, and culture. They also chided the older German immigrants publicly, eventually making a political split among the Germans inevitable. A sample of their bluntness can be taken from an editorial by Bernhard Domschke in the *Wisconsin Demokrat* in 1854:

The idea of forming a union of foreigners against Nativism is wholly wrong, and destroys the possibility of any influence on our part; it would drive us into a union with Irishmen, those American Croats. In our struggle we are not concerned with nationality, but with principles; we are for liberty, and against union with Irishmen who stand nearer barbarism and brutality than civilization and humanity. The Irish are our natural enemies, not because they are Irishmen but because they are the truest guards of Popery.[26]

These attitudes of the Greens mixed religion with politics and succeeded in isolating the German Catholics from the Protestant German element in the United States. German Catholics retreated from public affairs as they grew more suspicious of the Forty-eighters, and most fundamental Protestant Germans soon followed their example. Another complication for the Forty-eighter was his image — as a rule he tended to be a southern German who felt antagonistic toward his northern German countrymen according to the age-old tradition of north-south regionalism in Germany.[27] Seemingly, then, nothing could unite the Germans in the 1850s into a unified political bloc.

In 1856, a contemporary wrote that the Germans isolated themselves and nourished "their strongest passions, love of beer and hatred of the Irish." He was also struck by the intense hatred Germans were capable of exhibiting toward each other. "The Republicans have a deadly hostility to the Roman Catholics, and many of them dislike the Lutherans almost as bitterly. They regard the established churches of Germany as the greatest enemies to civil liberty, and they stamp kingcraft and priestcraft with a common brand of infamy."[28]

It is hardly surprising, then, that the political impact made by the Germans prior to the Civil War was at best mixed, and at worst, ineffectual. Some scholars credit the Germans with electing Lincoln and abolishing slavery. But such claims are difficult to sustain with statistics.[29] True, the Germans avoided the slave-holding South, but whether they did so for moral reasons or because the economic system in force there compelled them to move north is far from clear. Undoubtedly the immigrant Germans responded to all the environmental pressures, whether ethnic, economic, or climatic.[30]

Scattered attempts to establish a German state within the United States always met with failure. The *Giessener Auswanderungsgesellschaft* was the most vocal in favor of such a state, but dissenting opinions were frequent, mostly among the German immigrants themselves. Calls to the Germans to unite in a political party were also issued by the Forty-eighter editors, for example, in the St. Louis *Westliche Post* in 1858:

If the nativists have a right to found a party which is all Anglo-Saxon, we must have a right to have ours all German. . . . Such a German national union would send delegates to the great American party conventions, American parties would be informed as to the wishes, temper, and numerical importance of the German element. . . . All reformers and progressives would unite with the Germans in a great party of social and political reform. . . . The German element should take the initiative, become the leverage of reform in American politics. The German would hold the balance of power in

American politics and become the guardian of both German national and American national interests.[31]

Strong as the political plea was, editors from other parts of the country were calling for different panaceas. New York's Steuben Association wanted to establish a German educational system from primary through the university level. But instead of action in the political or educational fields, editors quickly lapsed into arguments that tended to follow sectional patterns, the East against the Midwest, the North against the South, in short, a pattern that has been used to explain why the Civil War itself was unavoidable.

German-American political conventions were frequent — in Pittsburgh in 1837, in Missouri several times during the 1850s, in Louisville in 1854, in Chicago in 1860, and in Cleveland in October, 1863. None led to the acquisition of political power. Resolutions were advanced and opinions marshaled, but they yielded little action or results at the polls.[32] Nor did the German Forty-eighters line up immediately behind Lincoln. Even Carl Schurz, as head of the Wisconsin delegation to the Republican Convention in Chicago in 1860, held fast for William H. Seward until the last ballot. Once nominated, however, Lincoln enjoyed the full support of Schurz who stumped everywhere in the German belt of the North. From the East he wrote home: "The old Pennsylvania Dutch follow me like children, although they can only half understand me. The Democrats are furious, and wherever I have spoken they telegraph like mad in all directions for German speakers to neutralize my speeches."[33]

In the late nineteenth century, the Germans proudly claimed that without the German bloc vote, Lincoln could not have been elected. But such boasts have now been called into question. Probably the issues of prohibition and nativism influenced the German vote in 1860 far more than did all the pro-Lincoln Forty-eighters who lectured on the stump and wrote in the newspapers. In Iowa, for example, the Germans were concentrated in townships that were almost solidly Democratic. If these townships did not vote for the Republican Lincoln, then the conclusion would be justified that there was no German bloc vote for Lincoln in Iowa. In 1860, none of these Democratic townships of Iowa gave Lincoln the lion's share of its votes.[34]

There was some evidence of German voting for Lincoln in Minnesota, but not as an overwhelming bloc.[35] In those townships where Germans amounted to more than half of the total population, twelve returned a Republican and only two a Democratic majority. Of those townships where the German population accounted for 30 to 50 percent of the total, ten returned Republican and eight Democratic majorities. Seemingly, then, rural Germans in Minnesota did turn out positively but not solidly for Lincoln.

Clearly, Lincoln was not elected by any grand strategy executed by German voters. More likely, Lincoln was elected by a coalition of American Protestant church members — Presbyterians, Congregationalists, Methodists, and Baptists — who were urged by their leaders to condemn the immorality of slavery. The Germans of Catholic persuasion probably joined the Irish in voting for Douglas and against Lincoln because of mutual feelings concerning the issue of Nativism. Faced with their own brand of discrimination, the German and Irish citizens were not troubled by slavery in the South. German Lutherans of the Missouri Synod were not antislavery, for they justified it on biblical grounds.[36] In the final analysis, therefore, it can at best be maintained that the Germans made some contribution to the election of Lincoln and that the Forty-eighters were somewhat influential in ridding the country of institutional slavery.

There were other achievements of the Forty-eighters. Personalities like Mathilde Franziska Anneke justify the claim that they were among the founders of the women's liberation movement. When Mathilde Anneke arrived in Milwaukee in the 1850s she began publishing the militant *Deutsche Frauen-Zeitung*, which she and her husband had begun in Cologne in 1848. Later she moved to New Jersey to find a more receptive audience for her views. No copies of the paper are known to exist, but one of her speeches, delivered in German at a stormy Tabernacle Meeting in New York in 1853, has been included in *The History of Woman Suffrage* by Elizabeth C. Stanton and Susan B. Anthony.[37] Karl Heinzen, another vociferous Forty-eighter, campaigned vigorously for women's liberation. Turner groups, such as the Davenport *Turngemeinde*, strongly promoted the cause of woman suffrage with lectures and public discussions.

Judging by the comments of ordinary Germans in America at the time, the Forty-eighter view on women was not shared by all German immigrants. Letters to relatives in Germany were critical:

The husband must buy the groceries, start the fire, and milk the cows. Outside of doing the wash, the American wife is more or less free. The general respect for womanhood causes parents to spoil their daughters and neglect teaching them the necessary skills for managing a household. It is little wonder that they often attend such ridiculous women's rights conventions where they praise woman's noble position in society, even though one can find nowhere else so few good housewives as in America. . . . The husbands let the wives become rulers of the house and they tend to control all household affairs. The conduct of American women is somewhat more free than in Europe. Marriage seems to be more of a business than anything else to them.[38]

Forty-eighters also campaigned against what they considered to be oppressive Puritanism in American thought. They sowed the seeds of the American labor movement which erupted late in the nineteenth century,[39] and they deplored America's squandering of natural resources. A leader in the drive to save virgin forests was the Forty-eighter Carl Schurz, after he became Secretary of the Interior in 1877.[40] Forty-eighters also set the pace for education, particularly vocational training and postgraduate schools. The kindergarten was a genuine German transplant to America.

In sum, the German nation lost more than a chance to acquire democracy when the revolutions of 1848 failed. It also lost the Forty-eighters whose talents were sorely needed at home.

CHAPTER 5

The Germans in the American Civil War

In general, the Germans as an ethnic group sided with the North in the American Civil War. The reasons have been alluded to in the previous chapter and may be labeled idealistic, economic, and emotional.

In the first place, the Germans saw in the North a haven for the downtrodden immigrant. That the immigrant was discriminated against by Know-Nothings and nativists was unfortunate, but it was more or less tolerated by the Germans. To them the North represented democracy. It offered the ideal of equal opportunity for the little man and held no man bound to a station or class of citizenry such as that which slavery imposed on the black man in the South. Furthermore, in the South the landed aristocracy continued to thrive in a manner that reminded the lowly German immigrant of the European nobility system which he had fled. Idealistically, the Germans were opposed to secession and "states' rights" because they had known all too well the disadvantages of many small, petty states pursuing their own objectives to the detriment of the nation as a whole. In spite of this general feeling among the Germans about the North-South difference, there is no reason to claim that, as an ethnic group, they had a very clear knowledge of their feelings or that they acted accordingly.

The economic factor was probably the strongest of the three reasons why the Germans favored the North on the Civil War issue.[1] Most Southern plantation owners were opposed to European immigration because the economic system in the South did not require new blood and did not depend on an influx of low-paid, unskilled labor. Southerners *owned* their unskilled workers and had no place in their system for mass production except as performed by their black field hands.

Proximal

Toward the joint of attachment of a structure on the body;

(hip proximal to knee)

In reality, the aristocratic upper class in the South was small. There were only 2,300 large, family-owned plantations which had a slave population numbering over 100, and none had over 1,000 slaves. The middle class in the South was also small, and, unlike the upper class, it had little influence.[2] Furthermore, this middle class was urban, and therefore the small German farmer did not fit into the pattern of Southern economic life. Even in the one new territory of the South — Texas — which opened up for colonization after 1845, it was a difficult struggle for a German immigrant livestock farmer to compete economically with the large plantation owner who used Negro slaves.

Added to this situation was the emotional factor. The Germans favored liberty and equality and therefore they did not identify with a system that depended on slavery for its livelihood. This fundamental fact would have remained latent in the minds of the Germans, even if the Forty-eighters had not kindled abolitionist feelings among the German-Americans. Without the Forty-eighters, however, the Germans probably would not have entered politics on the side of the North in regard to the issue of slavery. They would have remained silent and neutral. Immediately after their arrival, the Forty-eighters plunged vehemently into politics and illuminated the slavery question as one that stood in sharp contrast to the other liberal ideas prevalent in America.

Abolition undoubtedly presented a golden opportunity for the Forty-eighters. Without the slavery issue, these German intellectuals might have been dismissed as disillusioned visionaries, unacquainted with the American way of life. In pleading this cause, however, they aroused a marked response among the liberals of the North and built a bridge of moral responsibility to their fellow Germans in America. With few exceptions,[3] the Forty-eighters expended their fire in the North. Their effectiveness in the German area of Texas and in the industrialized, borderline city of Baltimore was also substantial.[4]

Recalling that the Forty-eighters were often engaged in journalism, it is significant that of the 265 German-language newspapers in the United States in 1860, only three favored secession.[5] By and large, then, the Germans were led to support the Union and they contributed more heavily to the cause of the North than to that of the South. This fact was recognized by President Theodore Roosevelt who paid tribute to the Civil War efforts of the Germans in a speech delivered in 1903.

"In the Civil War it would be difficult to paint in too strong colors what I may well-nigh call the all-importance of the American citizens of German birth and extraction toward the cause of the Union and liberty, especially in what were then known as border states. It would have been out of the question to have kept Missouri loyal had it not been for the German element therein. So it was in Kentucky — and but little less important was the part played by the Germans in Maryland."[6]

The story of how the Germans saved Missouri for the Union has been repeated enthusiastically every time German-Americans wanted to put themselves in a good light.[7] The supportive remarks of Theodore Roosevelt were based on the following incident.

Before the Civil War broke out, the Republican leader, of Missouri, Francis P. Blair, began recruiting militia companies among the eighty thousand Germans of St. Louis. When they took to drilling in their *Turnverein* halls, they were aided by Captain Nathaniel Lyon, a West Pointer stationed in St. Louis to command a company guarding the United States Arsenal at St. Louis. Apparently it was the pro-Confederate Secretary of War, John B. Floyd, who had seen to it that the arsenal was well stocked with a collection of 60,000 muskets, 1,500,000 ball cartridges, cannon, and lathes for gun-barrel making. Floyd envisioned that the cache would fall into the hands of secessionists or their sympathizers who would then seize Missouri, cut off Southern Illinois, and thus secure the southern Mississippi Valley for the Confederacy.

The Germans in St. Louis were openly pro-Union, but they represented only one side of the city's popular opinion triangle. One segment of the population favored secession. Another portion wanted nothing more than to remain neutral in the whole affair. The Germans favored the Union but were surrounded by slaveowners and their proponents. The latter Missourians produced enough votes to elect the prosecessionist governor Claiborne Jackson. Jackson, it appears, wished to secure Missouri for the Confederacy by capturing the local arsenal exactly as happened at Harpers Ferry in Virginia.

The pro-Union Germans were catapulted toward armed conflict when a brewery wagon was driven into the arsenal with beer barrels and left loaded with arms and ammunition to be used by students of the near-by Humboldt Institution in their round-the-clock surveillance of the arsenal. When Fort Sumter fell on April 14, 1861, and Lincoln called for volunteers, Governor Jackson responded by declaring, "your requisition in my judgment is illegal, unconstitutional, and revolutionary in its object, inhuman and cannot be complied with."[8] Only threats by members of the German Turner Society to put up a tenacious struggle dissuaded Jackson's state troopers from pouncing on the arms cache immediately.

As their enthusiasm mounted, the Germans vowed that they would either occupy the arsenal or, if that proved impossible, they would march out of St. Louis in a body to join the Union forces in Illinois. Under this ultimatum, Blair and Lyon permitted the German volunteers to occupy the arsenal on April 22, 1861. In retaliation, Governor Jackson ordered state militia into a camp outside of St. Louis on May 3. Pushed to the brink, Captain Lyon marched on Camp Jackson and imprisoned the state militia on May 10, 1861.

If it had not been for an anti-Union mob looking on, all might have ended without incident. But, in the heckling, someone began shooting and the German troops retaliated by opening musket fire. At least fifteen members of the crowd and two of the soldiers fell dead on the pavement. More were wounded. It looked as though St. Louis and all of Missouri would become engaged in an internecine Civil War on its own, but after hit and run skirmishes throughout the early summer, the threat of violence subsided. When General Fremont arrived in St. Louis to take charge of operations, General Lyon was assigned the task of driving Governor Jackson and his regiments south out of the state. Assisted by his second-in-command, German-born Franz Sigel, they met with disaster on August 10, 1861, at Wilson Creek. A flanking maneuver against the Jackson forces by Sigel was poorly executed, ending in a Bull Run kind of catastrophe for the Missouri Germans.[9]

As usual in major conflicts involving ideologies, the facts were blurred by the immediacy of the situation. No one could claim that the Germans as an ethnic bloc had consciously saved Missouri for the Union, and thereby tipped the balance in favor of the North. More likely, neither the Germans nor any other group knew exactly what they were fighting for. The struggle in and around St. Louis happened to start there. Also, the presence of the pugnacious Connecticut-born Lyon, whose horse bolted at the wrong moment, touched off a riot which escalated into a battle. Still, the actual presence of the German Turners in St. Louis at that time probably was a fortunate coincidence for the North.

In later Civil War actions, the Germans played many active roles. On various fronts, their performance was mostly average and sometimes cowardly. Occasionally they distinguished themselves for bravery. Surely as an ethnic group they were neither identifiable for their courage nor for their lack of it. They stand out, however, in one respect, and that is with regard to the total number of soldiers they contributed to the Union Army. Quantity may not have spelled quality, but surely the large number of Germans in the Civil War warrants a look at the statistics.

A few years after the conclusion of the Civil War, Benjamin A. Gould, actuary of the United States Sanitary Commission, compiled summaries of enlistments according to places of birth.[10] At first, the army did not record place of birth for the enlistees, and therefore less than half of the 2.5 million soldiers bore papers which indicated where they were born. However, the nativity of nearly 300,000 others was ascertained by written inquiries to regimental officers. In addition, all reenlistments after the first three months were duly recorded, thus greatly increasing the data on place of birth. In cases where the country of birth could not be determined, Gould distributed the nationalities in direct proportion to the numbers of soldiers whose places of birth were known. According to this calculation, there were 176,817 German-born soldiers in the Civil War on the Union side. The state of New York furnished the largest number (totaling 36,680 German-born) followed by Missouri (30,899), Ohio (20,102), Illinois (18,140), Pennsylvania (17,208) and Wisconsin (15,709).

Gould goes on to illustrate what manpower each nationality might have furnished if the enlistments had been calculated in exact proportion to the population of each foreign-born nationality in America as reported by the 1860 census. In all cases, foreigners of every nationality enlisted in numbers larger than would have been expected of them in comparison to their percentage of the total population. Statistical comparisons may not warrant weighty conclusions but the relative number of Germans versus the Irish is interesting. Comparing the two nationalities we find Gould reporting that the Irish supplied only 5,169 men in excess of the number expected on the basis of their percentage of the total population, whereas the Germans sent 58,169 more men than were called for by their percentage of the population. Some readers of these statistics have argued that the Germans simply deserted in large numbers and reenlisted for the bounties offered. But this theory does not take into account that the areas where the largest numbers of desertions occurred were not those from which the Germans volunteered in greatest numbers.[11]

A more plausible explanation of why so many Germans were found in the Union army is that German immigration to the United States at that time included a preponderance of males of military age. Such young men often arrived without jobs and with no family ties. Bounties for enlistment seemed to be the perfect interim solution to their financial and domestic problems. Moreover, immigrants arriving during the Civil War were often met by recruiting officers who induced them to sign up at once for military duty. In one case, Senator Wilson of Massachusetts boasted about having imported 1,000 Germans to serve in four of the required Massachusetts regiments.[12] Another deciding factor was the belief that service in the army meant full American citizenship without the fuss and delay of papers and applications — which in fact became a federal edict after the war. Finally, there was the factor that many Germans, particularly if they had arrived after the 1848 revolutions, were familiar with, and fond of, military life. Some writers even charged that, because their militaristic careers had been frustrated in Europe, America became a kind of overseas orphanage for cracked-up German officers. It is probably true that immigrant Germans had a natural inclination for military life and it is equally true that the Union Army needed their expertise particularly in the artillery, in the engineering corps, and in the cartographic units.[13]

For these reasons, the Germans, especially those from the middle western states, participated in the Civil War in proportionately large numbers. They were among the first to volunteer when Lincoln sent out his initial call for enlistments: 6,000 Germans from New York, 4,000 from Pennsylvania, and after the first six months of the war, thousands more from most states of the Union. As the war went on for years instead of lasting but a few months, entirely German regiments were recruited, in which German was the only language spoken. Faust lists some thirty of these: from New York, the Steuben Regiment, Blenker's Battery, and the United Turner Rifles; from Pennsylvania, Ohio and Indiana, variously numbered "German Regiments"; from Illinois, Hecker's Regiment; from Wisconsin, also several German Regiments with numerical designations, for example, the Wisconsin Ninth, which was all German.[14]

On the whole, the Turner or German athletic societies were quick to volunteer, frequently as a bloc. Thus the Ninth Ohio Volunteers and the 20th New York were made up exclusively of Turners. Other cities in which the Turner membership joined the military in large numbers include St. Louis, Washington, D.C., New York, Williamsburg, Newark, Boston, Philadelphia, and, especially, Cincinnati, Chicago, and Milwaukee.[15] Eyewitnesses from among the German soldiers participating in the conflict depicted their experiences with great exuberance. Ferdinand Cunz, for example, wrote home to his Protestant minister father, formerly of Giessen, Germany, about the attack of the *Merrimac* on March 8, 1862:

The southern slave holders have a good opinion of our regiment [Seventh, New York Volunteers, Steuben Regiment] ever since the battle of Big Bethel. . . . Our present uniform is dark blue coats, hats a la Tyrol and light blue overcoats. . . . Our Major von Schack, a Prussian officer, . . . is without doubt the best officer and has the entire confidence of the regiment. . . . Across Norfolk Bay comes a ship flying the rebel flag. . . . All bullets from our batteries fell like peas from the side of the ironclad *Merrimac* and in half an hour our beautiful frigate *Cumberland* with 200 men aboard was sunk. . . . From all directions now came enemy gun boats and opened fire on our camp. . . . Until 6 o'clock at night the firing continued but the rain of bombshells went over our camp. This was surely the greatest spectacle ever before witnessed in the world. I would not have missed it for five hundred dollars. . . . I bet we 880 Germans would have repelled 10,000 foes.[16]

But not all the Germans were as enthusiastic about participating in the war. In several rural counties of Wisconsin, the Germans remained loyal to the Democratic party which was against the war. Antidraft riots occurred among the Germans of Ozaukee and Washington Counties, and the densely German city of Milwaukee voted for McClellan in 1864. Disgusted with the proceedings of the war and Lincoln's slow pace ending it, German-Americans of a radical mind held a convention in Cleveland in 1863 at which fourteen states were represented. During the deliberations, they advocated the candidacy of John C. Fremont for president and a tough program of reconstruction for the South.[17] In short, therefore, the uncritical statements of some writers, who insist that the Germans automatically supported the Union cause during the Civil War, are in error.

It might be well to cite two typical examples of intimate antiwar sentiment. The first comes from a letter written by Edward Barck of Saginaw, Michigan, who penned the following words in 1863:

The Administration and with it, the Abolitionists, will not listen to suggestions for peace, for they insist on submission. . . . The people are getting tired of it. But we are in a dilemma now, and Mr. Abraham Lincoln, with all of his jokes, will not be able to get us out of it if we do not do it, that is, to force him to do it legally. Having 1,200,000 volunteers is no proof of Patriotism.[18]

In another letter dated 1864, Henry Frank wrote from Greenfield, Wisconsin:

... You will find out about the miserable war in the newspapers. August, brother-in-law Edward, and Louis have the prospect of being drafted at the next conscription (4 - 6 weeks). The worst is that no substitutes can be found any more. If he could find one, August would gladly give him $1,000 for a year's service. I can say freely that since I have a family, I am no longer a friend of soldiers, and least of all do I wish to be shot to death for Lincoln and his Negroes. Also, this is no way to carry on a war, it is butchery. Everything suffers as a result of the war, the great increase in prices, the high taxes, the broken families, the eternal fear. . . . One must have respect for the Southerners, for if we had half of their officers and could exchange ours for theirs, the blood bath would soon be ended. But enough of politics for now.[19]

Yet, willingly or not, the German-Americans did participate extensively in the Union army's efforts. Historians have reported the words of Robert E. Lee, "Take the Dutch out of the Union army and we could whip the Yankees easily."[20] Lee may never have uttered these words, but the spirit of his statement is surely correct, for a total count of the German-born and German stock who served as soldiers exceeds 750,000. While the conflict was raging, Yankee critics generally underestimated the Germans and frequently called into question their very patriotism. Bruce Catton points out, for example, that Know-Nothingism was still so widespread both in the civilian population and in the army that in reality "a country which hated foreigners almost as much as Negroes was now using the one to enforce freedom for the other and was suffering from emotional indigestion as a result."[21] The fight to end slavery, then, was simultaneously a fight by the immigrants for social acceptability on the part of the native population.

In discussing the role of the Germans in the Civil War, a word should be added about the interest of European nations in the American situation. It is well known that England sided with the South and even produced ships for the Confederate government, because England favored a weakened North America nation. France exploited the debilitated American Monroe Doctrine when Napoleon III meddled in Mexico. The Austrian Government was also implicated in the French adventure, for Maximilian was an Austrian prince.

Germany at the time was in such a divided state of affairs that it could not qualify as an overseas power of significance. In small ways, however, Germany sided with the North. Prussia's King Wilhelm opposed secession on principle and Bismarck had personal friends in the Union government. Thus, among other advantages, the North found a ready market for its bonds on the Frankfurt exchange.[22] Sentimentalizing about Germany's support of the Union in later years, leaders of German-American organizations, the American ambassador in Berlin, and even Bismarck himself commented fondly on the fine Civil War relationship Germany and the Union had cultivated. Carl Schurz seems to have said it well with a tongue-in-cheek remark: "During the Civil War, America was a friend in need whom her friends across the Atlantic did not abandon — and Germany was rewarded in gold for its idealism and trust in America to the tune of 7% interest."[23]

No matter how pro-Union Germany's official position on the Civil War may have been, large numbers of German immigrants were ensnared by the immediacy of life within the Southern states during the Civil War. In August, 1861, the Confederacy passed a law banishing from the Confederacy citizens fourteen years and older who were not prepared to take the oath of secession. The law worked to force hesitant individuals to make up their minds and it compelled neutral ethnic groups to take a stand on slavery and secession. The Germans were not solidly antislavery, even in the North, and in the South they had many reasons to be reticent about both slavery and secession.[24]

In looking at the Germans in the South, a sample area is Texas where the Germans were living largely on their own cultural islands. When a referendum was held in Gillespie County in 1861, the German inhabitants voted almost unanimously against secession and in the heavily German county of Medina there was also strong opposition to withdrawal from the Union. Yet in the most thoroughly German of the western Texas counties, Comal, the vote was emphatically in favor of secession.[25]

The *New-Braunfelser Zeitung*, which was no doubt the most influential German-language paper in Texas, supported secession. A recent reinterpretation of the antisecession vote of Gillespie County indicates that the Germans, in voting against secession, were not voting in favor of the Union. Rather, they were well aware that secession would mean war and that war would bring a withdrawal of the U.S. Army from the western frontier. In the event of war the local military posts which comprised the major market for agricultural products from the area would wither away, and the military barrier to Commanche Indian molestation of their agricultural lands would be removed.[26]

On the other hand, nowhere in the South was resistance to serving in the Confederate army as strong as it was in and around the German city of Fredricksburg, Texas. Whether or not the antidraft riots indicated pro-Union sentiment is difficult to ascertain. Nevertheless, on July 15, 1862, Confederate troops had to be dispatched to Gillespie County where German irregular soldiers clashed with the Confederates in what has come to be known as the Battle of the Nueces.[27] Atrocities and summary court martials of the arrested Germans resulted in the sudden execution of perhaps twenty-five Germans, not counting those who died later of hunger and exposure.

Another incident in the Civil War experiences of the Germans in Texas was a plan that called for the liberation of Texas from the Confederacy. Anthony M. Dignowitz, a physician and soldier, on December 24, 1861, petitioned for military action to protect the citizens of Texas. Dignowitz had invited Germans to settle in the state with the promise that Texas would become a free state. Claiming that there were 65,000 German-born soldiers serving in the Union army, he called on Washington for military occupation of Texas to transform it into a free state. Dignowitz submitted his plans for invasion to President Lincoln who referred them to a Committee on Military Affairs. Although the proposal seems to have died there, the strategy envisioned a two-pronged attack, one northward from Corpus Christi, the other southward from Kansas, which was to conquer much Indian Territory en route. The amateur strategist wanted a wing of these armies to be composed of Texas soldiers of German birth.[28]

The area of the South other than Texas where the Germans were easily identifiable and therefore an area which is worthy, of attention in assessing the involvement of Germans with the Southern cause, is Virginia. As noted in the case of Texas, the Germans in Virginia were occasionally praised for being to-a-man anti-Southern in sentiment. Closer investigation reveals that the German population in Virginia reflected virtually all shades of opinion regarding the Southern cause. To the Virginia Germans, slavery had become a tolerable and acceptable institution. Many a civic leader of German birth who lived and worked in the South during the Civil War years espoused the cause of the South wholeheartedly.[29]

The *Sociale Turnverein* of Richmond was an organization harboring typically Northern abolitionist sentiments. But these Germans represented an elitist and therefore exceptional point of view. More typical was the *Anzeiger*, a German-language newspaper of Richmond which criticized the North for its viewpoint on Negro emancipation, claiming that Negro rule would be the result and that the blacks would eventually dominate the country. This, the editors felt, would be sacrificing the cultured South and its people to the terrorism of an uneducated and inferior race.[30] As Southern German-language editors flailed the German editors of the North for their abolitionist views, the German immigrant-on-the-street grew increasingly annoyed at the whole political turmoil — one of the very issues which had prompted him to flee Germany. Yet, a crucial matter was brought home to ordinary Germans when the *Virginische Zeitung* posed a problem raised by secession, namely, that the naturalized Germans in the South had in fact sworn an oath of allegiance to the United States, not to the Confederacy or the state of Virginia.

When the war began, many Germans fled north. Others took refuge in West Virginia. Those not yet naturalized hastened to the Bremen Consul in Richmond to update their German nativity papers. As early as 1862, action was taken by the Confederate Congress to put foreign subjects under conscription. Willy-nilly, Southern Germans signed up, forming entire German units, sometimes with roll calls that sounded identical to the rosters of a gymnastic or singing society. The *Anzeiger* continued to bring news of battles to its German readers in full sympathy with the Confederacy. Moreover, when it decided to cease publication as a German-language newspaper, the Confederate government took unprecedented action by purchasing the *Anzeiger* in 1864. Perhaps the move was an indication of just how sensitive the Confederacy felt about the potential flight to the North of skilled German craftsmen and ablebodied citizens. Nevertheless, it is well known that the Germans flocked to Union-controlled Alexandria. German clubs mushroomed, the Jewish congregation expanded, and the *Alexandria Beobachter* began publication with a strong circulation.[31]

The number of Germans who lived in the Confederate States at the opening of the Civil War is estimated at 72,000. Except for the concentrations in Texas and Virginia, the only other area where the Germans could have acted as a cohesive element was Louisiana, where, by 1861, most of them lived in the city of New Orleans. There they numbered at most 15,000 thus forming an impotent minority in a city whose population was over 80,000. It is apparent that the Twentieth Louisiana was largely a German regiment and there is evidence to indicate that perhaps as many as eleven German military companies came from Louisiana in 1861.[32]

Georgia, too, had German units in the Civil War, and, although there may not be much that is distinctive about their service, a story is told about the Georgia Germans at the front. When a Northern, German unit from New York was attacking Fort Pulaski, the soldiers often sang German songs on the neighboring island of Tybee. In response the Georgia Germans defending the fort sang the same melodies.

Apparently this was not the only instance where Germans in opposing armies joined in singing the songs of their Fatherland. Concerning an evening in the Kanawha Valley of West Virginia, it was reported that:

when the firing was over, as night came on, nothing was to be heard but the roaring of the waters, intermingled now and then with snatches of song from some of the German soldiers on either side, which produced a touching effect at such an hour. Ofttimes one of our Germans could be seen leaning on his rifle, listening to the sounds of his mother tongue as they were wafted over from the enemy's camp. At times, one of the sentinels would shout across — "From what part do you come, countryman? I am a Bavarian."[33]

With the exception of a Prussian named Heros von Borcke, few Germans on the side of the South won distinction as military leaders. Von Borcke was a dashing baron who identified with the "chivalrous" Southern cause. To join the staff of Jeb Stuart, von Borcke had to run the Union blockade, but he was rewarded by being commissioned a major and given the title of "Inspector General" of J. E. B. Stuart's Cavalry. He rode gallantly with Stuart until the latter fell, cut to pieces by midwestern plough boys, many of whom were of German ancestry. They felt little appreciation for von Borcke's colors and plumes. In 1865, von Borcke's *Memoirs of the Confederate War of Independence* were published by William Blackwood in London and years later, it came out in Berlin in a German-language edition, *Zwei Jahre im Sattel und am Feinde* (Two Years in the Saddle and on the Enemy's Heels).[34]

On the Northern side, there were many well-known names of German-born officers. High on the list are those of August Willich, Ludwig Blenker, Friedrich Hecker, Karl Salomo, Alexander Schimmelpfennig, Franz Sigel, Max Weber, Peter Osterhaus, and not least, Carl Schurz.[35] A brief listing of where a few of them were engaged would show General Blenker commanding a German detachment at the first Battle of Bull Run. When his division was attached to McClellan's army, it became the subject of heated controversy which led to Blenker's early retirement in 1863. Sigel was active in Missouri, in the Shenandoah Valley, and at the Second Battle of Bull Run. At Shiloh, Colonel Willich fought with distinction, and Hecker won the respect and loyalty of his German troops for service at Chancellorsville and Chattanooga. Fifteen of the twenty-six regiments in the XI Corps were listed as German. Sometimes called the "Cinderella of the Army," the XI Corps was for a time commanded by Sigel, giving rise to the phrase "I fights mit Sigel." Within the corps, Schurz, Schimmelpfennig, and von Steinwehr held commands. Discredited earlier, the corps regained its honor in the battle for Lookout Mountain.

Other German detachments served steadily if not always with distinction in the various war theaters. Long before the end of the Civil War, however, the many German units were scattered, regrouped, or reorganized out of existence, and in fact they were being reconstituted all along by incoming non-German recruits. Early in the war, the Germans had been blamed by commentators for military failures, eliciting calls from Horace Greeley and others for the dissolution of the German regiments. Protests in the streets of New York led by Friedrich Kapp, the German-born U.S. Commissioner of Immigration,[36] slowed precipitous action, but eventually it happened anyway. Diffusion rendered it almost impossible to trace the performances of the Germans in later war records.

In the final analysis, the Civil War probably did as much for the Germans in America as the Germans in America did for the Union. Whether by design or by coincidence, the majority of the Germans happened to fight on the right side of the slavery issue. For many years after the war, editors of German-language newspapers could proudly place their ethnic brothers behind the cause of equality, justice, and reform, customarily asserting that the Germans were solidly aligned with Lincoln's principles. Identified with the Great Emancipator, they could forever see themselves as having formed a bulwark against the immorality of slavery, against the illegality of secession, and not least, against the xenophobia of Know-Nothingism. For they had fought hard, if not always well, for the Great Union, and as immigrants they had earned a right to participate in the golden years of industrial growth and boom that emerged after the Civil War.

CHAPTER 6

The Post - Civil War Period and Emigration from Germany

AT THE CONCLUSION OF THE CIVIL WAR, PEACE RETURNED TO THE land, but there was precious little tranquillity. American industry had sown seeds during the military conflict which would yield a harvest when the firing ceased. Increased capacity for machinery output, improved river transportation, and, especially, a zeal for railroad building spurred the nation to vigorous activities. Guns were not melted down to make plowshares, but the industrial might for producing the plows and other machines of peacetime was a by-product of waging war.

This new bustle accelerated the westward movement and gave new credibility to the frontier thesis. Belief in unlimited opportunity farther west was also embellished by a romantic lure to tame the wilderness and to bring civilization — for some individuals, to bring God and organized religion — to the "savages." In a matter of months, the "American Frontier" became a catch phrase which appealed to New England farmers, midwestern older stock immigrants, and eastern speculators alike. Further romanticized by stories of the American cowboy, the "Frontier" gained popularity among European peasants, especially when it was packaged and "sold" by state immigration commissioners and railroad agents in search of people to settle the wide-open spaces. Needless to say, new German immigrants as well as older naturalized Americans of German extraction participated in penetrating deeper into the West.

In dealing with the post - Civil War period of German immigration, at least three phenomena ought to be kept in mind. The first was the existence of outmoded laws of heredity in Germany, whereby farms continued to dwindle in size to the point where no one could make a living on them. Another, closely related to the first, was the occurrence of crop failures and famine in Germany. A third was the enactment and implementation of the Homestead Act in the United States. Other factors which gave impetus to German emigration to the United States after the Civil War were improved conditions of ocean travel, better guarantees for safe travel both on land and on sea, and the passage of laws in the United States to protect the new immigrant from the abuse of unscrupulous entrepreneurs and speculators.

Until about 1850, English-speaking immigrants dominated the social and political institutions of America. They knew the language and therefore comprehended the intricacies of govenent. They also captured most of the elective positions, gained the most influence, and left an imprint in excess of their numerical strength. After 1850, however, candidates for political office came to realize that there was much Teutonic influence in Middle America. Even Abraham Lincoln tried to learn German grammar and for a time owned a German newspaper.[1]

In contrast to the English, the Germans were gregarious. They lived with a "stockade mentality," building German-language islands throughout the Midwest. In one respect the "stockade" was a figure of speech; but in another, it was a subconscious defense mechanism erected against the all-too-rapid acquisition of the "English vogue" and the English language by their children. Occasionally the Anglo-Saxons resented the German clannishness, sometimes they admired it,[2] but usually they ignored it.

With this introduction, we can turn to the conditions prevailing in Germany which fostered heavy emigration to the United States during the second half of the nineteenth century. In his book *Germany and the Emigration*, Mack Walker has included two graphs which show the numbers of Germans who emigrated to the United States between the years 1820 - 1910.[3] He presents two lines, one drawn on the basis of official German figures on emigration and the other on official U.S. figures. The deviation between the two is not great enough to be of concern here. What is more significant, however, is the existence of three major crests interspersed by two corresponding valleys in the curve lines. The first pinnacle occurs between the years 1852 - 1855, at which time the immigration of Germans to the United States for the first time exceeded 215,000 (250,000 according to the German data) in one year, 1854. The valley between this pinnacle and the next found its nadir in 1862, the midpoint in the American Civil War. In 1862, immigration from Germany had declined to under 30,000 annually. After 1865 it rose sharply again, so that the eight-year period following the Civil War averaged in excess of 125,000 new German immigrants per year. Then the panic of 1873 stifled the economy of the United States to such an extent that immigration from Germany fell precipitously from its previously high plateau to an average well under 50,000 per year from 1874 - 1880. Thereafter, however, it skyrocketed to reach the all-time high of 250,630 in the year 1882.[4] Large migrations continued annually until 1885, but then leveled off around the 100,000 per year mark until after 1892 when immigration from Germany fell to the rate of about 20,000 annually until the First World War cut it off abruptly.

In reflecting on the statistics as shown by the line on Walker's graphs, one's interest is drawn immediately to the three major crests: 1854, 1865 - 1873, and 1882. The question arises as to what lay behind these three swells. The answers are complex. However, a few general indications can be assembled to provide a roughly drawn estimate. One might think the 1854 crest came on the heels of the major revolutions that swept Germany, particularly in 1848. Yet, on closer scrutiny, it is apparent that emigration from Germany from 1848 - 1853 was about what one might have expected had there been no revolutions of 1848 at all. The years 1846 and 1847 were years not only of potato crop disasters, but also of general crop failures in southwestern Germany.[5] In those years emigrants departed precipitously, forced to dispose of whatever they possessed for what they could get in order to avoid starvation.

Emigration in the late forties had its desired effect. As land values declined, so did the labor supply, with the result that wages climbed. Land could be bought again and life seemed to improve at precisely the time when political unrest made shipping, passage, and the whole idea of emigration less attractive. Seemingly, then, rather than forcing the common man to flee Germany, the revolutions of 1848 may indeed have convinced him to stay. However, from 1850 - 1853, crop failure recurred in Germany with the result that official action was taken. The export of food was forbidden, potatoes could not be converted into alcohol, and the German press was full of pessimism. All of this stood in contrast to reports of prosperity on the other side of the Atlantic. Characteristically, the areas worst hit by depression in these three years were the same ones that had supplied the largest numbers of emigrants in the past — southwestern Germany. Between 1850 - 1853, nearly 3 percent of Württemberg's population emigrated.

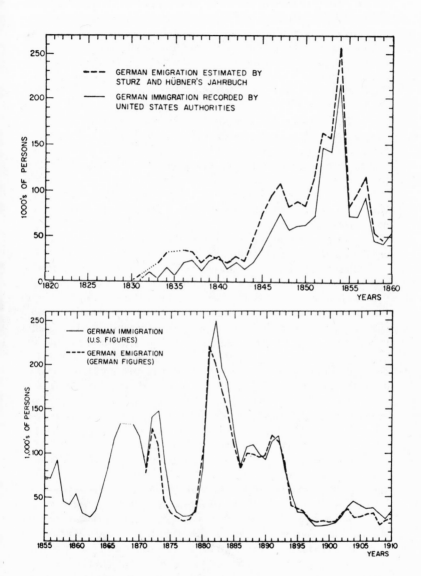

Nearly 10 percent of the Rhenish Palatinate emigrated and Württemberg, Hessen and the Palatinate experienced absolute declines in population during the 1850 - 1855 time span.[6]

In America, the 1850s showed a net immigration larger in relation to the existing population than that which occurred in any other decade of American history. There was an excess of arrivals over departures totaling approximately 12 percent of the 1850 population.[7] During this same decade, the foreign-born population in the United States grew by 84 percent; the German-born population increased by 118 percent; the state of Wisconsin added to its German-born population by 225 percent.

Although much attention has been showered on the 1848 intellectuals who arrived in the years following the miscarried German revolutions, the bulk of German immigrants between 1850 - 1855 were farmers and simple workers. Well-educated people — journalists, teachers, and so on — accounted for but a small number in the total German immigration during the period in which the Forty-eighters gained such prominence.[8]

Facing up to the facts of hunger and starvation, German provincial governments established commissions on emigration. They provided information on the climate, the working conditions, and the costs of travel to the United States. Other topics usually covered were the status of medical care, schools, churches, and the danger from Indians in the various regions of the United States.[9] Officially, the government of Baden, for example, systematically got rid of political offenders. Prisoners were pardoned on condition that they leave the kingdom and that if they returned, they would have to serve their entire prison terms. Not only thieves, beggars, and vagabonds, but also mothers of illegitimate children were shipped off in droves to the United States.[10] Due to these legal provisions of the German state governments, whole villages and rural districts in southern and western Germany were decimated.

To give some idea of the services provided by the government agencies, it might be well to look at one such organization — the *Nationalverein für deutsche Auswanderung und Ansiedlung*.[11] It was founded by private individuals in cooperation with government officials in Darmstadt, Karlsruhe, Stuttgart, and Munich in December, 1847. The very establishment of the society with government support gives evidence of the officially recognized need for emigration and the necessity felt by the governments to meet this need. Administratively, the society was based in Darmstadt, but it had agents in each German state, such as Bavaria, Alsace, Baden, Württemberg, Bremen, Hamburg, and even in Switzerland.[12]

Services rendered by the society can be summarized as follows. Primarily, the organization furnished transportation by German ships from German ports. Allegedly, the American ships bringing freight to Europe docked most frequently at Le Havre, Antwerp, and Rotterdam, where they disgorged their wares and took on German emigrants for the return journey. To foster the continued use of these three harbors, according to claims of the German Emigration Society, the French, Belgians, and Dutch gave a 30 percent reduction on railroad fares for emigrating passengers and/or their baggage from Germany to the point of departure. In order to counter this pattern of movement, the German National Society fostered steamer-train connections on the Rhine and Weser Rivers to the ports of Bremen and Hamburg.[13]

The society divided emigrants into three classes: the rich, the semi-independent (those having over 1,000 florins), and the poor. Naturally the first group was self-sufficient and could fend for itself. The second group consisted of artisans and farmers, "the core of our people who frequently take up the invitations of relatives to join them." The third group was the problem class, a potential burden on the citizens of any harbor city where they might land. For the first two classes, the National Society advised settlement in the states where Germans were well-established — Missouri, New York, Wisconsin, Iowa, and California — thus assuring them an easy transition and contacts for immediate employment. For the third group, the society suggested the establishment of poor colonies, somewhere in the newer western states, but admitted that such a plan could not be carried out effectively.

Therefore, the society proposed a two-pronged traveling system. One line led from New York along the Great Lakes to Wisconsin, Iowa, and Illinois. The other stretched northward from New Orleans along the Mississippi and Missouri to the heartland of the inner United States. The system was to operate by the cooperative efforts of "German Societies" in all the major cities of America. Each organization would collect money from its members to assist the immigrants from group to group until they reached their destinations. They were also to be helped in finding work. Exactly how much these societies accomplished for their poor immigrating German countrymen has never been determined, but throughout the years, several active immigrant aid groups existed in various states where the poor were benefited in exactly the way prescribed by the society.[14]

The *Nationalverein für deutsche Auswanderung und Ansiedlung*, as it was known officially, also made other provisions. Before departing, every emigrant was supplied with the following items: (1) a travel guide in which the journey was explained in German and provision was made for the emigrant to register any complaints he might have at the nearest office of the society so that discomforting situations would be remedied; (2) a map of the United States on which the territorial boundaries and divisions as well as railroad lines were marked; (3) a historical primer on all states in the Union with travel routes marked; and (4) tables which showed the equivalents of German and American money.

Beyond this, the society stationed officials in Bremen and Bremerhaven to assemble all members of a party on a given ship before their departure. The travelers then elected representatives who would be their negotiators with the ship captain concerning problems that might arise during the journey. Also, for the purpose of follow up, the emigrants were to keep travelogues and turn them in at the society's office upon arrival at their destination. These notebooks could then be used as evidence in confronting government agencies and shipping companies if they had failed to fulfill their commitments.

The National Society also provided other services, including (1) a clearing office in the United States for gathering and distributing information about the professions in the United States; (2) a bookstore in Darmstadt which offered materials in German on the main topics of concern for the emigrant to America;[15] (3) a list of settlements where Germans lived, namely in Missouri, New York, Wisconsin, Iowa, and California; (4) an emigrants' bank which facilitated financial arrangements for emigration; and (5) a business bureau that assisted emigrants with the legal problems of inheritance and many others.

In addition to official encouragement of emigration from Germany, there was plenty of mercantile stimulation prompted by the profit motive which led shippers to traffic in emigrants.[16] Commercial interests recruited immigrants to the ports by special rates and promises. Agents sent by companies traveled the German countryside preaching the "gospel" of emigration. Others established ticket agencies in Bremen, Frankfurt, and other cities. During the winter months, returnees from America were also enlisted to make the rounds from tavern to tavern praising America.

However, official and unofficial encouragement, even when coupled with rural overcrowding and economic depression, did not of itself bring about mass emigration. These preexisting conditions were wedded to other factors which have been defined elsewhere as "the *freedom*, the *desire*, and the *means* to move."[17] By *freedom* was meant a loosening of the feudal bonds, namely, a change in the land tenure which brought about a relaxation in the rigid community structure that had formerly chained the individual within it. The *desire* to move presupposed political, social, and psychological motives which always had to be accompanied by the *means* to leave, namely, the development of land and sea transportation.

When the masses began leaving Germany in the 1850s, both Europe and America were going through a period marked by the rapid construction of canals and steamships, posts and telegraphs, banks and travel agencies. Emigration, then, was intimately connected with the quickening of communications, markets, commerce, and capital flow between Europe and America. One might say that the commercial forces eroded the customary European community and increased social mobility. Some scholars point out that the greatest migration of the nineteenth century was not the movement to the grasslands of rural America. Rather it was a migration of the labor forces to the concentrations of coal and iron in every country where industries were being established.[18] Even within the United States, once the farmland was largely taken up by homesteaders, the migration from the farms to the cities continued — a process that in the 1970s is still in progress.

While these principles may be applied to all the migrations to America, they applied particularly to the three crests of immigration from Germany that occurred between 1853 - 1855, 1866 - 1869, and 1881 - 1883. In many respects, what has been said thus far in this chapter has applied largely to the first crest. Yet, as we turn now to the latter two, it will be obvious that the stimuli had long-term significance. In summary, they were land fragmentation, the decline of the handicrafts and the home industries, and the shift from an agricultural to a money economy. Coupled with these factors were the social changes which created a dissolution of personal ties, and changing political conditions. The constantly developing transportation systems remained an additional spur.

The second crest of German immigration hit America immediately after the conclusion of the Civil War. Even as warfare in America was ending, it was beginning in Germany, first with Denmark in 1864, then with Austria in 1866, and finally with France in 1870. This does not mean that the wars by themselves affected the flow of immigration except in temporary and obscure ways. During the American War, the Bavarian government concurred with Austrian schemes to get surplus German-speaking peoples to move into the Danubian lands which were part of the greater Austrian Empire. In this same period, South American agents seem to have had their heyday soliciting Germans for their countries. Brazilian recruiters were successful in Pomerania, where, apparently, local officials received fees for each German citizen they talked into emigrating.[19] However, in 1861, the Prussian Government interdicted the flow of emigrants to Brazil because it disapproved of the conditions under which German immigrants lived in the coffee plantations.[20]

Whether German government actions of this nature slowed emigration cannot be determined. It is a fact that emigration to the United States declined during the Civil War. Two factors that undoubtedly accelerated emigration to America after the Civil War were passage of the Homestead Act and a marked increase in German conscription as the German wars of unification got underway. Under the provisions of the Homestead Act of 1862, up to 160 acres became available without charge to the settler, provided that he bound himself to dwell on the land for a period of at least five years and to improve it. As regards the threat of conscription in Germany, several German states were annexed by Prussia at this time, and thus young men came under this constant threat of disruption in their lives.

Another factor influencing the flow of German immigrants into the United States was the highly stimulated condition of American industry immediately following the Civil War. To a remarkable extent in post - Civil War America, the immigrants represented an influx of labor to areas of high demand. They were attracted to the booming economy of the United States, which desperately needed their services, a situation that prevailed again in the late 1870s and the early 1880s. It has been pointed out that in the post - Civil War decades, the economic cycles in the United States and Germany were roughly parallel, with the German cycle sometimes lagging about a year behind the American. German immigration, however, was more closely tied to the American business cycle than to the German.[21]

If one considers the circumstances under which families migrated from Germany to America, a somewhat different picture unfolds. When emigration rose and became more characteristically rural, the proportion of families also rose, as did the number of children. Lone emigrants were predominantly male, whereas family emigrant groups were made up of considerably larger numbers of females. Perhaps some statistics are needed. Between the years 1820 and 1850, German immigration to the United States was well above 60 percent male. After 1850 the percentage of males hovered near 60 percent and it remained above 55 percent until the end of the century. The cause of the decline of male German immigration after 1850 is not necessarily due to an increase of family emigration (it could reflect an increase in single females who emigrated), but an expansion of families appears to be the case. Tables showing the statistical age spread for U.S. immigrants from Germany indicate that children under fifteen years accounted for an average of 25 percent between 1870 and 1890 but that this average percentage fell significantly — to about 17 percent — after 1890.[22] Thus it seems fair to conclude that the period of family emigration from Germany was between 1850 and 1890. In this framework, it is perhaps also worth noting that this period approximately overlaps the time when the Homestead Act was in effect (1862 - 1890).

As a rule, German farmers were welcomed by states which had unclaimed land waiting to be brought under cultivation. The word spread in Germany that Teutonic farmers in America seldom ended in the poorhouse or lived on public charity and that they were willing to take up farms which the Yankees had left behind in their move westward. For the Yankee, a farm was a place to milk out a living until the soil was depleted, at which time he simply headed west where he could again find more virgin soil. By contrast, the German farmer generally looked upon his holding as something permanent, something to be handed down from generation to generation.[23]

The Homestead Act was not the only American legislation that appealed to German emigrants. Just as German states offered to help their population to emigrate by means of legislation and semiofficial emigration societies, so too the United States came to the defense of the immigrant. As early as 1847, New York created a Board of Commissioners of Emigration, whose membership included a distinguished leader of the German element in the United States, Friedrich Kapp. Kapp's writings about the problems and harsh realities of immigrant life are an invaluable source of eyewitness information.[24] The Board of Commissioners gave advice, found employment whenever possible, inspected ships, and compelled the captain of each vessel to file complete data for each voyage at the mayor's office. This board also bought and held the old fort facility at the tip of Manhattan Island, which was converted into the famous immigrant station, Castle Garden. These New York state facilities served the purposes of immigration until 1892 when federal authorities took over responsibility for immigration and established Ellis Island.[25]

After 1870, the characteristics of emigration from Germany to the United States changed noticeably. There were fewer peasants and more industrial workers and artisans. In the earlier periods, the farmers left because there was no hope of making a living on agricultural lands under the system that prevailed in Germany. After 1870, farmers and small townsmen alike often left in search of industrial work. Consequently, in regions of Germany where workers could shuttle back and forth between their jobs in a factory and their homes on a farm, emigration rates remained steady. But in the exclusively rural areas, incomes could not be supplemented by work in a factory. The peasant had to make a break in search of industrial employment in a big city. Once uprooted, the decision to proceed to the United States followed. Thus, when the panic of 1873 abruptly created economic stagnation in the United States, emigration from Germany fell precipitously, until it reached its nadir in the period from 1877 - 1879. Thereafter, as the American economy recovered, so — predictably — did emigration from Germany.

In the last crest of German emigration, 1882, and for years thereafter, industrial growth in Germany seems to have worked as a major stimulant to emigration. The time when emigration to the United States was highest was also the time when Germany imported the largest number of emigrants from other European countries to replenish the labor force depleted by those who had left for America. Bismarck probably put his finger squarely on the pulse of the matter when he said: "The volume of emigration is a most exact index of our growing well-being; the better it goes for us, the higher the volume of emigration. . . . There are two kinds of emigrants . . . those who emigrate because they *still* have money enough, . . . and those who emigrate because they *now* have money enough."[26]

Imperial Germany never promulgated laws to sanction the concept of emigration but the Reichstag (Parliament) produced one. In 1878 the German Progressive party, in a bill drafted by Friedrich Kapp, sponsored legislation to recognize the right of German citizens to emigrate. This was the same Kapp who, years earlier, had served as a leader of the New York German-American Society and as a member of the New York Immigration Commission. Having returned to Germany, he was serving as a member of the Reichstag in 1878. Parenthetically, it might be recalled that this politically liberal *Rückwanderer* ("returning emigrant") had a son named Wolfgang who led the reactionary Kapp putsch against the Weimar German Government in 1920. The Kapp bill was domestically oriented. It had no grandiose provisions for the settlement of Germans in colonies or for establishing states in America as had been attempted earlier. It only provided that emigration was the constitutional right of German citizens.[27] Though the Reichstag passed it, Bismarck refused to implement the bill.

With such views prevailing in Germany, it is not surprising that these latter-day immigrants held political views different from those who had come previously. The late arrivals were much less critical of the German government than, let us say, their 1848 countrymen. Likewise, they seldom espoused the cause of political liberalism, whether it pertained to Germany or America. Earlier, too, the German-American press had been bitterly critical of the German government and participated vociferously in American politics. In later years this criticism was muted. In the 1880s and thereafter, the German-American press tried only to reflect the views of its constituency. With this in mind, it reported with pride on the events of the Franco-Prussian War and hailed the success of Bismarck's policies in Germany.[28] That Bismarck never enacted the proposals fought for by the Forty-eighters no longer seemed to matter.

In proportion as Germany was successful, it was characteristic for the Germans of America to glory in the achievements of the new German Empire. News of its success spread, in part because many of the new editors and intellectuals were imported from Germany. Also, American physicians, scientists, and artists were drawn to study in the distinguished universities of Germany to augment their professional training. In the process, the whole tone of German-American relations improved. Contrary to the hopes of many a staunch German-American that the German tradition and its language in America would be strengthened through such interchanges, the new atmosphere of mutual respect accelerated the process of Americanization among the young. No longer were the Germans in America a beleaguered ethnic group. Always numerically smaller than the English-Yankee coalition of Americans, the Germans steadily and readily merged into the preexisting English-language culture.

In concluding this chapter on German emigration to the United States, it might be well to note that between 1847 and 1910, fully 90 percent of all the Germans who emigrated overseas chose to settle in the United States.[29] The closest competitor in attracting them was Canada, which drew an annual average of less than 4 percent, with the remaining 6 percent going to various other countries around the globe. Toward the end of the nineteenth century, German politicians and a substantial segment of the public began to view German emigration with an eye toward German colonization.[30] They observed that the only place where a chance existed for establishing a "*Deutschtum* overseas" was in the United States. But the Germans in America by the end of the century had traveled far in the direction of assimilation. As a result, they no longer paid much attention to pockets of *Deutschtum* in the middle northern states. Whenever the notion of building an overseas *Deutschtum* was mentioned in the first decade of the twentieth century, German-Americans generally responded with a yawn. When it was orchestrated by German imperialists during World War I and in the 1930s, the Germans in America recognized it for what it was, rejected it, and sped ever more swiftly (if not entirely willingly) along the road to assimilation. This facet of German-American history shall be the subject matter of Chapters 14 and 15.

CHAPTER 7

The Post - Civil War Period: States, Railroads, and Industries Solicit Immigrants

DURING COLONIAL TIMES, THE GERMANS CAME TO AMERICA LARGELY for religious reasons. In the middle of the nineteenth century, however, political reasons supplanted religion as the chief cause for German immigration, especially for the freethinking political refugees of 1848. After the Civil War and for the remainder of the nineteenth century, Germans came because they were recruited! For the first time since the days of William Penn, German immigrants were not only welcome but were actually invited. Under recruitment is subsumed propaganda by governments as well as campaigns by railroads and by industry. Also there was the romantic appeal of a new land with a widely publicized frontier myth. It included the glowing letters sent back by relatives and friends who had done well in the New World.

To a certain extent, the solicitation of German immigrants intensified in proportion as the German nation acquired respect abroad. In this regard, the unification of Germany in 1871 dispelled the mockery of Germany's *Kleinstaaterei* ("tiny little states"), and Germans in the United States erupted in celebration. Chicago's Germans, for example, spent $200,000 commemorating Germany's achievement. One float bore a gigantic Arminius flanked by Teutonic riders and soldiers.[1] In Columbus, Ohio, the German peace festival of May 1, 1871, depicted "Peaceful Germania" and the notable contributions of Germans like Kepler, Dürer, and Gutenberg. The city's German paper, the *Westbote*, claimed that the Franco-Prussian War had improved the status of German-Americans by 50 percent, "so that one can have a little hope that before long the name Dutchman may be changed into German."[2]

Mutual respect led to a higher regard for the German immigrant. Even the tough-talking Forty-eighters mellowed as a result of the new prestige Germans enjoyed in the world, and soon they turned to

85

reminiscing. They responded to appeals from Germany to contribute funds for erecting a monument in the old homeland to martyrs of the 1848 revolution.[3] As a different way of showing their pride, the Forty-eighters of Davenport founded the society of *Schleswig-Holstein Kampfgenossen* and erected a monument in their American hometown in Iowa.[4]

The twenty-fifth anniversary of the 1848 revolutions was nostalgically celebrated in a number of American cities in 1873. In Cincinnati, Friedrich Hassaurek reviewed the history of the Forty-eighters, characterizing them as romantic, youthful dreamers who entertained impracticable ideals. In Chicago, the once belligerent Forty-eighters displayed the flag of the new German Empire alongside their symbolic black-red-gold colors which had become famous as the banner of the 1848 revolutions and a battle cry for democracy.[5] The Cincinnati Forty-eighters celebrated their fiftieth anniversary in 1898 by noting that in their opinion the Wilhelminian Empire had achieved the goals for which they had once fought so vigorously.[6]

More than attitudes changed. For one thing, the flow of money between Germany and America quickened. During the Franco-Prussian War, for example, the Germans in America responded generously to a campaign for contributions to widows and orphans. Chicago's Germans collected $35,000. In St. Louis, they pledged $50,000, and in New York they accumulated $64,000 for the cause.[7] This relief work was administered through a national organization which held a convention of Patriotic Relief Societies at Chicago in 1871. There German-Americans designated Friedrich Kapp, the former head of the New York State Immigration Board, to become their liaison in Berlin. More than a million and a half dollars were forwarded to the Fatherland from German organizations in the United States.[8]

In reporting about this American aid that flowed into the German economy, Kapp dwells on the fact that the Germans who had emigrated to the United States were, on the whole, far better off financially than those who had chosen to remain behind. Yet Kapp expressed the hope that in the future, prospective German emigrants would consider settling in the less populated northeast provinces of the German Empire, such as Pomerania and Posen, rather than migrating across the ocean to the United States. As the figures given in the previous chapter illustrate, Kapp's admonition was never more than a wish. Emigration to the United States continued until it reached its maximum annual flow of over 250,000 in the year 1882.

Another kind of financial flow from America to Germany occurred in the form of the "prepaid" ticket. After 1850, increasing numbers of Germans came to the United States because friends or relatives sent them steamship tickets. There is some indication that German shipping firms wooed this business by advertising their services in German-American communities. Apparently the "prepaid" business was particularly active after the conclusion of the Civil War. Without it, reportedly, the majority of shipping firms in Bremen would have run annual deficits.[9]

To be sure, money did not flow in one direction only. By way of the Christian churches in America and their affiliates for the propagation of the faith, substantial sums found their way from Germany and Austria into the American economy. Two well-known mission societies were founded to advance missionary activities in North America. First, there was the *Leopoldinen Stiftung* ("Leopoldine Foundation"), which was initiated in Austria in 1829 as a result of a personal visit to Vienna in 1827 by Frederic Rese, vicar general for the bishop of Cincinnati. Secondly, there was the *Ludwig Missionsverein* ("King Louis Mission Society"), which was founded in Bavaria in 1838 at the suggestion of Rese, now bishop of Detroit. Both organizations sent financial support to the fledgling American Catholic Church.[10] The funds were used for the erection of churches, rectories, and charitable institutions as well as for the financing of seminaries and schools. As the annual reports to the missionary societies show, the German priests succeeded in making the cash flow from Germany and Austria to the United States. Bavaria's *Ludwig Verein* sent an estimated 3,339,343 marks to the American Catholic Church, much of it from the coffers of the royal family.[11]

To a lesser extent and in a more indirect fashion, capital funds also flowed into the United States economy by way of such organizations as *Der St. Raphaelsverein zum Schütze katholischer deutscher Auswanderer.*[12] Although the *St. Raphaelsverein* focused on helping the emigrant before sailing, during his voyage, and at the ports of debarkation, most of the financial support for these activities came not from America but from contributors in the Catholic dioceses of Germany.[13] In 1883, the *St. Raphaelsverein* acquired a base in

America under the tutelage of Bishop Wigger of Newark. In that year, Peter Paul Cahensly (whose program will be discussed in detail in the chapter on religion) attended the convention of the German-American Catholic *Central Verein* and aroused American church leaders to respond to the needs of German immigrants. Not until 1887, however, did the German-American clergy actively support the American branch of the *St. Raphaelsverein*. Thereafter they raised money, established the Leo House in New York (named in honor of Pope Leo XIII), and greatly aided German immigrants right up to the World War I period.[14]

Protestant groups were not as a rule supported by the established churches of Germany. Usually they departed the Fatherland under protest and therefore were hardly in a position to request financial help from their mother churches. In addition, Protestant church leaders who sought funds in Germany were often plagued by the popular response, "das reiche Amerika könne sich selbst helfen" ("let rich America take care of itself").

The money they did raise usually came from the established Lutheran centers of Ohio, Missouri, Indiana, and Michigan, rather than from anywhere in the old homeland. Exceptions were the agencies for pastoral care in the embarkation centers of Bremen and Hamburg as well as at reception centers in New York. Likewise, there were scattered Protestant communities and societies which waxed and waned throughout the nineteenth century, but these seldom contributed much money, concentrating their resources instead on furnishing pastoral services. The one Prostestant churchman who, more than any other, contributed to the fledging German Lutheran Church in America was Johann Konrad W. Löhe of Neuendettelsau, Bavaria. Löhe not only saw to it that German immigrants in America benefited from the church's ministry, but also organized mission societies, some of which raised money in Germany to be given as aid to the German Protestant Church in America.[15]

Capital from Germany was also available in the United States in more traditional ways. Arriving immigrants were certainly not all destitute. Some had sizable savings which they brought along, particularly those who left for religious reasons rather than in order to improve their economic opportunities. In fact, government officials in Germany protested that emigration would eventually deplete the country of its economically stable middle class, especially middle-class farmers. In a few local districts, officials said it was the wealthy rather than the poor who were emigrating.[16]

As one example of wealthy German immigrants, we have the reports of Carl B. Schmidt, the former Commissioner of Immigration for several railroads, who recounts his work among the affluent Mennonites of West Prussia, many of whom were settling in the United States.[17] Schmidt tells of a German Mennonite bishop then living in Russia who entrusted him with 80,000 rubles ($56,000) in the form of a draft written on a Hamburg bank, with the request that he invest the sum in land-grant bonds of the Atchison, Topeka, and Santa Fe Railroad Company.[18] By 1883 at least 15,000 Mennonites from Prussia and Russia had settled on the lands of the Santa Fe Road, and they were joined by additional well-to-do Mennonite immigrants from southern Germany and Switzerland.

However, exact statistics on the outflow of capital from Germany to America due to emigration are difficult to obtain. Several sources indicate that between 1835 and 1839 German emigrants took twenty-five million talers (a taler was worth 71 cents in 1900) out of the country. Between the years 1832 and 1855, the total is put at 200 million talers. Calculating the outflow on an annual basis, German officials in 1860 reckoned that between twenty and thirty million talers left the country each year in the pockets of emigrants, most of whom went to America. Two decades later in 1881, the 200,000 German emigrants passing through the port of Bremerhaven that year alone officially declared more than thirty million marks for currency export.[19] While these figures are not definitive, they make one point clear: the popular belief that the typical German immigrant was a pauper is a misconception.

Capital exchange took place between Germany and America in still other ways. As noted in the chapter on the Civil War, the Union government sold stocks on the Frankfurt exchange, both during the war and thereafter, thus raising some of the capital needed for America's developing industry during and after hostilities.[20] Occasionally a more spectacular capitalization project found backing in Germany as when Henry Villard (born Heinrich Hilgard in Germany) refinanced the bankrupt Northern Pacific Railroad in the early 1880s. Through personal contacts with Georg Siemens of *Die Deutsche Bank*, Villard was able to secure financial assistance from the latter bank for the construction of the cash-hungry Northern Pacific line.[21]

The period immediately following the Civil War was also the time when middle western states officially lured north European immigrants to America. Even prior to the war, some state legislatures had passed laws establishing commissions of immigration. Each had a budget with which to pay commissioners and agents who maintained offices in various U.S. ports as well as in the European countries.

In 1894, the Michigan legislature took steps to promote immigration by establishing an agent and a German-language booklet with a press run of 7,000 copies. As a result, the American consul in Stuttgart, Charles L. Fleischman, planned to purchase $600,000 worth of Michigan farmland for resale to German immigrants. The project fell through, but the immigrants came anyway, infusing at least $150,000 into the state's economy.[22]

Many other states had their commissioners as well. Each competed with neighboring states to lure immigrants. Interestingly, the Germans were always a prime target. When Wisconsin established its office of commissioner of immigration in 1852, the first appointee was a Dutchman, Gysbert Van Steenwyck, who immediately employed as his assistants, one Norwegian, two Germans, and an Englishman. With $1,250 to spend on publications, Van Steenwyck issued pamphlets to describe opportunities for the settler in Wisconsin. Of these, 20,000 copies were printed in German, 5,000 in Norwegian and 4,000 in the Dutch language.[23]

Minnesota created its Board of Immigration in 1867. Commissioner Eugene Burnand tried hard to secure German immigrants for the state, but at this time made little effort to induce Scandinavians to make their homes in Minnesota.[24] Iowa was a relative latecomer to the business of luring immigrants to its lands. But in 1870, as a result of a bill introduced by Mathias J. Rohlfs, a native of Germany, Iowa did establish a Board of Immigration patterned on the Wisconsin model. Agents were sent directly to Europe, equipped with pamphlets, maps, and cash for advertisements.[25] Iowa felt compelled to get into the act, reportedly because large windfalls of capital were bypassing the state when well-to-do immigrants settled in neighboring states. A report for the year 1856 shows that the passengers listing Wisconsin as their destination(10,-457 in all), brought cash with them amounting to more than$1,045,-600. The Iowa-bound tallied only 1,855 persons with a mere $248,-300 in their pockets.[26]

In addition to these states, Nebraska, Kansas, Missouri, Oregon, and eventually Montana operated immigration commissions. Dakota Territory also established an office in March, 1885. Political leaders of the territory proposed the idea of having an "emigrant agent" much earlier, but a fuctioning state bureau of immigration did not come into being until January, 1871. The particular European immigrants who commanded most of the attention of Dakota Territory officials were the Russian-Germans, especially those of the Mennonite faith. For a time during the early 1870s, provisions were being made to ticket the Russian-Germans for direct transportation from Odessa on the Black Sea to Yankton in Dakota Territory.[27]

Although efforts to attract immigrants were characteristic of the states in the Middle West, the South after the Civil War was not far behind.[28] Governor James L. Orr of South Carolina in 1866 appointed John A. Wagener, a native of Germany, to be the state commissioner of immigration. Wagener was successful, for, in 1880 the Germans formed the largest immigrant group within the state.[29] A few states on the eastern seaboard, Maine, for example, invited German and Swedish immigrants to settle in that state.[30] The West Coast states did not become involved in the procurement of immigrants from Europe, preferring instead to concentrate on older immigrants from states farther to the East.

While the individual states went through considerable expense to entice immigrants to their free lands, there is little evidence that anything comparable happened on the federal level. During the Civil War, however, the Union procured immigrants to relieve the labor shortage caused by demands for men at the front. In 1862 William H. Seward wrote to consular officials directing them to make known to desirable persons the attractions of the American labor market. He warned, however, that the United States Government could not offer precuniary inducements to foreigners. Nevertheless, Europeans charged that the Union promoted immigration in order to replenish its decimated armies.[31] After the Civil War the federal government retreated completely from encouraging immigration, despite efforts by state governors to induce it to return to the recruitment business.

Unfortunately no statistics are available to evaluate what was accomplished by state boards of immigration. The lack of information is even more acute when the focus is on the Germans as a specific immigrant group. As a general rule, however, the boards were successful. Furthermore, the German element was by far the largest immigrant nationality arriving in those states of the Middle West which had boards of immigration. Since the German immigrant received the largest advertising attention of the agents, and since the Middle West received the lion's share of German immigrants, it could be argued that state efforts were successful in luring Germans to settle there.

Inasmuch as the boards succeeded, we might take note of how they accomplished their tasks. Most relied heavily on the printed word. Wisconsin, for example, published 20,000 copies of its German-language pamphlet in 1882, its most active year. It also advertised in forty-two foreign newspapers, all but one in Germany. Frequently, the boards sent agents to Europe to arrange for advertising, and, not least, answered letters from prospective immigrants. The man employed to handle Minnesota's letters of inquiry claims to have answered no less than 220,000.[32]

The personal touch of the on-site immigrant agent should not be discounted. What his activities entailed can be illustrated from a report which Minnesota's Albert Wolff sent to Governor Horace Austin in 1870.[33] From Bremen, Wolff recounted how he fulfilled his duties by answering letters, advising transportation agents, and contacting shipping companies. He also made personal contacts with editors of newspapers and periodicals, "inquiring of them what my chances would be for interesting their papers in the humanistic and public minded effort to *concentrate German emigration* to Minnesota, where Germans were most likely to find healthy and congenial climate, the greatest supply of unoccupied lands and the best chances for investments in enterprises of industry."

Wolff told of visiting emigrant boarding houses, observing that in previous times the emigrants had already made up their minds where they intended to settle in America. "But no sooner had I commenced to enter into conversations with them, than I found, that whole *groups* of them, belonging sometimes to the best class, too, were perfectly free yet, to go where they pleased, having no relatives or friends in America but having been induced to emigrate by a presentiment of the horrors of the war. . . . Never before I beheld [sic] such crowds of emigrants, whose wealth shone forth in their dress and baggage. . . ."

In the days before the departure of vessels, Wolff would visit the emigrant houses in Bremen and make the rounds of some twenty-three freighter offices. In 1870, for example, there were seventy boarding houses, and by all indications the demand for housing outstripped the supply by a large number.[34] As Wolff explains, the emigrant was usually "preyed upon by blacklegs and confidence men, here called *Bauernfänger*, which means trappers of 'green horns,' from the moment he starts from his native city or village down to the day of arrival at his final abode." The counterpart to the *Bauernfänger* on the American side of the Atlantic was the runner — middle man for various services available to the immigrant, at an exorbitant price.

Turning now to the efforts of the railroads, a slightly different picture emerges. The railroads, too, needed immigrants, sometimes to do the physical work of laying the tracks but more often to occupy the lands which the railroads received from the Federal Government as a subsidy for constructing the lines. Railroads did not just want to sell their lands. They wanted products to haul, and this meant settlers.

Usually railroads had their own immigration agents. In rare circumstances, however, a state agent and a railroad agent were one and the same person. Such was the situation in Wisconsin when the Wisconsin Central Railroad Company got the Wisconsin Board of Immigration to appoint the agent of their own land department, Kent K. Kennan, to the position of Wisconsin state immigration agent in Europe.[35] The Burlington system first worked the port of Liverpool, but soon expanded to Hamburg where it established good relations with the state agent from Nebraska, Frederick Hedde. In 1871 the Burlington shipped 10,000 circulars printed in German for distribution by their representative, George Harris.[36]

Among the railroads campaigning abroad, the Northern Pacific probably used the most intensive methods of any in Germany. It established two newspapers of its own, the one in Gotha and the other in Frankfurt. Nebraska's Hedde commented that this company was "sagacious enough to know the importance of using money in the right way."[37] Two years after its incorporation in 1866, the company initiated "a Bureau of Emigration for the purpose of settlement of the lands of the Company" and proposed sending a director of the Bureau straight to Germany.[38] At the Vienna Exposition of 1873 the Northern Pacific was represented by its German agent, Colonel von Corvin, who displayed exhibits of agricultural and industrial products from Minnesota. He also erected a huge map of the world positioning the lines of the Northern Pacific and pinpointing the city of Bismarck, North Dakota.

Bismarck, in fact, got its name because of a promotional stunt perpetrated by the Northern Pacific to inveigle German immigrants and investors of capital to seriously consider the prospects of North Dakota. When the city first sprang up in 1872, it was given the name of Edwinton in honor of a railroad engineer, Edwin F. Johnson. One year later, Samuel Wilkinson, secretary of the Railroad, proposed changing the name to Bismarck with the hope that the International Trade Exposition in Vienna and press coverage in Berlin would draw the attention of Germans to North Dakota.[39] For a time promoters believed the Iron Chancellor himself could be persuaded to dedicate the new city, but he declined. However, immigrants from Germany and from German-speaking Russia got the message and streamed into North Dakota to take advantage of the land offered by the Northern Pacific. It totaled 10.5 million acres, 22 percent of all the land in the entire state. The Germans are still the largest ethnic group in North Dakota. As late as 1920, the census reports show that the German-born numbered 23 percent of the state's total population, a percentage that rises considerably when the German-speaking, but Russian-born, immigrants are included.

The railroads employed various techniques to induce immigrants to establish farms on their lands. A common one was the rate reduction. In some cases the full fare applied, but if the settler purchased land, then the entire fare was credited to the purchase. Often free tickets were available for families of settlers when they took up residence on property purchased from the railroad. The Northern Pacific even allowed a reduction of the regular rate for all freight shipped over its lines to the point of settlement. The St. Paul and Pacific granted reductions on both passenger and freight rates to those who would settle on its lands.[40]

Other land-merchandising devices of the railroads were the immigrant houses. They were maintained by the railroads at town sites near the settlers' destinations.[41] Usually, these houses provided the immigrants with information as well as food and clothing if necessary. Importantly, they accommodated families while the men selected and bought their farms. They had their own kitchens, laundry facilities, bedding, and furniture as well as company-staffed hospitals to care for the sick and the undernourished.

During the Henry Villard ownership of the Northern Pacific, the line was especially German-oriented. In 1882 he maintained 124 active general agents plus a host of local agents of the railroad at work on the European continent, where they distributed 623,590 copies of Northern Pacific publications. In 1884 the company was advertising in sixty-eight different German newspapers. Villard's chief agent was Adam Roedelheimer, a German native and former agent for the Kansas Pacific. Under Roedelheimer, the company also developed close relations with the German immigrant societies in the United States.[42]

In addition to the official railroad agents, there were also private individuals who wrote semiofficially on behalf of the railroads. In his countless publications lauding the opportunities of the state of Minnesota, for example, Eduard Pelz, the Saxon-born German Forty-eighter, often carried advertisements for the lands of the St. Paul and Pacific Railroad. After 1870 he seems to have cooperated with the Northern Pacific in establishing a monthly journal called *Der Pfadfinder*, which bore the subtitle "A Monthly for the Evaluation of German Emigration and Immigration." The unexpressed purpose of the monthly was to promote German settlement on the lands of the Northern Pacific.[43]

From these examples it is clear that the railroads like the state immigration boards played significant roles in making the upper Midwest into a belt of German settlers.

Prior to regular steamship traffic between Germany and America in the 1850s, sailing-ship companies handled emigration through the ports of Bremen and Hamburg. But much traffic also passed through foreign ports in Holland, France, and England. In hopes of winning more freight markets away from foreign competitors, especially the Americans and the English, German sailing firms turned to agents for a steady supply of German emigrants. The agents formed independent companies which signed contracts with the shippers for a specific number of passengers to embark on a certain date. Since the middlemen were at liberty to charge emigrants what the market would bear, business was profitable and, between 1830 and 1850, a large number of agencies sprang into existence. Due to the abuses they practiced, however, the senates of both Bremen and Hamburg passed strict laws regulating their rates and commissions with the result that many of the middlemen disappeared. When the North German Lloyd initiated regular steamer service for North Atlantic passengers, the improved service was its own advertising. Middlemen were no longer needed.[44]

Finally, a few remarks should be made about the efforts of

American manufacturers to attract German immigrants to the United States. As with the states and railroads, American industry campaigned for emigrants in Europe, sometimes in cooperation with the official state organizations. No system devised by industrial management for the importation of labor received official American sanction, however, until the Thirty-second Congress passed a bill and the president signed it on July 4, 1864.[45]

It was the labor supply crisis of the Civil War that brought American industry to seek skilled immigrants abroad. However, the main target for this phase of immigrant recruitment was the pool of skilled British workmen. Also, the main thrust of recruitment remained in the hands of private companies who enjoyed Government approval but no support. By way of organizations like the American Emigrant Company, founded in Connecticut in 1863, the work of soliciting immigrants was successful in England. However, in Germany, at least during the early 1870s, agents acting for American manufacturers were summarily evicted.[46]

Soon the German press turned against emigration to America in general and against the 1864 Act to Encourage Immigration in particular. Editorials commented that now the American government was willing to sanction the swindling of German workers, which previously had been characteristic only of private companies. Subsequently, only two of the German-based emigrant journals, *Der Ansiedler im Western* of Berlin and the *Deutsche Auswanderer-Zeitung* of Bremen looked favorably on the federal law. Eventually even the latter turned negative with an article that was excerpted and quoted widely in other German papers:

The craftiest of the proposed arguments is the advance of passage money to needy emigrants — the repayment of which is to be made good by the labor of the emigrant brought over. This is just what the Brazilian emigrant agents resorted to in order to cheat the German proletariat into slavery, much the same system as the infamous coolie trade. . . .[47]

Immigration agents were regulated by the German states and arrested if they violated these regulations.[48] German societies in the United States also warned that under no circumstances should emigrants sign labor contracts before leaving Germany. When the American Civil War ended and with it the critical shortage of skilled labor, the need for industrial immigrants also ended. So did the Act to Encourage Immigration, which was repealed by Congress in

1868. In 1885 Congress passed the Foran Act, which explicitly prohibited the importation of contract labor.[49]

During the period when Congress remained neutral (1868 - 1885), American manufacturers continued to attract German immigrant labor indirectly. One of these methods was the publication in German of data available from the Treasury Department which gave details on the high wages paid for skilled workers in America. Another was exemplified by managers of the Slater Woolen Mills of New England who hired a New York agent to notify them of the approach of ships from Bremen or other German ports so that they could send employment clerks directly to Castle Gardens to interview German workmen as soon as they disembarked.[50] Still another method was to work through the established state agencies, as when Wisconsin's Kennan advertised in Germany that the state offered "just as cordial and ready assistance to the mechanic bound for Milwaukee as to the farmer who proposes to buy lands."[51]

Perhaps more significant than the states, railroads, or industries was the "America letter" which reinforced the desire, especially in the Ruhr and in Silesia, to follow relatives and friends to America. In due time whole districts had established links to the New World through former acquaintances. Private letters then supplanted all types of the immigrant agent.[52]

Often, employment was also arranged for the new immigrant by relatives or friends. In the event that a German immigrant arrived in New York without a job, however, a number of agencies existed to which he could turn for help. There was, for instance, the *Deutsche Gesellschaft* which maintained an office on lower Broadway. This organization quickly pinpointed employment possibilities through its many branches in such German cities as St. Louis, Chicago, Baltimore, New Orleans, and elsewhere. Likewise, there was the German Mission at Castle Garden which was managed by a Lutheran pastor, Robert Neumann, of Brooklyn. After 1873, there was also the Lutheran German immigrant house opposite Castle Garden which offered help in finding employment. Somewhat later, the Catholics provided similar services through the New York branch of the St. Raphael Society. Not much is known about the German *Arbeits-Nachweisungs-Bureau* of New York, but at least it existed. In the last two decades of the century, it appears, the distribution of immigrant laborers was handled largely by private employment agencies that dealt with industrial employers who specified which immigrant nationalities they wanted to hire.[53]

To recapitulate, there were three currents of German immigration: the colonial, when Germans came for religious and economic reasons; the 1848 period, when they came for political and economic reasons; and after the Civil War, when they came once again for economic reasons but also because they were invited, nay, recruited officially by the states and unofficially by the railroads, by industry, and by friends already in America.

CHAPTER 8

The Forces of Religion

THE GERMANS DID NOT EASILY SHED THE CUSTOMS OF THEIR Fatherland even after several generations had lived and died in America. Several factors account for this retention. Among them are the German-language press, an outlook on life that contrasted with American puritanism, the German theatrical, musical, and singing societies, the German-language schools, and, in particular, the churches. Undoubtedly the most important factor in perpetuating German culture in the United States after 1880 was the church. To be sure, German-language churches would not have endured without German schools, but the majority of these schools were parochial or church schools. We see, therefore, that religion and ethnic identity were closely intertwined. Late in the nineteenth century when temperance and Sunday closing laws drew the Germans into political battles with Yankee Americans, it was as much a difference of religious opinion as of national traditions that nourished what, at first glance, seemed to be opposite cultural viewpoints.[1]

Toward the end of the nineteenth century, there was an unbelievable proliferation of German clubs — *Vereine* as they were called. Sometimes the Germans criticized each other for paying too much attention to local *Vereine* instead of uniting into national organizations to promote German interests. All too often the local societies bred factionalism in the German-American community, which led to schisms and duplication of effort. As often as not, however, these schisms had religious roots. Particularly the mutual aid and benevolent societies were not only German, but also German Catholic, German Lutheran, or perhaps German atheist. Usually the gymnastic societies or *Turnvereine* had religious characteristics. A key tenet of the North American *Turnerbund* was the propagation of a freethinker's philosophy of life.[2] The Turners espoused socialism and proselytized for the common ownership of property. As time wore on, the federated Turners toned down their missionary zeal, but they never relented in their belligerence toward the Christian churches. Temperance, prohibition, nativism, and extreme wealth were targets for their scorn, but nothing was ever more despised than *das Pfaffentum*, the organized clergy.

The following pages shall provide thumbnail sketches of the German churches as they participated in the evolution of German-American culture. From the settlement of Germantown, Pennsylvania in 1683 to the Bismarck May Laws of 1873 - 1887 (which initiated a persecution of Catholics under the banner of a *Kulturkampf*), Germans had looked to America as a refuge from religious persecution. Broadly speaking, we can present the German churches under three main headings — the pietistic sects, the Lutherans, and the Catholics. The pietistic German sects came to occupy the lands which William Penn had pledged would retain freedom of religion for all time.[3] The Lutherans, the Moravians, and the German Reformed were also numerically significant in colonial times, but with the exception of a few settlements in Pennsylvania and Maryland, Catholic Germans did not migrate to America before the revolutionary war.[4]

There are historical reasons why the pietistic sects predominated in the colonial German element. One provision of the treaty which ended the Thirty Years' War (1618 - 1648) stipulated that only three religious confessions were to be tolerated in Germany: Catholic, Lutheran, and Reformed. Sects other than these basic three were outlawed. Catholic, Lutheran, or Reformed members often had to move to a new duchy, but religious nonconformists had to emigrate. Thus the largest percentage of colonial Germans were members of dissenting sects. They rejected fixed doctrine, they were more or less dedicated to a communal way of life, and virtually all of them opposed military service.[5] By contrast, Catholics and legal Protestants found that their faith would be endangered more by emigrating abroad than by staying close to organized spiritual life at home.

After the colonial period, the smaller sects were never again numerically dominant among the incoming Germans. At the peak of German immigration in the early 1880s, roughly half of all German-Americans were Roman Catholics.[6] Since the smaller sects contributed so much to the mosaic of American life, let us turn first to a few representative groups that came from Germany.

Among the earliest were the German Baptist Brethren, also known as the Dunkards, Dunkers, or Tunkers (from the German word *tunken*, "to immerse"). The first German Baptists to arrive in America came from Krefeld in the Rhineland and settled in Germantown, Pennsylvania, in 1719, to be followed by the entire congregation in 1729. As the German Baptist Brethren expanded into other parts of the United States and Canada, some were converted to a belief in celibacy. Led by Johann Conrad Beissel, this offshoot founded the celibate German community at Ephrata, Pennsylvania, in 1732. A well-known tourist attraction today, the original cloisters of Ephrata disbanded in 1830. Another branch, the Seven Day German Baptists, maintains churches and a publishing house at New Enterprise, Pennsylvania. In 1881 a further split sent the Old Order Dunkers to establish their church in Covington, Ohio, while the more progressive Brethren Church moved on to Winona Lake, Indiana, founding Ashland College en route. The main body, the Conservative Dunkards, today has central offices in Elgin, Illinois.

Like the German Baptists at Ephrata, the Rappists believed in communal ownership of property, communal work, and, after 1807, celibacy. The society of Rappists was founded by Johann Georg Rapp, born in Württemberg in 1757, who brought his group to the United States in 1803, purchased land near Pittsburgh, and named it Harmony.[7] By 1815 the colony had moved from Pennsylvania to southern Indiana, where a new settlement called *Harmonie* was established. The 9,000-acre townsite in Pennsylvania was sold for $100,000 to a Mr. Ziegler in 1815. To New Harmony, located on the Wabash River near the Indiana-Illinois line, came an influx of new German immigrants. Germans not belonging to the society also settled nearby to take advantage of the many luxuries and conveniences which the society's managers made available. After a few years, the members not only carried considerable weight in politics but on occasion made loans to the state government of Indiana.

But in 1824 it was determined that New Harmony on the Wabash was to be sold. The total land amounted to 20,000 acres, and an earlier court suit had placed an appraised value of $368,690 on the property.[8] After a few months, the communist philanthropist from Scotland, Robert Owen, purchased the entire package for the asking price of $150,000. The Harmony Society moved back to Pennsylvania, where a third settlement was established at Economy, a townsite downstream from Pittsburgh. Applications for membership poured in from would-be members who were motivated by the alleged existence of great wealth. Others sought to learn a valuable trade or to gain social prestige from association with the society's factories and schools.

When Father Rapp died in 1847, the church fund was estimated to contain a half million dollars in gold and silver, all of it hidden in Rapp's house. Thereafter the society declined from one of communal work and ownership to one of corporate investments. For the balance of the century, the Harmonists pioneered in oil, built pipelines, and constructed railroads. Provisions restricting use of the wealth to religious purposes were ignored. In spite of stipulations that prohibited the funds from being inherited, "except by the state of Pennsylvania as an aid in the payment of her heavy debt," the entire common holdings were converted to the property of individuals by a court decision of 1916.[9] Today, the very name of the society has been expunged: Economy is now known as Ambridge, an abbreviation for the American Bridge Company which bought the lands and built the world's largest structural steel plant on the site.

There were other nonconformist Germans who came to the United States to establish communistic societies called by some "small oases of cooperation in a wide desert of competition." In 1817, some 300 separatists emigrated from Württemberg, Baden, and Bavaria to Tuscarawas County, Ohio, where they founded the communal town named Zoar, in honor of the biblical city to which Lot fled when the cities of the plain were destroyed. Like the Zoar in Genesis, the little Ohio town was intended as a refuge from the evils of the world.[10] Under their leader, Joseph M. Bäumeler (mispronounced Bimeler by the local citizens, hence the name Bimelers for the society), the community was financially successful and acquired new members, although the total never exceeded 500. A charge brought by the state that Bäumeler could not retain the property in his own name was rejected by the U. S. Supreme Court in 1852. It declared that "Bäumeler's holding of property was not only *not* fraudulent, but above reproach."[11] Less than one year later, however, Bäumeler died, and, while his will assigned all property to the society, disintegration set in immediately. The mills and furnaces were first mismanaged, then abandoned. In response to a petition by the members in 1884, the village of Zoar was dissolved and the land incorporated by the local county.

Still another example of a German-American communistic society rooted in religious mysticism was the Amana Society of Iowa. Situated on the Iowa River twenty miles south of Cedar Rapids, the community originated when 800 members of a pietistic sect left Germany under the leadership of Christian Metz in 1842 and settled in Ebenezer, New York. In 1855, the Community of True Inspiration, as the colony was officially known, moved west to Amana, Iowa.[12] By 1858 the society owned about 26,000 acres of land. Legally incorporated in 1859, the membership reached 2,000 by 1900 when a nonmember brought suit charging that the society exceeded its franchise in holding property. In 1906 the state supreme court held in favor of the community.[13] The county auditor in 1908 assessed the property at $1,843,000, demonstrating the extent of the financial success of these religious communities. Communally held property remained in force until 1932 when the society's assets of over $2,000,000 were divided into common stocks and distributed to the members. While the German flavor and German language of their forbears remain alive today, private property is the rule, and even the famous Amana Refrigeration Company no longer belongs to the community.

Amana is not to be confused with Amish. The Amish originated as a sect of the Mennonite Church, and in North America they are formally known as Old Order Amish Mennonites, numbering at least 50,000. The Amish trace their heritage to Jakob Ammann, a Mennonite bishop of Bern, Switzerland, who separated from his parent church in a controversy over *Meidung*, a form of severe excommunication meted out to individuals who offend against the society's codes.[14] Persecuted in Europe, the Amish began migrating to the New World in 1728. At first they lived on fertile farmlands in Pennsylvania, then expanded to Ohio, Illinois, Iowa, and of late to Wisconsin, Minnesota, and Canada. Today the Amish Church exists only in North America and, despite being marooned on an English-language "sea," the members continue to use High German in their religious services and a dialect of German in family speech. Virtually all of them also know English.

Known as the Plain People, the Amish divorce themselves from the mainstream of modern American life. They dress in the tradition of their forefathers, and occupy homes without mirrors, radios, telephones, or electric lights. Forbidden to own automobiles, they travel by horsedrawn vehicles and resist the social changes which modern conveniences have brought to American society. Education, too, centers on the practical, and as a rule, is limited to their own schools. In 1871, the U. S. Supreme Court decided, in a suit brought against the Amish by the state of Wisconsin, that the members were exempt from compulsory public school attendance laws, because their way of life *is*, in all practical respects, their religion. Compelling them to attend public schools would be tantamount to denying them freedom of religion.[15]

Although the Amish are known as Old Order Mennonites, the name Mennonite comes from Menno Simons, a Roman Catholic priest born in Holland about 1496. Converted to the Anabaptist movement, he preached personal sanctity without the dogmatism and violence of the original Anabaptists. Although the sect developed mainly in north Germany, especially near Lübeck and Hamburg, the strong leadership of Menno Simons eventually caused all Anabaptists to be known as Mennonites.[16]

Mennonites emigrated to the United States in five major periods: (1) to Pennsylvania before the revolutionary war; (2) to Ohio, Indiana, Illinois, and Iowa after the Napoleonic wars; (3) to the prairie states of North and South Dakota, Nebraska, Minnesota, Kansas, and Manitoba, Canada, during the last three decades of the nineteenth century, when at least 20,000 migrated from South Russia to avoid military conscription; (4) to the western Canadian provinces after World War I, when another 20,000 arrived from South Russia; and (5) to Canada, the United States, and South America after World War II, when about 15,000 left Russia, Prussia, and Pomerania. While there are at least 300,000 members of the Mennonite Churches in the United States, they are widely fragmented, some as a result of controversy over use of the German language in their religious services. To many, English means the language of the world.[17] For these Mennonites, the German language was not only the vehicle of worship but the means of keeping Mennonite life intimately associated with religion.

In the case of the Hutterian Brethren or Hutterites, a different set of circumstances prevails. Anabaptist in origin, the Hutterites do not employ the term Mennonite, but take their name from Jakob Hutter of Austerlitz, who led their congregation during the Reformation and died in 1536.[18] For more than a century, the Hutterites lived in a German-language enclave in the midst of slavic Moravia. During the late eighteenth century the Hutterites accepted the invitation of Czarina Catherine the Great (1762 - 1796) to settle in Russia, where they sojourned for approximately a century until 1874. At that time the Russian government made the Russian language mandatory for all schools and made military service compulsory. As a result, all of the Hutterite colonies left to settle, first in Dakota territory, and later also in Canada. Today there are at least 17,000 members in North America.

To this day the Hutterites maintain their German language, employing a Tirolean dialect for everyday purposes and High German in school and in services. They also practice *Gemeinsinn* ("devotion to the common good"). During and immediately after World War I, the Hutterites suffered persecution from American neighbors who resented their use of the German language. Concomitantly, the federal government indiscriminately drafted conscientious objectors. As a result, a majority of the communities left southeastern South Dakota and settled in Manitoba, Canada.[19] Many have since moved back. At present, fully two thirds of the Hutterite colonies in the United States lie east and north of the Missouri River. South Dakota remains the North American home of the Hutterites. Here, in 1874, with an original population of 443, they established their first settlement, Old Bon Homme. In 1935 the South Dakota Legislature passed the Communal Corporation Act which encouraged the colonies to incorporate their farmlands as a religious community. Seven of South Dakota's newer colonies represent reentrants from Canada, whereas others are the offspring of older colonies in South Dakota.[20]

The Hutterites maintain their own German-language instruction for children of public-school age. Pupils attend classes in the community schoolhouse during the morning before nine and after three-thirty in the afternoon. They learn Hutterite history, religion, and German before and after hours. During the main part of the school-day, a certified teacher employed by the district comes into the school for regular instruction in compliance with compulsory school attendance laws. After age fifteen, pupils serve as apprentices to learn a trade within the community. In South Dakota, no Hutterite children attend schools with children from outside the community. In all cases, public-school boards provide for the education of colony children on colony property. In 1968, only five out of the twenty-seven schools in Hutterite colonies of South Dakota were parochial schools supported exclusively by a colony. The remaining received tax money to pay expenses, often in the form of a district returning to the colony all of the revenue collected from it for education.[21]

In spite of the interesting character of the German-language sects, the vast majority of German immigrants have been members of the more traditional Protestant and the Catholic churches.[22] There was a German Baptist Church, a German Presbyterian Church, and, especially worthy of note, the Moravian Church, which had German origins. Today there are two Moravian bodies, one located in Bethlehem, Pennsylvania, and the other at Winston-Salem, North Carolina.[23] The German Reformed Church remained strictly German during the nineteenth century in America. Originating with the Swiss reformers, Huldreich Zwingli, John Calvin, and others, the Reformed Church had deep roots in the Palatinate, and because these were the Germans who came to colonial America, the German Reformed Church was a strong force in the United States ever since the first synod was formed in 1793.[24] A national synod of the German Reformed Church came into being in 1863. It was this church that established the missionary organization known as *Deutscher Evangelischer Kirchenverein des Westens* (German Evangelical Church Syndicate of the West) in 1840. After 1877 the church began using the name German Evangelical Synod of North America, by which it was known until 1925, when the word "German" was dropped.[25]

The German Methodists owe their existence in America to the great partriarch William Nast, a descendant from a long line of Swabian pastors of the Lutheran Church in Würtemberg.[26] Initially, Methodism was extended to German immigrants in the United States by the Methodist Episcopal Church. When Nast arrived in the United States after seminary training in Germany, he taught German at West Point and at Kenyon College in Ohio before being appointed a Methodist German missionary in Cincinnati in 1835. By leaps and bounds, the German Methodist Church grew after the Civil War into a church with 138 churches, 200 Sunday schools, 165 circuit riders, and over 20,000 members. Not until 1924 did the Methodist church take steps to phase out its German wing of the church.

The German Lutherans in the United States date from colonial times when the Salzburgers settled in Georgia and when Pastor Heinrich Mühlenberg established the first Lutheran Synod of America in Pennsylvania. Suborganizations of these early German Lutherans were at work in Ohio and Tennessee since 1812. By 1900 the largest of the Lutheran general bodies was the Synodical Conference, popularly called the Missourians, which dates from 1838. In that year, some 800 Saxon Lutherans, *Alt-Lutheraner* as they were called, chose to leave their native land rather than combine with other Protestant sects (Lutherans and Reformed churchmen) into one state church. They departed from Bremerhaven in five chartered ships, one of which was lost at sea. Traveling via New Orleans and the Mississippi to Missouri, they purchased land in Perry County. Thus, once again in 1838, America became the land of refuge for Germans in search of religious liberty.[27]

At a Chicago meeting in April, 1847, the Lutherans of the Midwest united into the German Evangelical Lutheran Synod of Missouri, Ohio and Other States. In this achievement the great leader, Carl Walther, was aided by the Reverend Frederick Wyneken of Indiana and the Reverend Wilhelm Sihler of Ohio. Subsequently the Missouri Synod expanded, spreading into Wisconsin, Michigan, and later Minnesota and Iowa. As time passed, it also spread to California, New Orleans, Texas, and eventually throughout the United States.[28] Everywhere the church went, it developed a progressive program which usually included German-language parochial schools.

By the outbreak of World War I, German Lutherans of the mid-nineteenth century were federated in the Synodical Conference.[29] Other German Lutheran churches at the time were the Joint Synod of Ohio, the Buffalo Synod, and the Iowa Synod. For the most part, German Lutherans in the eastern United States were Americanized by World War I. Not so in the Middle West. Predictably, the Midwest German Lutherans were sympathetic to the German cause between 1914 and 1917. The Missouri Synod vigorously denounced America's arms trade and voiced the conviction that "anything that touches moral issues is within the sphere of the church."[30] In turn, the Lutherans of German extraction were vilified by superpatriotic Americans. There were charges that the German-Lutheran churches were hotbeds of treason, were harboring enemy agents, and were loyal to the kaiser. German-language church services were disrupted and pastors threatened. Major newspapers like the *New York Times* and the *St. Louis Globe* urged them to drop German from their worship and from the curriculum in their parochial schools.

As a result, not just the Germans, but all of the foreign-heritage

Lutherans became convinced that German and other languages should be replaced by English in both worship and work. Not that German had always been preferred to English. In fact, the Missouri Synod witnessed considerable controversy over this matter almost from its inception in the late 1830s. German was always the language for conventions and official proceedings, but provisions were made for those who knew only English.[31] Lutheran leaders in the nineteenth century were ambivalent about the desirability of maintaining German, because a century earlier, the Pennsylvania German Lutherans had lost the second generation by not abandoning German in worship when the young adopted English in their daily speech.[32] The Missouri Synod's Statistical Yearbook reports that services conducted in German had dropped from 62 percent in 1919 to 46 percent in 1926. Ten years after the close of World War I, the language question ceased to be an issue in synodical discussions.

The story of German Catholicism in the United States parallels that of German Lutheranism.[33] The difference is that German Catholic immigration in the nineteenth century coincided with the influx of Irish Catholics.

The Irish furnished the clergy for the Catholic Church in the United States. The Irish were urban and skilled in the art of politics, whereas the Germans were more rural and ill-suited by virtue of speaking a foreign language to seize the political initiative. Thus the Irish held a decided edge in maintaining an Irish hierarchy in America.

German Catholicism gained its first hierarchical toehold in the figure of John Martin Henni, who was appointed bishop of Milwaukee in 1844. In the decades that followed, Henni became the patriarch of German Catholicism by building a solid foundation for a German-American clergy in his Midwest archdiocese. During his time it became something of a policy to appoint German-born bishops and to import German-speaking priests until seminaries could be built in the United States to train German-speaking priests. The policy was developed in Milwaukee where, it was calculated, German-speaking pastors were needed to hold the German immigrant church together. Almost half of all the German-Americans in the 1880s were Roman Catholics. But as Sir Shane Leslie wrote in the 1918 *Dublin Review*, "The Germans are a pillar of the Church in America, but the Irish have always held the rooftop."[34] Of the sixty-nine American bishops in 1886, thirty-five were Irish and only fifteen were German-speaking, including those of Swiss and Austrian descent. Up to 1900, 210 bishops had been appointed in the United States. Of these, 174 were of foreign birth or parentage. Ninety-three were Irish, thirty-five French, seven Austrian, and four Swiss. Only nine were German.[35]

Understandably, then, the Midwest Germans made efforts to secure their own clergy in their own churches. In many a small town, even today, it is common to find two or more Catholic churches, often only a block or two apart. Each bears the name of a national patron saint, but among the townspeople the churches are known simply as "the German church," "the Polish church," or "the Irish church". In rural areas where only one church was a feasibility, a compromise was occasionally reached whereby the parish was called "St. Boniface," but the statues of St. Patrick and St. Boniface shared opposite but equal positions on the High Altar. The Irish resented that the Germans as well as the Polish and Italians clung to their mother tongues in America. Non-Irish clergy promoted retention of the foreign languages, as a rule, in order to create islands of Catholicism which would be isolated from contact with non-Catholics. Irish clergy had the same objectives, but, because they spoke English in an English-speaking country, they never understood the importance of a mother-tongue ministry for the non-English speaker. It may have been an exaggeration, but a priest from Albany, New York, reported in 1881 in a paper read at Liege, Belgium, that out of 25,000,000 Catholic immigrants to the United States, fully 20,000,000 had lost their Catholic faith.

Around the middle of the nineteenth century, Irish and German Catholics found a more or less common rallying point in self-defense against the nativists who hated all foreigners in general, and Catholic foreigners in particular. Allegedly Catholics were foreign by birth and by virtue of their allegiance to the Vatican. When nativism died down in the last third of the nineteenth century, Catholic immigrants were less dependent on each other. German Catholics were also appalled when certain Irish clergymen, for example, Archbishop Ireland of St. Paul, became militant prohibitionists — failing to perceive that liquor may have been a curse to the Irishman, but to the German it was a balm and a "living bread."

Tensions between these two ethnic wings of the Catholic Church in America emerged in the 1880s and eventually erupted in open conflict in the 1890s. The battleground was the so-called "German triangle of the West," the area embraced by the archepiscopal sees of Milwaukee, Cincinnati, and St. Louis. Strife began when Archbishop Henni reiterated that all priests in his diocese must be German.[36] He also petitioned Rome to appoint a German coadjutor bishop who would automatically succeed him on his death. Irish members of his clergy wrote to Cardinal Gibbons of Baltimore objecting to the Germanizing of the Catholic dioceses in Wisconsin.

While the Milwaukee commotion continued, at the other end of the triangle in St. Louis, Archbishop Peter Richard Kenrick created German, Bohemian, and Polish parishes which did not enjoy all the rights and privileges of the English-speaking parishes. Pastors were not juridical pastors. In 1884, therefore, eighty-two priests in the St. Louis diocese petitioned Rome to upgrade the succursal foreign-language parishes. The case for this petition was prepared by the Catholic German-language newspapers, especially by Father Henry Mühlsiepen, the Cologne-born editor of the *Pastoral Blatt*.[37]

When the petition was received at the Vatican, lobbyists for the Irish-American clergy reported back to their bishops comments such as these: "There is evidently a powerful German influence active in Rome. . . . The breach between the nationalities is widening every day, and if the German influence at Rome is allowed to hold sway, it will, I fear, be the entering wedge of a grave breach. . . ."[38] Bishop Gilmour of Cleveland charged that "the Germans demand absolutely that the priest and the school should be German. To keep the peace with the Germans, injustice is often done to other nationalities."[39] In the thick of this, a Milwaukee priest named Peter M. Abbelen set out for Rome with petitions from German priests in Milwaukee, St. Louis, and Cincinnati. Bishop McCloskey of Louisville rushed a note to his Roman lobbyist, "If these German prelates are allowed special legislation as Germans, great injury is likely to follow to the interests of religion. We will be looked upon as a German church in an English-speaking country."[40]

With tempers ruffled, the Catholic bishops of America poised for battle. Ominously, Bishop Gilmour prophesied that if nothing dramatic was done, then in twenty-five years it would be too late and "the Church in the Mississippi Valley would be bound hand and foot to the wheel of Germanism."[41] Through the years 1886 and 1887 the controversy continued.

Eventually arguments for relenting on the German question came from Father John Gmeiner, editor of the German weekly *Der Seebote*. In part, he wrote:

The Catholic Church is no literary club to foster peculiar linguistic tastes, nor an ethnological society to advance any particular national cause, but a divinely instituted organization to bring men of "all nations, and tribes, and peoples, and tongues," to eternal salvation. She, indeed, encourages the study of languages, as she uses other temporal means, in their relation to her God-given mission — not for the sake of the languages themselves.[42]

Gmeiner claimed that the Germans were better represented in the American hierarchy than they were in national or state legislatures. The Irish, he said, lost their original language when English was imposed upon them, yet they remained faithful to their religion. Besides, he pointed out, modern English is substantially Germanic and akin to the language spoken by the Angles and Saxons living along the Elbe River in Germany. "Let our German infidels who ignore the One True God worship their idol *Deutschtum*. To us as Catholics our German language is not an object of religious veneration."

Taking up where Gmeiner left off was the Reverend Anton H. Walburg of Cincinnati, who in 1889 wrote on the question of nationality to the German American Priests' Society.[43] Walburg argued that people can change languages just as they can change political parties. But changing does not make them better or worse Americans. One who speaks English cannot be considered a better American than one who speaks German just because English predominates in the United States. In fact, a rich mixture of languages, Walburg was convinced, would result in a richer American culture.

But Walburg startled everyone when he concluded that denationalization is demoralization.

A foreigner who loses his nationality is in danger of losing his faith and character. When the German immigrant . . . seeks to throw aside his nationality . . . the first word he learns is generally a curse, and the rowdy element in his preference to the sterling qualities of the Puritans . . . like as the Indians . . . adopted the vices rather than the virtues. . . ."[44]

Slowly the voices of reason were heard, however, as when Archbishop Ireland maintained that people had the right to practice their religion in the language of their choice: "Yes, speak the German language and teach it to your children. But permit me to add in very earnest words, whatever be your conclusion as to your own selves, see that your children learn well, and speak well, English."[45]

Out of the language controversy there arose a further complication. The philanthropist member of the Prussian Parliament and later of the *Reichstag*, Peter Paul Cahensly, who sponsored the St. Raphael Societies in Germany and in the United States to aid German immigrants, expanded his organization throughout Europe to provide for all Catholic emigrants to the United States. Representatives of the St. Raphael Societies assembled in 1890 in Lucerne, Switzerland, to suggest policy. No delegates from the American branch of the society attended. Nevertheless, the meeting generated a set of resolutions called the Lucerne Memorial, which was signed by fifty-one Catholic delegates from seven nations and presented to Pope Leo XIII. Disregarding all other signers, the American press and the Irish hierarchy charged Peter Paul Cahensly with authorship of the document.

Essentially the memorial called for the establishment of separate churches in the United States for each nationality, with priests of the same nationality as the faithful. Likewise, parochial schools were to be set up and maintained separately for each nationality with the language of each native country included in the respective curriculums. Also, Catholics were to be organized into social societies and mutual aid unions according to country of origin. Most offensive was the seventh provision, which stipulated that "Catholics of each nationality . . . have in the episcopate of the country where they immigrate, several bishops who are of the same origin."[46] Finally, the Holy See should sponsor seminaries in the mother country where priests could be trained for service in the United States.

The provisions of the memorial were published in the United States for the first time when the Associated Press released the story from, of all places, the imperial city of Berlin on May 27, 1891. The chief irritant to the Irish-American Catholic hierarchy was the proposal regarding episcopal appointments, since proportion to nationality would have divided control of the Church in America almost evenly between the Germans and the Irish. As expected, the German Catholic press in America agreed with the Cahensly proposals, whereas the public press saw it more or less as an attempt by a foreign power to mingle in internal American affairs, and the Irish hierarchy saw it as a threat to their existence.

While the matter was considerably threshed over, Cardinal Gibbons of Baltimore exhibited a level-headed approach to the problem. Through his suggestion, the Vatican wrote to Gibbons explaining that the Holy Father was willing to assist organizations such as the St. Raphael Society, but he did not find the plan opportune. On August 20 of the same year Gibbons came to Milwaukee and spoke out boldly,

Woe to him who would breed dissention among the leaders of Israel by introducing the spirit of nationalism into the camps of the Lord! Brothers we are, whatever may be our nationality, and brothers we shall remain. . . . Let us glory in the title of American citizen. We owe all our allegiance to one country, and that country is America. . . .[47]

Americanization thereafter proceeded at a rapid pace, although not without incidents in St. Louis, Buffalo, and elsewhere. Attempts were made to erect nationality parishes for the Germans in several cities but with only partial success. Meanwhile in Wisconsin, compromises on the appointment of bishops were reached when German-speaking candidates received appointments: James Schwebach of Luxembourg was appointed bishop of La Crosse, and Sebastian G. Messmer of Switzerland became bishop of Green Bay.

On the floor of the Prussian House of Representatives, Cahensly reviewed his twenty years of work with the *St. Raphaelsverein.* He stressed that the society had spent over four million marks for emigrants of all faiths at no obligation to the emigrants and with no compensation from commercial sources, states, or shipping companies. He urged the German government itself to take the initiative in drawing up emigration laws. He spoke out against having the state give money to private emigrant societies. As for his own *St. Raphaelsverein*, he rejected government help, stating that although the society

cares for 30,000 emigrants yearly, and helps all emigrants without differentiating religion, [it] is at the same time primarily directed toward Catholics. It is, for religious considerations, not in a position to accept these 30,000 RM for fear that they would not be equally distributed. We cannot fulfill the task nor accept the grant that the Reich offers.[48]

By 1910 the storm between the Irish and German Catholics in

America had all but blown over. A tone of ethnic nostalgia emanated from the lips of the Irish bishop of Peoria, Edmund M. Dunne, when he addressed the German *Central-Verein* of his district.

Most of my student companions were Germans, and I always am happy to visit German parishes because I find all there in beautiful order. I especially rejoice at the good parochial schools in German parishes. I cannot encourage you Germans enough to teach your children as much German as possible; for a German who values his language lightly, as a rule abandons his religion without thinking. Hold to your language, and I will make it a point to see that there will be instruction in German conversation in the parish schools.[49]

German Catholics in the early twentieth century were first Catholic, then American, and thereafter German. Overcoming feelings of mistrust toward the German element, the Irish-American hierarchy developed plans to induce German Catholics to come to America.[50] In St. Louis, St. Paul, Green Bay, and other cities, Irish prelates joined the St. Raphael Society and the *Central-Verein* to foster such projects. In 1910 Archbishop John J. Glennon of St. Louis founded the Catholic Colonization Society to promote similar endeavors. Behind the dream lay the belief that "man made the city but God made the country," and therefore the Church would thrive if it would build its strength on the land.

In Germany, Cahensly worked with the Catholic Colonization Society in directing "his" immigrants to its lands. In 1910, Cahensly journeyed to the United States, where he was received warmly by the hierarchy and clergy. In his report, given orally at Augsburg in 1911, Cahensly stressed that the Slavic and Italian immigrants were in the unfavorable position in America once occupied by the Germans. He recommended the same medicine, that they be given spiritual succor in their native languages — proof, perhaps, that he never advocated the German language out of a desire to advance the interests of Germany in the United States.

One of the most important structures through which the Catholic leadership in America aided the German-American Catholic was the *Central-Verein*. It was a loosely structured vehicle through which German-American Catholics could participate in church and civic functions in the United States.[51] Although several bishops called upon the *Central-Verein* to take a stand on the Cahensly issue, it persistently refused. The *Central-Verein*'s period of greatest influence came between the time it was reorganized in 1909 and

America's entry into World War I in 1917. the battles over Cahenslyism were over, and yet, according to the data compiled for the *Catholic Encyclopedia*, in 1909, there were over 2,000 Catholic congregations in which the German language was used either exclusively or in combination with English. A few years earlier, there were 2,600 German-speaking priests in the United States. Fourteen of the twenty dioceses having fifty or more German-speaking priests fell within the triangle, Ohio on the east, Minnesota on the north, and Missouri on the south. After 1910 the society exercised a strong force through its organ, the *Central-Blatt and Social Justice*, published in St. Louis. The most important personality behind the society and its journal was its director and editor, Frederick P. "Fritz" Kenkel. Born in Chicago in 1863 of Forty-eighter immigrants, he studied in Germany, became a convert to Catholicism, and eventually edited the *Central-Blatt*.[52] Until his death in 1952, Kenkel worked tirelessly, if in later years, somewhat hopelessly, for fundamental changes in the American Catholic social order.

In Cahenslyism, unlike the *Central-Verein*, native Americans pretended to see the shadow of Pan-Germanism cast diagonally across the United States. They objected to the prospect but with no great vigor until World War I brought anti-Germanism to a frenzy in America. By the time this emotionalism had spent itself in the 1920s, there was litle "German" left in the German Catholic Church in America.

CHAPTER 9

The German-American Schools

WORSHIP IN THE GERMAN LANGUAGE AND PASTORAL CARE BY GERMAN-speaking clergymen were key factors in sustaining the German segment in America. Next in importance were German-language schools. Recognizing that all too often the loss of nationality consciousness meant the loss of faith, religious leaders encouraged German-language communities as a means of postponing assimilation and perpetuating the German-speaking colony, regardless of whether new immigrants arrived from Germany or not. Without German-language schools to nourish these communities culturally, however, the spiritual work of the pastors among second generation German-Americans would have been quite limited. The main thrust of German-language education, therefore, came from men whose primary concern was the preservation of the faith, not of German culture for its own sake.[1]

Until the close of the eighteenth century, virtually all German-language schools were parochial. At that time, however, the religious denominations were not as solicitous about maintaining the German language as they were about fulfilling the age-old duty of the church to educate children. Naturally the German language was used in these schools (most of which were in Pennsylvania, Maryland, Virginia, and the Carolinas), frequently to the exclusion of English. Practically every sect had its own schools.

The attitude of the Anglo-Americans toward these schools was by and large neutral. However, in Pennsylvania, Benjamin Franklin expressed concern that his fellow citizens of German descent should also learn some English. In 1753 he wrote to Peter Collinson, an English botanist:

I am perfectly of your mind, that measures of great temper are necessary touching the Germans. . . . They begin of late, to make all their bonds and other legal instruments in their own language (though I think it ought not to be) are allowed good in courts, where the German business so increases, that there is continued need of interpreters, and I suppose in a few years, they will also be necessary in the Assembly, to tell one-half of our legislators what the other half says.[2]

One of the objectives in founding Franklin College (established in Franklin's honor in 1787)[3] at Lancaster, Pennsylvania, was to curb the tendency toward Germanization. The statesman's fears were never realized because German-language instruction was seldom available at levels higher than grade and high schools in the New World.

The chief reason why German-language colleges did not develop in pre-Revolutionary America was that sectarian leaders in colonial times emphasized the simple life, not intellectual growth. To them, advanced learning was synonymous with rationalism, which they branded as atheism. Therefore higher education was at best suspect, at worst a sure pathway to the loss of faith.[4] By the time German intellectual leaders arrived after the 1830 and 1848 revolutions, they were too late to make significant inroads on behalf of German-language instruction at institutions of higher learning in the United States. Exceptions to the rule were the many theological seminaries that conducted classes in German.

This does not mean that the Forty-eighters and other German intellectuals were not concerned about education in America. Many were arrogant about the German as compared to the American educational system. Some even believed that German culture would be the savior of American social institutions, especially the schools. Expressing their hope of founding a German educational pattern on American soil, they reiterated the slogan "Am deutschen Wesen wird dereinst die Welt genesen" ("At the hand of the German system, the world will one day recover").

Many of the sectarian German-language schools founded during the colonial period were still operating during the nineteenth century. Lutheran and some Catholic parochial schools also sprang up in the first half of the 1900s, becoming in the latter part of the 1900s the mainstay of German-language education in the United States. Extant also were secular German schools supported by nonreligious, German-American organizations, for example, the radical freethinker societies. Broadly speaking, however, all of these fell into the category of parochial schools.

In addition to these "religious" schools, German intellectuals sometimes prodded German-American communities to organize a *Schulverein*, what might be called a community school system. Though private, the society functioned as any other school board, hiring German-speaking instructors to teach their children. In areas where the German element was not numerically strong enough to initiate its own "public" school system, German teachers could be found to serve as private tutors in the home.

German intellectuals also established schools, the primary purpose of which was not German-language instruction. For example, the Round Hill School at Northampton, Massachusetts was founded in 1823 for the purpose of practicing pedagogical ideas which had been developed in Germany and Switzerland. Two of the most prominent teachers at the school were the political refugees Carl Beck (born in 1798) and Carl Follen, who were expelled for their participation in liberal reform movements in Germany. Follen later left the school to become a professor of German at Harvard.

Beck and Follen were also strong exponents of the German Turner (gymnastic) movement which became a strong impetus for general education not only in German-American communities but throughout the United States. A sharp upswing of the Turner movement resulted from the 1848 revolutions. In 1851, the new refugees organized the *Sozialistischer Turnerbund* to unify the twenty-two local societies. When the Civil War claimed the bulk of the membership, the umbrella organization dissolved. During its first decade, however, the Turners promoted causes which fitted in with their views about socialism. Whole towns were founded to serve as nuclei for their utopian ideas. Perhaps their most successful venture was at New Ulm, Minnesota, which was intended as a settlement that would preserve its German character. For well nigh a century, the city remained socially, administratively, and financially in the hands of the Turners.[5]

Liberal in the extreme, the Turners propagandized for socialism, if not outright Marxism. They shunned the mention of God, lauded the forces of reason, and advocated radical reform programs. They championed welfare legislation, tax reform, the direct election and recall of publicly elected officials, and the expanded use of referenda in deciding issues. Along with their activism in social matters went anticlericalism, antinativism, and opposition to prohibition. Through lectures, discussions, reading rooms, libraries, concerts, and the theater, they advocated intellectual rigor and their brand of continuing adult education.

In 1865, the Turners reorganized without the heavy socialistic emphasis under the title *Nord-Amerikanischer Turnerbund.* Immediately they founded the Turnlehrer-Seminar in Milwaukee to train physical education instructors for clubs and for the public schools of America.[6] Gymnastics were performed with paramilitary precision, for over 60 percent of the members had volunteered for military service on the Union side during the Civil War. During the last quarter of the nineteenth century, the Turner societies became social organizations, in which there was ample exercise for the body and a great deal of instruction and stimulation for the mind.[7]

German refugee intellectuals also introduced the Rösler von Oels School in New York, the Zionsschule in Baltimore, and in Belleville, Illinois, the innovative pedagogical school system under the guidance of Superintendent Georg Bunsen, formerly of Frankfurt. In Watertown, Wisconsin, Theodore Bernhard organized a German school which was the first system in America to offer free textbooks — long a practice in Germany.[8]

Later, other German educational practices reached America. One was the report of Horace Mann who traveled widely in Germany to study the educational system and subsequently advocated that some German principles of pedagogy be adopted in American schools. There was also Cornell University, where its president, Andrew D. White (later an ambassador to Germany) tried to combine in one institution the dual German system, which prescribed that the humanistic and the technical universities should remain separate.[9] Also significant was the founding in 1876 of Johns Hopkins University, where an effort was made to transplant the German university system to America. This model of research-oriented, graduate and professional schools which could be attended only after attainment of the bachelor's degree, was immediately adopted by Harvard University and subsequently by all American universities.[10]

The United States also inherited the kindergarten system from Germany. Usually this contribution is credited to the wife of Carl Schurz, who founded the first one in Watertown, Wisconsin, in 1855.[11] The concept of kindergarten education, however, was not initiated by Mrs. Schurz but by Friedrich W. Froebel, who in 1837 established the first one in Blankenburg, Germany. Some reports indicate that one of his students, Caroline Louisa Frankenburg, started a kindergarten in Columbus, Ohio, as early as 1838.[12]

During the latter half of the nineteenth century, the private German school in America waned as public schools developed rapidly. Thus, the insistence on German-language education switched from maintaining independent German-language schools to insisting that German be taught in the public schools and that academic subjects be taught in German. In many communities the Germans had enough votes to compel state legislatures to pass laws which permitted the teaching of basic subjects in the German language. Pennsylvania seems to have been the first to enact such a law in 1839, followed shortly by Ohio. Within the next half century, the states of Wisconsin, Minnesota, Iowa, Indiana, Maryland, Michigan and others followed suit. In most cases, however, there were limitations on the extent to which German-language instruction was permitted.

In the 1850s, the Cincinnati Public Schools recognized the absolute right of pupils to receive instruction in either German or English, thus setting a precedent for many independent school districts in the nation. The motives of schools which followed Cincinnati were not always the same. St. Louis included German in the curriculum as a means of luring German children into the mainstream of American education and hastening their assimilation.[13] With this objective, the St. Louis board provided German-language instruction in reading, writing, and speaking. However, as soon as a pupil had progressed as far as the second reader and primary geography, he was to attend classes in English. The St. Louis plan proved popular. During its heyday, children from English-speaking homes availed themselves of the opportunity to learn German while their German counterparts were learning English. So integrative was the policy that German instruction in St. Louis died out long before World War I dealt it the coup de grace.[14]

Toward the end of the nineteenth century, opposition to teaching in German gained momentum. Various states passed laws restricting the use of German in one way or another. The two most famous were the Edwards Law in Illinois, which was passed in 1889, and the Bennett Law, which was introduced into the Wisconsin Legislature in 1890. A requirement of the law was that English be taught in the schools of Wisconsin for at least sixteen weeks during the school year. Furthermore, the law provided that no educational institution in the state could be regarded as a *school* unless the subjects of reading, writing, arithmetic, and United States history were taught in English.

The impetus for the Bennett Law did not arise out of opposition to German in the public schools. It became a public issue only because William Dempster Hoard, who was elected governor in 1888, learned that in 129 German Lutheran schools of the state, pupils were receiving no instruction whatever in English. Nor were they learning English as a special subject.[15] What the governor discovered in the Lutheran schools existed in the Catholic schools as well.

By coincidence, Catholics at the time were embroiled in the Cahensly controversy and thus the Bennett Law took on intra-Catholic ramifications. Irish clergymen were only too willing to nourish the Bennett Law as a device by which to reestablish their influence over the German clergy in Wisconsin. Bishops Heiss, Katzer, and Flasch of Wisconsin strongly opposed the bill, but it was warmly endorsed by Irish clergymen, of whom Archbishop Ireland of St. Paul was one. Either by intention or by coincidence, Ireland went one step further in aiding the Bennett Law. He devised a scheme known as the Faribault Plan, according to which the Catholic Church divested itself of the administration of its parochial schools by leasing them to local school boards in cooperation with the state. Implicit in the plan as the German clergy viewed it, was a treacherous plot for doing away with German-language education in the United States.

Naturally the German Catholic press attacked the Bennett school bill and Ireland's Faribault Plan with equal vigor, one paper going so far as to claim that Archbishop Ireland was a Freemason.[16] The secular press assailed both the Catholics and the Lutherans for injecting the specter of alien preponderance into Anglo-American Society.

For the short run the controversy did what no theological doctrine could ever have done, it united the German Catholics and Lutherans in a struggle to preserve their German-language schools. The outcome was total victory for the German schools. Governor Hoard was defeated and the Bennett law repealed in the Wisconsin Legislature.[17] In the long run, however, the spirit of the law prevailed and nobody won. Archbishop Ireland was defeated in his leasing plan while the German Lutherans and Catholics gradually lost the German language in their parochial schools.

Although the German school controversy came to a head in Wisconsin around 1890, legislative maneuvers to regulate the status of German were in progress for nearly a century. The Ohio law of

1839 granted the district superintendents the right to open German schools, but only in Cincinnati were German schools required by law.[18] A subsequent Ohio law in 1870 renewed the right to existence of dual-language schools. Not until 1912 was German downgraded to the status of a subject in Ohio's schools. Colorado legalized dual-language schools in 1867, Oregon in 1872. Wisconsin legislated that every Milwaukee school which taught English as a subject in 1846 would be a public school. In 1848 dual-language schools were authorized in all German areas of the state. A Texas law of 1856 allowed schools to receive tax monies only if English was taught, at least as a subject. After 1858, in order to qualify for tax support, English was required as the language of instruction.[19] In 1874 the Michigan Supreme Court heard arguments whether German could be the language of instruction in the high schools since it was permitted in the grade schools. Massachusetts prescribed English as the only language of instruction in 1873. In Illinois, the Edwards Law of 1889 was identical to Wisconsin's Bennett Law.

Where legislatures did not get involved, city school administrators adjudicated matters. In Baltimore, grade school pupils were given German-language instruction for one third of the instructional day. Baltimore's high schools did not allow German instruction, except in art and music, where it was the only language used. In geography, history, and physics, German or English could be used interchangeably. According to an 1866 public school regulation in Indianapolis, German could be used for all subjects, including American history and geography, except for grades six to eight, where German could be used only half of the instructional time.[20] Columbus, Ohio, designated specific public schools as German schools. This was possible because the German population of that city was rigidly defined on the south side.[21]

By and large, the use of German for instruction ceased in the big city systems before 1900. In small towns of the Middle West and Texas, however, German-language instruction persisted for decades, but it ended abruptly in 1917 when the United States entered World War I. In their heyday, the German schools enjoyed a high reputation for scholarship and pedagogical competence. The German teachers usually prided themselves on the good English they spoke and taught their pupils. Often German teachers were brought in directly from abroad. But there were also institutions of higher learning for training German-speaking teachers. There was a national German Teachers Association with administrative offices in

Philadelphia. German normal schools operated in Cincinnati, St. Francis, Wisconsin, Addison, Illinois, Seward, Nebraska, Elmhurst, Illinois, and, last but not least, there was the National German-American Normal Seminary in Milwaukee.[22]

The National German-American Normal Seminary had considerable influence on German-language instruction in the United States. It was promoted and in part funded by the German Teachers Association. Opened on September 1, 1878, the institution provided a curriculum for the techniques of teaching kindergarten and primary school in the German language. By the time it disappeared in 1919, it had trained a total of 335 German-speaking teachers. All of the German teachers had the benefit of athletic training at the Milwaukee-based school of the *Nord-Amerikanischer Turnerbund.*

Perhaps the German normal schools outlived their need. By 1900 German was used less and less as a vehicle of instruction. As a subject studied by the general school population, however, German steadily increased until 1915 when fully 25 percent of all high school pupils were enrolled in German. As a result of World War I, however, this percentage plummeted virtually to zero in the fall of 1918. Only then was much thought given to the problem.

In 1901 the National German-American Alliance had been formed to promote various causes of the Germans in the United States, but few overtures were made initially on behalf of language maintenance.[23] As its convention in 1903, however, the alliance briefly took up the cudgel for German-language schools. It articulated its programs in its official publication, the *German-American Annals:* "Only through the preservation of the German language can our race in this land be preserved from entire disappearance. The principal aim should be the founding of independent parochial schools in which the language of instruction would be German, with English as a foreign language."[24] In reality, the cause was more ambitiously expounded than implemented. When World War I broke out in 1914, the energies of the German-American Alliance were diverted from fostering schools to defending the German identity. Little time remained for the school issue.[25]

As a result of the American entry into the war in 1917, laws were passed not only forbidding the use of German for instruction but also the teaching of German. Most were phrased to prohibit all non-English languages, but in Ohio, Louisiana, and others they were explicitly written to outlaw German. It was in Nebraska where the anti-German school controversy was most sharply focused during

World War I. In 1913, the Nebraska Legislature had passed the
Mockett Law, which was masterminded by the state's chapter of the
German-American Alliance. It required that every high school, city
school, or metropolitan school give instruction in the grades above
the fourth in those modern European languages which were re-
quested by the parents of at least fifty pupils. As World War I
propaganda increased, opponents pointed out that the German
language was the only one that was benefited by the act. During
1917, pressures for repeal of the Mockett Law mounted. In 1918, the
state legislature held a special session in which Governor Keith
Neville said of the law: "Such legislation is vicious, undemocratic
and un-American and its repeal will be universally endorsed by the
people of Nebraska."[26] Driven to action by popular hysteria, the
legislators obliged without a single dissenting vote.

Although the war ended in 1918, the hysteria did not. Caught up
in the mood of the times, state legislatures carried the ban on German further. Eventually, all states required the exclusive use of
English in all schools. Oklahoma, South Dakota, and West Virginia,
for example, passed laws making it unlawful to teach in any other
than the English language in any public, parochial, denominational,
or private school or institution. Some states like Oregon, Wisconsin,
Idaho, and Maine made similar laws, but exempted the teaching of a
foreign language as a subject from the proscriptions.[27]

Many new anti-German laws were passed under the guise of
patriotism and merchandised under the name of "Americanization."
States had to drop their former practice of publishing legal
notices in German papers. New Jersey required courses in community civics. South Dakota ordered all private educational institutions to give one hour of instruction each in patriotism.
Connecticut created a department of Americanization in its state
board of education. Oklahoma established an Americanization
committee. Flag laws prohibiting the German and the Communist
flags were passed in Wisconsin, Oklahoma, Arizona, Maine, and
Connecticut.[28]

Although anti-German activities continued on a wide scale after
the armistice, it was once again the state of Nebraska where the issue
of German in the schools was most sharply contested. Sentiment
against the use of German was so strong that one out of every ten
bills introduced into the Nebraska Legislature during January, 1919,
reflected the German-language concern. The bill finally enacted on

April 9, 1919, provided that "No person, individually or as a teacher, shall, in any private, denominational, parochial or public school, teach any subject to any person in any language other than the English language."[29] Furthermore, it specified that no pupil be permitted to study any foreign language until he had passed the eighth grade.

Priests and ministers, particularly of the Missouri Synod, testified that their people could not receive proper religious training unless it was in German. But in the legislature, the mood prevailed that English was the only conceivable language for a patriotic American. One representative typified the majority when he said: "If these people are Americans, let them speak our language. If they don't know it, let them learn it. If they don't like it, let them move. . . . I would be ashamed to face my boy when he returns from France . . . [if I] had to tell him that I had done nothing to crush Kaiserism in this country."[30]

In the course of time, the churches maintaining parochial schools brought suit in district court to nullify the effects of the 1919 act. When that failed, they appealed to the State Supreme Court. Attorneys for the churches argued that the law penalized parents for providing their children with supplementary instruction and that the German language was a valid academic subject. Furthermore, they contended that knowledge of the language was neither harmful to the state nor to the individual. To no avail, for the State Supreme Court of Nebraska also upheld the legality of the act.

However, the supreme court sympathized with the arguments of the church leaders that German might be taught before or after regular school hours. To prevent even this use of German, the 1921 Nebraska Legislature amended the 1919 law to make it clear that no instruction in any foreign language was to be given in schools at any time. The intent of the original law, said the amendment, was to forbid all German instruction, not merely during regular school hours.

Shortly thereafter, Robert T. Meyer, a teacher in the Zion Evangelical Congregation of Hampton, Nebraska, was found guilty of violating the statute and fined $25. In moving his case through the courts, the anti-German language law was held to be constitutional by the Nebraska Supreme Court which supported its decision with the argument that "the legislature had seen the baneful effects of permitting foreigners, who had taken residence in this country, to rear and educate their children in the language of

their native land. The result of that condition was found to be in-
imical to our own safety."[31]

From this decision, an appeal went to the United States Supreme
Court where an opinion, written by Justice James C. McReynolds,
declared the Nebraska law to be unconstitutional. On the same day,
June 4, 1923, the court decided in similar fashion in the cases of
Bartels vs. Iowa, Pohl vs. Ohio, and Bohning vs. Ohio. In the opinion of the U. S. Supreme Court, the Fourteenth Amendment
prohibited any state from denying a person life, liberty, or property
without due process. Mere knowledge of the German language
could not be regarded as harmful. Moreover, the Court said, the
right to teach and the right of parents to have their children taught
in a language other than English was within the liberties guarantéed
by the Fourteenth Amendment.[32]

But court action came too late to rescue German-language education. State laws were declared unconstitutional, but they had
already accomplished their purposes. Once Nebraska had 137
German-language schools; there were seven counties in which all
the schools offered exclusively German programs. A few opened
each class day by singing the German national anthem. Adverse
public opinion, typified by the comment, "These schools should be
closed as this is not Germany and we don't care about any more
Kaiserism being taught to the coming generation," did not change
as easily as the law did. Consequently, all foreign-language schools
were duly expurgated in the name of "public safety."[33]

It is difficult to assess what ill-effects Americans of German descent endured because of laws against the German language. One
statistic dating from January, 1921, indicates that, up to then, a total
of 17,903 individuals had been arrested on charges of pro-
Germanism because of the inadmissible use of German in public. Of
these, 5,720 were convicted and sentenced, whereas 2,924 were
released without sufficient evidence. The remaining cases, as of
January 1, 1921, had not yet come to trial.[34]

During the 1920s some parochial schools, particularly those of the
Missouri Synod, retained German instruction in their curriculums in
states where it was allowed. In 1927, the Synod operated 1,368 grade
schools with over 80,000 pupils. Of these, 555 schools having 35,000
pupils still offered German-language programs. In the subsequent
years, however, the use of German in these schools declined rapidly,
especially in states such as Nebraska, Iowa, Indiana, and Ohio,

where German had been suppressed between the years 1917 and 1923. By 1936, Missouri Synod programs in German had shrunk to 281 schools and only 17,800 pupils.[35] After 1940, German-language parochial schools amounted to a mere handful.

German continued to be the language of religious instruction in many Sunday schools well into the 1940s. Such schools were possible only where a specific church retained the use of German in religious services. Studies show that as late as the 1950s, a considerable number of parishes using German in their services kept it in Sunday schools, but that the number of these parishes had diminished in an "in-gathering fashion." That is to say, where German-speaking populations still existed, churches catering to them continued securely in their use of German, whereas the peripheral parishes were forced to drop German-language worship by 1940. The parochial schools always followed suit.[36]

German-language schools survived after World War I only where language islands existed. These were isolated enclaves where German was the principal tongue used in daily conversations by at least four-fifths of the population. The larger the island the greater was its ability to resist assimilation. If it was large, then linguistic assimilation did not occur unless efforts were made by the community leaders to bring it about. If small, then vigorous language maintenance efforts were necessary if assimilation was to be avoided.[37] As the communications media affected every part of America toward the middle of the twentieth century, the requisite size of a minority language island increased. Soon mass communication, aided by improved transportation, caused a breakdown of the rural community, rendering German-language islands obsolete.

The parochial German schools were of paramount importance in maintaining the language. By the middle of the twentieth century the Catholics and Lutherans had abandoned German completely. Only the community-conscious sectarians such as the Amish and Hutterites have succeeded in maintaining German schools, and then only because German is a tenet of their faith. Importantly, the latter use German beyond the level of primary school, for thinking, for diversified occupations, and for ideas. In other words, once the use of German was no longer an everyday occurrence among adults as well as children, it slowly died, as illustrated by what happened after grade school education among the Catholics and Lutherans.

Today bilingual schooling is once again possible as a result of the

1968 Bilingual Education Act.[38] It was designed not to reintroduce German, French, or Polish but in recognition of the right of those children to an education who are not conversant in English. The chief benefactors of the act are the Spanish-speaking citizens and some Indian and Chinese minorities. This legislation was reenforced by the United States Supreme Court when it reiterated the principle handed down with reference to the Nebraska case of 1923. Going far beyond that decision, the Supreme Court on January 21, 1974, ruled unanimously that public school systems were required by federal law not only to allow the teaching of subjects in a foreign language, but were obliged to take positive steps to help children receive an education. Merely providing the same education to all does not satisfy the law when some pupils are "effectively foreclosed from any meaningful education" by a language barrier, said the Court.[39] The decision, though reached on behalf of the Chinese children of San Francisco, was felt far beyond the city's borders.

In concluding we should be conscious of the 180 degree shift in government policy and popular attitudes. The xenophobic monster unleashed by World War I has finally been chained. In 1910 there were approximately nine million German-speaking Americans. All had been reared in homes where German was natively spoken and a large percentage had been educated in schools where German was the medium of instruction. Very few descendants of those German speakers can speak the language today. Nor do the 800,000 German-born living in the United States (as reported by the 1970 Census) significantly affect the status of German, because the new immigrants no longer form language islands. Whether the new permissiveness in regard to foreign languages will retard assimilation and with it economic equality for the foreign-tongue speaker remains to be seen. Without question some nine million German speakers were linguistically eliminated within a mere fifty years, and perhaps they benefited economically in the process. It seems unlikely that any other nationality group of equal numerical strength has ever before been so completely and so quickly absorbed in any country on the globe.

CHAPTER 10

German-American Theater and the Musical Arts

THE GERMAN-LANGUAGE THEATER IN AMERICA WAS SCARCELY KNOWN in colonial times. Its birth was delayed until approximately 1840 for two reasons. One is that the colonial Germans were largely religious dissenters who considered the theater too worldly. The other reason follows from the first: the Germans who came to the United States for economic rather than religious reasons did not arrive in sufficient numbers and lacked the means to support a German-language theater until about 1840.[1]

An early center for German stage productions was New York City. *Kleindeutschland,* as the New York colony was fondly called, could be defined as the district south of Houston Street, west of Attorney, north of East Broadway, and east of Lafayette. In this "Little Germany" there was no mention of a German theater before 1837 and not until 1840 did a *Deutscher dramatischer Verein* come into existence.[2] Beginning its first season in 1840, the German theater of New York lasted for the balance of the century and beyond. The first fifteen years of activity took place in tiny, rented quarters of the Franklin Theater. When this theater proved unsatisfactory, productions were shifted from pillar to post until 1854 when New York's Forty-eighters upgraded both the quality and the domicile of German theater by founding the New York *Stadttheater.* Immediately they introduced plays by classical German writers, especially those of Goethe and Schiller.

As a rule, New York theater directors experienced the same dilemma in selecting dramas that plagued German-American theater directors in other localities. If they chose plays of solid dramatic and literary worth, they usually ran the risk of drawing small audiences. If they sought to attract large audiences — a necessity for the financial health of the theater — they had to be satisfied with inferior

129

quality. Thus a pattern developed whereby the directors put big-name actors, frequently traveling experts, on the stage for a brief period in the fall or spring to stimulate attendance. Buoyed by large box-office figures and laudatory press reports, they would stage a few classical plays. With a German-speaking public, of whom only a small minority (like the Forty-eighters) was educated, the diet of classics soon turned sour and enterprising directors quickly reverted to plays of lower quality.

All across America, German immigrants who arrived in the second half of the nineteenth century were quick to start amateur theater activities. Felled tree trunks still littered the fields and mudholes scarred the streets when groups of Germans would begin to assemble a singing society and a drama club. Before mass communication and entertainment, every town supported a theater or opera house, and plenty of coarse comedy and ghost dramas were played. Frequently, a group of businessmen or town boosters contrived to have theater, opera, and musical organizations in their "city" in order to lure a more educated class of people to their latest boom towns.

In such cities as Cincinnati, Chicago, Philadelphia, St. Paul, and Milwaukee, the German theater achieved professional status. Chicago started on a high plateau, opening its long history of German theater with a performance of Schiller's *Kabale und Liebe* in 1856.[3] Throughout the 1870s and 1880s operations rose and fell. Frequently, there were exchanges or cooperative ventures with the German theater companies of Milwaukee. As elsewhere, the English-language press was not always friendly to German theater endeavors, and often English-language churches objected when the Germans scheduled their performances on Sundays. Another problem in Chicago was that the city's German population was widely scattered. Consequently the Chicago Germans found more cohesion in their local Lutheran or Catholic churches than in such a purely cultural organization as a theater.

The prominent German-language actors who enjoyed a good reputation in Chicago, Christian Thielmann and his wife, were the founders of German theater in Cincinnati.[4] Due to Thielmann's early efforts, Cincinnati's German theater began in 1846 and lasted with some interruptions until 1918. In April of that year, a cold winter, an epidemic influenza, and a financial deficit teamed up with a severe case of anti-German propaganda. Many German-speaking actors were arrested, and the German theater in Cincinnati ended abruptly.

In many respects the German theater of Cincinnati was characteristic of others. It always waged some kind of battle for survival by tempering idealism as expressed by appreciation for classical German authors, with realism in the face of threatening deficits at the box office. Likewise, directors battled to satisfy their own clientele's preference for the "joy of life" by offering Sunday performances and refreshing beer, which always had to be "explained" to the Anglo-American critics. For a brief period in the 1880s, Sunday closing laws forbade regular German performances in Cincinnati.[5] By 1889, however, the ban had been lifted or circumvented, and in that year Cincinnati finally dedicated its own *Germania-Theater*. Deficits forever plagued the directors and prevented a golden age of German theater from materializing in Cincinnati.

Columbus, Ohio, had a German stage which brought forth its finest drama when guest troupes or individual actors came from Cincinnati to perform. It is worthy of note that in 1854 the Thielmann family performed in a number of plays in both German and English during that Columbus season.[6] Typically, Columbus had its Thalia Club, but it lapsed during the Civil War. All too frequently thereafter, the Columbus Germans opted for colorful operatic extravaganzas staged in cooperation with the local singing society *(Männerchor)* and for popular plays and pageants.

Baltimore had German theaters as did Cleveland and Buffalo. In St. Louis, German theater was spearheaded by Heinrich Börnstein, a former Austrian actor.[7] San Francisco developed German-language performances in the 1860s[8] and Milwaukee's German stage achieved prominence when the Pabst brewing family provided it with a permanent home.[9] German theater reached its apogee in St. Paul during the 1920s when its new facility was erected near the state capitol.[10]

Such all-German towns as New Jersey's Egg Harbor City, Iowa's Davenport, Illinois' Belleville, and a host of others in Ohio, Wisconsin, and Minnesota also enjoyed fledgling German theaters.[11] The spread of German theater characteristically took place along the waterways, especially on the Mississippi and the Ohio Rivers and on the Great Lakes. Between the years 1857 and 1890, in the relatively unpopulated state of Minnesota alone, there were over 1,600 different performances of German plays on that state's German-American stages.[12]

A rough survey of the plays staged indicates that the Germans in

America lagged perhaps thirty years behind the Europeans in their selections. Seemingly it took about that long before a budding German author achieved prominence on an American stage, if he did at all. Classical plays by Goethe seldom moved across German-American stages. The reason for Schiller's acclaim was his thematic depiction of political freedom, which had become ingrained in the average German-American's consciousness.[13] The most popular of Schiller's entire collection was *Wilhelm Tell*, a play which even today is performed annually in German on an open-air pasture in the Swiss-American community of New Glarus, Wisconsin.

In many respects, *der Gesangverein* ("singing society") was closer to the hearts of Germans in America than the German theater. As with the theaters, these singing societies waited for the second wave of German immigrants, which arrived in the 1840s. Colonial German sects did not take readily to celebration, whether it encompassed acting or singing, although there was much sacred music in the German settlements of colonial America.[14] The first German singing society was organized in Philadelphia in 1835 and Baltimore followed the next year. Within the next two years these new organizations visited each other's bailiwicks and enacted what may be regarded as the first *Sängerfest* in the history of the United States.[15] Soon New York had its *Liederkranz*, organized in 1847. Through its distinguished history it boasted the membership of famous German-Americans, most prominent of all, Carl Schurz. In 1876 the *Liederkranz* gave a commemorative concert on the anniversary of the American Revolution, under the direction of Dr. Leopold Damrosch. Later, under the leadership of William Steinway, the society had its own building, where it staged everything from annual balls to Wagnerian opera.[16]

Shortly after the founding of the New York *Liederkranz*, Cincinnati established its *Liedertafel* and Charleston its *Teutonenbund*, while other German-American cities were not far behind. Several cities in Texas, notably Galveston, San Antonio, and especially New Braunfels, were widely known for their German music festivals.[17] Columbus, Cleveland, St. Louis, Milwaukee, Buffalo, Pittsburgh, and many others had singing societies which offered both light musical fare and an opportunity to socialize.

The notion of singing societies and competitive gatherings did not arise with the Germans in America. The practice goes back at least to the fifteenth century in Germany where middle-class poets and singers joined in societies similar to those of the handworker guilds. However, rather than competing to increase the quality of their "products," these societies strove for more perfect renditions of their musical scores. Presentations by the Meistersingers were judged according to an elaborate set of rules. By passing the tests, individual singers improved their social status in the community. Attention was called to the practice of competitive singing during the nineteenth century when Richard Wagner wrote his opera *The Meistersingers of Nürnberg*, which premiered in Munich on June 21, 1868, and in New York's Metropolitan Opera House in 1886. In America, the competitive meeting of singers, known as a *Sängerfest*, did not depend on Wagner to gain acceptability. The first to be undertaken in earnest was by the societies of Cincinnati in 1849.[18] Soon the tradition became an annual affair.

Sängerfest programs sometimes included German folksongs and *Heimatlieder* ("songs of the old homeland") but more often they were composed of serious music — cantatas, oratorios, overtures, and excised operas. In a typical offering, the audience might hear the *Messiah*, the *Creation*, the *Magic Flute*, some four-part performance of a Brahms arrangement, a Haydn or Beethoven number, and perhaps one sentimental or patriotic American piece. The renditions appear to have been creditable — at any rate, they received much publicity. Enjoying group rates on the railroads, the Germans traveled far and wide not only as participants in the competitive singing but also as listeners.[19]

Closely allied to the singing societies were other musical organizations. While several German-American communities pioneered in organizing symphony orchestras, most had smaller musical activities such as a Cecelia club, a Schubert society, or a Beethoven *Verein*. Larger German settlements, such as the ones in Cincinnati and Milwaukee, secured for their cities the title of "Athens of the West." In some cases, the Germans in America were quick to claim that without the German influence, American music would have remained in the Dark Ages.[20] Prior to 1850, however, German musical activity in the United States was slight, or even nonexistent. Critics in the Fatherland kept referring to the United States as a country without music.

Thanks to its German heritage, Philadelphia was the first American city to support an orchestra. Organizational talent for an orchestra came from the city's Musical Fund Society, begun in 1820.

It arranged both sacred and secular programs and combined instrumental and vocal musical renditions for its concerts. Later, the society founded a school, built a music hall, and gave concerts until 1857. New York's Philharmonic Society also had the benefit of German leaders — Theodore Eisfeld, Carl Bergmann, and Henry Timm among the earlier ones. The Philharmonic Society gave its first concert in December, 1842, with about sixty performers, twenty-two of whom were Germans. Subsequently, under the baton of distinguished conductors, Leopold Damrosch, Theodore Thomas, Adolph Neuendorff, Anton Seidl, Walter Damrosch, and Emil Paur, membership in the orchestra increased to eighty-one musicians in 1865, of whom seventy were Germans. A quarter century later, there were ninety-four players, only five of whom were non-Germans.[21]

Significant advances were registered in the art of orchestral music by the arrival of refugees from Germany's revolutions of 1848. During 1848 and 1849, a traveling orchestra called the Germania Orchestra, made up of members of Berlin's distinguished Gungl Orchestra, visited several American cities: New York, Philadelphia, Washington, Baltimore, Boston, and others. During the following six years, they presented 829 concerts, and some of the world's best soloists appeared with them: Ole Bull, August Kreissmann, Jenny Lind, and Henrietta Sontag. Worn by the pressures of too many performances, the Germania disbanded in 1854, but the fires of the organization refused to go out. Wherever a member of the Germania settled, he established a nucleus of musical performers. Several former Germania members achieved distinguished careers, among whom was Carl Zerrahn, who served forty years as director of Boston's Handel and Hadyn Society. Carl Bergmann became director of the New York Philharmonic; William Schultze was appointed head of the music department at Syracuse University; Carl Sentz conducted in Philadelphia, and Carl Lenschow directed in Baltimore.

Several German-Americans tower above their many talented countrymen in the field of music. One of them was Theodore Thomas, born at Esens, East Friesland, near the North Sea.[22] Thomas came to America in his youth with his parents. By 1848 his father had enlisted in a U.S. Navy band and young Thomas immediately followed in his footsteps. Thereafter he pursued a career as a traveling soloist in the South, performed for orchestras in New York and, by 1864, recognized that New York was large enough to support two orchestras. Initially he met competition from the Philharmonic Society. He countered his rivals with several tactics, one of which was the practice of open-air garden concerts in the European tradition. Another was the orchestral tour which revived the custom initiated by the Germania Orchestra.

Thomas' New York career came to an end in 1879, when he was appointed head of the new Cincinnati College of Music. When he returned to New York two years later, it was as conductor of his former rival organization, the New York Philharmonic Society. Thomas' orchestral talent had an impact on all of America. New orchestras sprang up in several large American cities and those that had been in existence prior to his time were spurred to greater heights. In 1891, Thomas was invited to Chicago, where he established an Opera Company and developed an orchestra known today as the Chicago Symphony. Soon musical interest was strengthened in Philadelphia, Pittsburgh, San Francisco, Kansas City, and elsewhere.

It was in New York City, however, that the other towering German-American musical family made its mark on orchestral music — in the father-and-son team of Leopold and Walter Damrosch. Born in Posen, Leopold lived for years in Breslau, where his son Walter was born.[23] In 1871, the Damrosch family settled in the New World. Leopold founded the New York Symphony Society in 1879, and, when he died in 1885, the baton passed to his equally gifted son, Walter J. Damrosch. Writing in 1937, Walter recalled the difficult days when at the age of twenty-three he assumed the conductor's podium in place of his father. In the first years he successfully supported himself and his orchestra by giving six concerts and "public rehearsals" during the winter. In addition, his orchestra was employed for seven years by the German Opera Company of New York until it gave way to Italian opera. Deprived of this income, Damrosch boldly began a tradition of Sunday afternoon concerts — something only the Germans were ready to tolerate at the outset.

Damrosch also took his orchestra on long spring tours, penetrating the South, Middle West, and later the Far West. Most communities on these tours had never heard a symphony orchestra, and thus Damrosch filled a major gap on the contemporary musical stage. In time, he was invited to play at the Exposition of Louisville, at a festival in Oklahoma City, and in Canada.[24]

Like so many other German-Americans, Damrosch lived under

the shadow of suspicion during World War I. In this predicament, former president Theodore Roosevelt wrote a letter testifying to Damrosch's loyalty:

Mr. Walter Damrosch is one of the very best Americans and citizens of this entire land. In character, ability, loyalty, and fervid Americanism, he, and his, stand second to none in the land. I have known him for thirty years; I vouch for him as if he were my brother.[25]

During the year 1920, Damrosch took his New York Symphony Orchestra on an invited tour of European cities, starting in Paris and moving through southern France to Italy and Rome. On the way north, the orchestra played in cities of Belgium and Holland, and concluded in London. Thanks to men of Damrosch's caliber in the 1920s, America could no longer be referred to as the land without music.

Damrosch also deserves credit for bringing highly talented musicians to America. Take the case of Victor Herbert, who was born in Dublin in 1859, and his wife, Therese Foerster. Herbert's mother married Dr. Wilhelm Schmid and took the seven-year-old boy to Stuttgart, where he was educated as a musical prodigy. Herbert's half-brother, Willy Faber, was a famous actor in the German theater. During his middle twenties, while performing as first cellist with the Stuttgart Opera, the Irish-born Herbert fell in love with the company's prima donna, Miss Foerster. At about the same time (1886), Walter Damrosch was on a tour of Germany in search of talent for New York's Metropolitan Opera and offered a contract to Therese Foerster. She refused to sign until Victor Herbert received a similar offer to serve as leading cellist in the Metropolitan Opera. An immediate marriage followed and both journeyed to the United States, where Therese Foerster was gradually overshadowed by her husband.

Following his appearances with the Met, Herbert became conductor of the Pittsburgh Symphony Orchestra and wrote operettas on the side. One night in 1902 at a home concert in Pittsburgh, Herbert had the pleasure of conducting for a guest soprano, Fritzi Scheff, a twenty-two-year-old veteran singer from the Metropolitan Opera. In Fritzi, Herbert discovered the magnetism of a daring, lively personality who could deliver what his light opera demanded. Born in Vienna in 1879, Fritzi spent three successful years at the

Frankfurt Opera and performed in various German opera houses before being recruited for the Met in 1900.[26] Her greatest triumph came when she sang in Herbert's *Mlle. Modiste* at the New York Knickerbocker Theater in 1906. Fritzi became the dream girl of pre - World War I America. Songs like "Kiss Me Again," from *Modiste* lingered for decades, and in 1951 she sang it at the unveiling of a plaque in Lüchow's New York restaurant, where Herbert had spent so many happy hours dining on German food and beer.

The success of America's greatest opera company, the Metropolitan of New York, was not an immediate one. Nor was its greatness achieved by such men as Herbert or the Damrosch father-son combination alone. The Met's eventual success and the high caliber of its performances were attributable to many German influences. When the Met first started giving regular productions, the fashion was to select Italian opera. From the outset, the Met also presented German selections by Wagner, Beethoven, and Mozart — sung, however, in Italian. Beset by deficits during its first years of 1883 - 1885, the managers turned to Leopold Damrosch. His plan, which was to prove eminently successful from the artistic and economic points of view, called for organizing a cast of German singers who were equal to the talents of better-known singers but were not so widely recognized and therefore would not demand such high fees. With his all-German repertoire and singers, Damrosch undoubtedly reckoned with the unquenchable love of Germans for opera. At that time, there were a quarter of a million German-speaking immigrants in New York City and the surrounding area.[27]

When Damrosch died unexpectedly of pneumonia, his stunning breakthrough was carried forward under the direction of Anton Seidl, one of the world's most gifted Wagnerian conductors, and the first representative from Bayreuth to make an appearance in New York. During the early years of the twentieth century, the most influential director of the Met was Heinrich Conried, who gained fame not only for his talent, but because he produced *Parsifal* for the first time in the United States against the wishes of the Wagner family in Bayreuth. Similarly, Conried presented the modern musical dramas of Richard Strauss, causing lifted eyebrows when he staged Strauss' *Salomé*. The owners and financial backers of the Metropolitan Opera Company forbade further performances of *Salomé*, on the grounds of its "immoralities." During World War I, the strong German leanings of the Met were toned down and, as with most other interests of American life bearing a rich Teutonic flavor, the continuing German influence became less pronounced.[28]

Before concluding about the German contribution to development of American opera, the name of Oscar Hammerstein should be mentioned. His grandson, Oscar Hammerstein II, gained fame for his operettas written in cooperation with Richard Rodgers. The original Oscar Hammerstein was a businessman and a daring impresario. Born in Stettin in 1846, he spent his early life in Berlin where his father, a prosperous building contractor, determined to make his son into a man of art and erudition. At the age of fifteen, Hammerstein returned late one evening from ice skating and was chastised for failing to practice his violin. Filled with resentment, the young Hammerstein slipped away to Hamburg, where he boarded a cattle ship bound for the United States.[29]

Almost immediately, Hammerstein launched a cigar business from which he derived considerable income. In 1874 he founded the *United States Tobacco Journal,* composed music, and wrote plays in German. With his friend, Adolph Neuendorff, a conductor of some standing in New York, Hammerstein presented a short season of German opera at the *Stadttheater* in 1871. Hammerstein contributed financial backing and wrote the publicity. During the 1880s Hammerstein engaged in various real estate speculations and by the end of the decade constructed the Harlem Opera House on 125th Street. Subsequently he built the first Manhattan Opera House in 1892, the Olympia in 1895, and the Victoria in 1899. Then, in 1903, Hammerstein became convinced that the opera as presented at the Metropolitan Opera House under Heinrich Conried was a disgrace. As his biographer notes, Conried discovered at the Bremen *Stadttheater* that there was "no one . . . above him," and therefore he adopted "an imperious manner which instilled confidence in those under him, but which gained for him many enemies."[30]

In 1906, therefore, Hammerstein erected his second Manhattan Opera House on 34th Street and gathered a brilliant company with an intensely interesting repertoire which rivaled the Metropolitan Opera Company. In 1908, scenting success on a larger scale, he built the Philadelphia Opera House and ran it in association with his New York enterprise. His competition with the Met intensified. After proving that he could beat the Met at its own show, he entered into negotiations with the Metropolitan Opera Company which purchased Hammerstein's operatic interests in April, 1910, with the stipulation that he would not produce opera in the United States for a period of ten years. This took Hammerstein to London where he built the London Opera House. It opened in November, 1913, but failed shortly thereafter. On departing, Hammerstein is supposed to have said, "I'd rather be dead in New York than alive in London." Back in New York he built the Lexington Opera House on 51st Street but was prevented from starting opera there by his former agreement with the Metropolitan. In 1919, Hammerstein once again announced his intention of producing opera in New York during the year of 1920 when the restrictions imposed by the Met would no longer have been in force, but death plucked him from life's stage the same year.

No less dramatic than Hammerstein in the world of German-American musical productions is the personality of Ernestine Schumann-Heink. Born Ernestine Rössler near Prague in 1861 as the daughter of an Austrian army officer, Ernestine made her debut at fifteen in Beethoven's Ninth Symphony in the city of Graz. Soon thereafter she sang at the Court Opera in Dresden and from 1883 until 1898 at the Hamburg Municipal Opera. In 1898 she signed with the Berlin Royal Opera, but secured a leave of absence to perform in American engagements for the next four seasons. She then purchased a release from her German contract. Her American debut came in Chicago in 1898 and the following year she began four consecutive seasons with the Metropolitan Opera House. Eight months pregnant at the time of her New York appearance in *Lohengrin*, she named her new baby George Washington Schumann in honor of her adopted country. Three times married (to Ernst Heink in Dresden, to actor Paul Schumann in 1893 who died in 1904, and to William Rapp in 1905 whom she divorced in 1914), Mme. Schumann-Heink had an extraordinarily opulent and powerful voice. She claimed 150 operatic roles in her repertoire. Moreover, she mastered widely divergent roles and showed outstanding interpretative ability as a *Lieder* singer.

An American citizen since 1908, Schumann-Heink lost her eldest son who joined the Austrian army and was killed during an early battle of World War I. Her other four sons fought loyally on the Allied side. In the face of derogatory slurs on everything German, she refused to disown her dead son and demonstrated her sincere patriotism for her adopted country by giving many concerts for Red Cross benefits and for American Army camps.[31] Later it was said of Schumann-Heink: "Many another prima donna has successfully mothered a large family. But she has gone further. She has mothered audiences, mothered towns and cities, mothered the A.E.F. and now mothers the American legion."

Other German-born musicians exerted their influences in developing America's music during the nineteenth century. Such a man was Konrad Merz whose 200 compositions and arrangements were significant, but whose greater contribution may well have been his dedication as a teacher and writer. While an instructor at Oxford Female College in Ohio, Merz wrote choral music. Later in 1882 he began his duties as director of the Wooster Conservatory. From 1873 to 1890, he enjoyed profound influence on the American musical scene as editor of *Musical World*. From his pedestal as editor, he campaigned with all his energy for appreciation in America of German classical music from Bach to Wagner. Finally, in 1889, when Theodore Thomas and his orchestra were making plans for a tour abroad, Merz could confidently claim that America had come to the end of her apprenticeship period and that she could now take her place in the world of music.[32]

During the first half of the twentieth century, there were many distinguished German musicians who made their way to the United States, the majority as political refugees. Mention should be made of several famous names, proceeding alphabetically.[33]

Kurt Herbert Adler was born in Vienna but directed mainly in Salzburg and in German cities before coming to America, where he conducted the Chicago Opera from 1938 - 1943. Thereafter he conducted the San Francisco Opera and eventually the New York Metropolitan Opera. Adolf Georg Busch, internationally known for his Busch quartet, was a violinist, composer and music professor who came to America in 1938. The conductors Fred Cohen and Heinrich Jalowetz taught at Black Mountain College; later Cohen taught at the Juilliard School of Music.

Perhaps the most famous German-American musician of recent times was Paul Hindemith. Born in Silesia, Hindemith, a composer, conductor, and musicologist, had been a professor at the Berlin Hochschule für Musik before being expelled for his "degenerate art, and for being a cultural bolshevist," according to the Nazis. Hindemith came to the United States in 1940 to become a professor at Yale University. After receiving American citizenship in 1946, he was elected to the National Institute of Arts and Letters, served as visiting lecturer at Harvard, and in 1949, guest-conducted the Berlin

Philharmonic in a program of his own works. After 1953, he settled in Switzerland. Historians have written that Hindemith's impact has been stunning. Both in terms of total works and effectiveness, Hindemith has scarcely been equaled in the twentieth century.

Otto Klemperer never took out American citizenship, though he lived for years in the United States and conducted many concerts with the New York Symphony from 1933 - 1939 and later with the Los Angeles Philharmonic Orchestra. Erich Leinsdorf, Viennese by birth and training, became conductor of the Metropolitan Opera in New York from 1937 until 1943, when he was made conductor of the Cleveland Orchestra. He then served in the American army, conducted in Europe after World War II, and returned to the Rochester Philharmonic in 1947. His career eventually took him back to New York and, from 1962 - 1969, to the Boston Symphony Orchestra as conductor. Arthur Schnabel, pianist and composer, was Austrian-born and long a resident in Berlin, where he taught at the Berlin Hochschule. Since 1921 he was a frequent visitor and guest performer in America.

Sharing the spotlight of importance with few others in the music world of the twentieth century was Arnold Schönberg. Vienna-born, Schönberg frequently resided in Germany and oscillated between the two German-speaking music centers of Berlin and Vienna. This revolutionary composer once responded to a music critic of the *Los Angeles Times* who had inquired what effect separation from Europe had had on his creative work by saying: "If immigration has changed me — I am not aware of it. Maybe I would have written more when remaining in Europe, but I think: nothing comes out what was not in. And two times two equals four in every climate."[34] One year later in 1951 when Schönberg died in Los Angeles, he had been living in the United States for seventeen consecutive years and had produced fifteen significant works climaxing a lifetime of masterpieces. His twelve-tone system, plus his overall stature, has not diminished since his death. It has been said that "almost single-handedly, he ensured the continuation of the art of music in the twentieth century, a time in which political and social upheavals [are] so full of danger not only for the survival of art but for the survival of man."[35]

Bruno Walter, whose real name was Bruno Walter Schlesinger, was born in 1876 in Berlin. His distinguished career as a conductor in Germany won him invitations to guest-conduct in New York between 1923 and 1925 and again in 1932 - 33. Bruno Walter, who had to flee Germany, became an American citizen and settled in California when World War II broke out. Concerning his first impressions of America, Walter wrote in his autobiography that New York was "a new city-type, never seen on the other side. . . . It was a city dominated by the vertical line instead of Europe's horizontal one. The European city lay, this one stood."[36] He referred to the New York orchestra as "Damrosch's orchestra" and boasted the privilege of having Arthur Schnabel as his soloist. To Walter Damrosch he gave the accolade: "His name and his activity in the musical life of America on behalf of German and Wagner's musical dramas had long been known to me. I was sincerely glad to salute the enthusiastic and youthful man of sixty."[37]

Reflecting near the end of his brilliant career on his experience when he arrived permanently in the United States, Bruno Walter has written:

Friends have given to my life in America the warmth without which there can be no feeling of home. . . . The country is becoming increasingly familiar to me through its literature, and I am acquiring a deeper understanding through my study of its history. To me, there stand out from the mighty epos the figures of Thomas Jefferson and Abraham Lincoln, whose lofty thoughts and immortal words have not only pointed the way to the American people, but are so wise, fruitful, and potent that they might well guide the whole world into a better future. To my discerning look, they were the first statesmen in responsible positions who used political wisdom and power for the attainment of humanity's goals.[38]

Finally, mention should be made of Kurt Weill, born in Dessau in 1900, whose lasting fame was assured by his composition of the music for Brecht's *Threepenny Opera*. Weill settled in America in 1935 and produced a series of musicals that revealed his amazing capacity to adjust to the style of American popular music. His *Knickerbocker Holiday, Lady in the Dark*, and *One Touch of Venus* all became major musical hits. In *Street Scene* and *Lost in the Stars*, Weill created a genre that combined serious music with operetta. Shortly after his folk opera *Down in the Valley*, composed in 1948, reached its peak of popularity, Weill died and was buried in New York in 1950. His wife was Lotte Lenya, star of the *Threepenny Opera*, who also performed in other works by Weill.

Maria Augusta von Trapp has made a different kind of contribution. Like a great many other musicians from German-speaking countries, Maria was born in Vienna. After studying at the Vienna Teachers' College, she joined a convent. As a novice in Salzburg, she found the life of a religious too rigorous and was allowed by her superiors to help care for the seven children of widowed Baron Georg von Trapp. Ever since 1927 when Maria married the Baron, the family has been singing. Their popularity drew them into concerts all over Europe, and in 1938 they toured the American Middle West and South before ending up in Manhattan. After a daring escape from Hitler's henchmen, the family returned to the United States in 1939 and continued their concerts for decades thereafter.[39]

Commenting about her first impressions of America, Maria Trapp summed up what must have been the identical impressions felt by hundreds and thousands of German immigrants to the United States.

The real America is not neon-sign-language; it is a state of mind. It is warm, spontaneous generosity — full measure, pressed down and running over. . . . A refugee is not just someone lacking in money and everything else. A refugee is vulnerable to the slightest touch: he has lost his country, his friends, his earthly belongings. He is a stranger, sick at heart. He is suspicious; he feels misunderstood. If people smile, he thinks they ridicule him; if they look serious, he thinks they don't like him. He is a full-grown tree in the dangerous process of being transplanted, with the chance of possibly not being able to take root in the new soil.[40]

In summing up, we should acknowledge that this chapter (and the next) contains more names than most of the others. Nor do all of the persons named come from the lands strictly defined by the German borders. Germany's share of immigrants to the United States has always been less than precisely understood because of the lack of an exact German territory. The German artists — broadly understood to include musicians, painters, architects, and others from all the German-speaking regions of Europe — not only shared their common German language but their artistic heritage. It is hoped that these two chapters on the arts will demonstrate the tremendous impact which the German immigrants in the United States exercised on the cultural growth of America.

CHAPTER 11

The Fine Arts, Architecture, and the Sciences

AMONG THE NINETEENTH-CENTURY GERMAN-AMERICANS WHO GAINED recognition for their paintings in the United States was Emmanuel Leutze, who completed his *Washington Crossing the Delaware* in 1851 and *Emigration to the West* in 1862.[1] The latter forms one of the panels in the Capitol staircase in Washington, D.C. Equally well known is Albert Bierstadt, who received a gold medal from the Berlin Academy in 1868 for his paintings from America. Western landscapes were his specialty. Born in Düsseldorf, Bierstadt studied in Germany and Italy, but he found his inspiration in the Rocky Mountains. Among his better known-works are *Looking Down the Yosemite, The Rocky Mountains, The Storm,* and *Starr King Mountain, California.*[2] Frankfurt-born Adolf Höffler was known for his landscapes, especially the Mississippi Valley.[3] Also acclaimed were German-born Carl C. Brenner of Lousiville[4] and Carl Nahl, called the father of Californian art.[5]

Other artists from the German-speaking countries included the Swiss-born Peter Rindisbacher, who made engravings of American scenes,[6] and the Austrian, Franz Hölzlhuber. The latter traveled through Michigan, Illinois, Minnesota, Wisconsin, Mississippi, Arkansas, Louisiana, and Tennessee sketching the changing scenes of early America.[7] Worthy of mention is Henry Lewis, an American who lived in Europe and in 1854 published *Das Illustrirte Mississippithal.* Printed in Düsseldorf, the German narrative was embellished with lithographs which revealed Middle America to the Germans. Recently the book has been translated into English.[8]

The folk art of Pennsylvania forms a category by itself. Pennsylvania German art means crafts and other artistic products that are lost in machine-oriented America. These handwrought articles of daily life have come to reveal a simplicity, freshness, and originality.

144

Utensils around the farm were decorated with colorful tulips and hearts, distelfinks and peacocks, doves and pelicans, unicorns and horses. Of particular interest are the hex signs which are painted on barns to ward off evil spirits. Birth, baptism, and marriage certificates, too, were customarily embellished with folk art. So were pieces of hardware, stove plates, latches, hinges, and weathervanes. Pennsylvania Dutch artistry is also evident in kitchen utensils: pitchers, sugar bowls, coffee pots, cookie cutters; and in wooden furniture: chairs, tables, chests, and bedsteads. Undoubtedly, the value of such art lies in the traditions it depicts of the Pennsylvania German way of life.[9]

The contributions of German-American painters were noteworthy, not because of the large number of paintings, but because of their importance. German-American sculptors are equally distinguished for the quality of their works, if not for their numbers. Among those who gained recognition was the Viennese immigrant, Karl T. Bitter who, in 1893, served as director of sculpture for the Columbian Exposition at Chicago. He produced works at Broad Street Station in Philadelphia and is acknowledged for his memorial to Carl Schurz.[10] Another sculptor was Frederick W. Ruckstuhl whose works are on display at numerous cities of America, in the Library of Congress, and in Washington's Statuary Hall. Finally, there was Albert Jaegers, born in Elberfeld, who came to Cincinnati, where he worked for a time as a wood-carver. Among his works is the statue of General Steuben in Washington, D.C., commissioned by the U.S. Government.

There was one famous German-American cartoonist, about whom Abraham Lincoln said, "Thomas Nast has been our best recruiting sergeant."[11] Nast was born at Landau, Germany, in 1840 and came to the United States as a boy. While still in his midteens, Thomas Nast came to the attention of Frank Leslie who employed him to cover events for *Leslie's Weekly*. A personal acquaintance of President Lincoln, Nast gained international fame for his depiction of Civil War battles. In the wake of the war, Nast made his mark as a political, satirical cartoonist for *Harper's Weekly*, then one of the most widely read magazines in the country. Both the Democratic and Republican parties owe their party mascots to Thomas Nast, who personally invented the elephant and popularized the donkey after the election of 1874.

In the twentieth century, exhibits of German art toured several

American cities. The Germanic Museum was established at Harvard in 1903 on a permanent basis. To initiate the collection, the German emperor made a gift of casts of sculptures from the Middle Ages and the Renaissance. The king of Saxony and the city of Nuremberg made other donations. Later, Adolphus Busch and Hugo Reisinger bequeathed money to enable the museum to erect a structure designed by a Dresden architect. Ground was broken in 1914 but the war intervened, preventing completion until 1921. Today it is called the Busch-Reisinger Museum in honor of the donors.[12]

German-American art was, however, much more dramatically affected by those German immigrants who arrived in the United States during the 1930s. Without doubt, it was from 1930 - 1941 that the arts in America benefited most from an influx of German refugees. Not only the visual arts, but the fields of music, writing, and especially architecture, received a large infusion of talent.[13]

It is a misconception that there were hundreds of thousands of refugees who came to the United States as a result of Hitler. Using statistics compiled by Donald Kent, we note that from 1930 - 1941, only 104,098 Germans (including Austrians after the annexation of Austria in 1938) were admitted as immigrant aliens.[14] Virtually all of them should be classified as refugees. They had something in common with the religious dissenters who left Germany prior to the American Revolution and with the Forty-eighters who left following the abortive revolutions.

The new refugees like those of earlier times tended to be older and often they were accompanied by families. The nineteenth-century German immigrant, by contrast, was relatively younger, unmarried, and over half were male. While the Hitler migration was an uprooting — a compulsory immigration — the waves of newcomers preceding them represented a transplanting. Out of the total number of Germans who passed through the United States Immigration Services during the 1930 - 1941 time, only 7,622 listed a specific profession. The largest number was medicine. There were also significant numbers in education (1,090), music (465), and art (296).[15]

To measure the full impact of the refugee intellectuals would require in-depth studies. An example of what is needed is Martin Duberman's book on Black Mountain College,[16] which employed German refugees who were composers, musicians, and artists. Not all the talent clustered at Black Mountain was German; Buckminster

Fuller was not. But a great many, including Richart Gothe, the economist, Erwin Straus, the psychoanalyst and Heinrich Jalowetz, the composer, were indeed refugees from Nazi Germany. Others thrown together at Black Mountain after hair-raising escapes from Germany were Frederic Cohen, a conductor and his dancer wife, Elsa Kahl, and occasional lecturers such as Lyonel Feininger, the artist, Hugo Kauder, another composer, and Alfred Einstein, the famous musicologist. Among the longest in residence, as well as one of the most famous German artists to emigrate to America was Josef Albers and his wife, Anni, both of whom spent fifteen years at Black Mountain College.[17]

The name Albers brings to mind an institution in America that was entirely German in origin, the Bauhaus, which was transplanted from Germany in 1933. To the art world, the Bauhaus is a household word. Bauhaus and *Bauhäusler* mean respectively a house of design and a person connected with it. A literal translation, however, does not explain the titles. They are catchwords and umbrella terms for the many concepts and trends in new architecture, new art, functional design, interior decoration, experimental theater, and innovative art education. The appellatives express the polarity between the master and his pupil, between the institution and the individual working in it, and between the idea and people attempting to transform it into life. Ludwig Mies van der Rohe, a longtime member of the Bauhaus wrote: "The Bauhaus was not an institution with a clear program — it was an idea, and Gropius formulated this idea with great precision. The fact that it was an idea, I think, is the cause of this enormous influence the Bauhaus had on every progressive school around the globe. You cannot do that with organization, you cannot do that with propaganda. Only an idea spreads so far. . . ."[18]

The genesis of the Bauhaus was France, and it came into Germany by way of Le Corbusier's "esprit nouveau" which challenged the sentimentality that characterized nineteenth-century art. Of equal importance was the cross-fertilization which reached Germany from America. Rejected in the United States, Frank Lloyd Wright found admirers in Germany, where he traveled in 1910. His first significant publications occurred there in 1910 and 1911, *Ausgeführte Bauten und Entwürfe von Frank Lloyd Wright* and *Frank Lloyd Wright-Ausgeführte Bauten*, similar but distinct titles. At a Wright exhibition in the Museum of Modern Art in 1940, Mies van der Rohe commented about Wright: "The work of this great master presented an architectural world of unexpected force, clarity of language and disconcerting richness of form. . . . The dynamic impulse emanating from his work invigorated a whole generation. His influence was strongly felt even when it was not actually visible."[19]

The Bauhaus came into existence when Walter Gropius was granted permission in April, 1919, to merge the former Grand-Ducal Academy of Art and the Grand-Ducal School of Arts and Crafts at Weimar into a single academy. Known subsequently as *Staatliches Bauhaus in Weimar*, the institute continued in Weimar despite political and financial problems. In 1923 the authorities asked Gropius to render an account of activities, which resulted in a widely publicized exhibition. For the occasion, Oskar Schlemmer wrote a pamphlet:

The *Staatliche Bauhaus in Weimar* is the first and so far the only government school in the Reich — if not in the world — which calls upon the creative forces of the fine arts to become influential while they are vital. At the same time it endeavors, through the establishment of workshops founded upon the crafts, to unite and productively stimulate the arts with the aim of combining them in architecture. The concept of building will restore the unity that perished in debased academicism and in finicky handicraft. It shall reinstate the broad relationship with the "whole" and, in the deepest sense, make possible the total work of art.[20]

After the exhibition of 1923, the Bauhaus seemed to enjoy momentary public approval which led Gropius to proclaim his thesis of "Art and Technology — a New Unity." A mere two years later, the rightist government of Thuringia reduced the budget of the Bauhaus and, although private industries promised help, the directors on December 29, 1924, dissolved the institute effective April 1, 1925. Gropius moved with his faculty and students to Dessau at the invitation of Mayor Fritz Hesse, where the institute reopened as the *Bauhaus Dessau, Hochschule für Gestaltung* ("School for Modeling"). Gropius continued to direct it until 1928 when Hannes Meyer took over, remaining in charge until 1930 when the mayor and city council of Dessau dismissed him.[21]

Ludwig Mies van der Rohe became director, but in 1932, the city legislators of Dessau closed the Bauhaus. Mies van der Rohe appealed the action and moved the institute to Berlin. Early in 1933, however, the Berlin police accompanied by Nazi Storm Troopers raided the facilities with the result that the faculty voted to dissolve the organization. The Bauhaus had lasted fourteen years — almost exactly as long as the Weimar Republic in which its genius had thrived. The *Bauhäusler* scattered taking the spirit with them into exile.

But, as Marcel Breuer concluded, "The Bauhaus idea as it really existed could not be transplanted."[22] Initial attempts to give it life in America were abortive. A fragile existence came at the Design Laboratory in New York, another try was at the Southern California School of Design. Two other endeavors, though more extensive, also failed. One was Black Mountain College, which generated enthusiasm but not a Bauhaus. This agrarian setting, far from metropolitan centers, was contradictory to the Bauhaus idea. Nevertheless, in 1939 Gropius and Breuer made models for an extravagant structure proposed for the ridge of the mountain but, unfortunately, nothing came of it.

The only genuine revival of the Bauhaus came in 1937 in the city of Chicago. Its new domicile was sponsored by the Association of Arts and Industries, and it was directed by the Hungarian-born, German-educated, longtime member of the Bauhaus, Laszlo Moholy-Nagy. Its chief consultant, however, continued to be the founder himself, Walter Gropius. Initially the Chicago Bauhaus was located at 1905 Prairie Avenue. But in 1939, Moholy-Nagy changed the name from "New Bauhaus" to "School of Design" and moved it to 247 East Ontario Street. Due to further evolution in 1944, the name became "Institute of Design," and the status of an American college was acquired.[23]

With these alterations in title and accreditation, enrollment at the Bauhaus increased. Success was guaranteed for the future when the Bauhaus was incorporated into the Illinois Institute of Technology in 1949, thus achieving university status. The new director after incorporation with I.I.T. was a German immigrant who had worked closely with Walter Gropius, Konrad Wachsmann. Under Wachsmann the institute shifted its emphasis toward solving problems through the application of art and design. It secured commissions from industries as well as from American government agencies, chief among which was an aircraft hangar system for the United States Air Force.[24]

During the 1960s, ideas of the Bauhaus reached countries which had not been affected by them previously. The Federal Republic of Germany was anxious to promote the Bauhaus as a contribution from the 1920s which had been suppressed by the Nazis in the 1930s. In the United States, the Bauhaus gradually was assimilated by a new generation of designers. Fully Americanized now, the design concepts radiate back to the Old World which is coming to terms with the American developments.

Relatively few of the Bauhaus staff members stayed with the institute after their arrival in America. Most started their own companies or traineeships. Several have become world-famous designers, affecting all areas of modern life. Marcel Breuer was one, and he was perhaps the greatest exponent of the Bauhaus tradition. He was born in Hungary in 1902 and was associated with the Bauhaus since the age of eighteen. His furniture, buildings, factories, and abbeys stretch the imagination in their creativity and their beauty.

Breuer's chapel at St. John's Abbey in Minnesota and his Y-shaped UNESCO headquarters in Paris are universally lauded. But he undoubtedly affected the lives of the average citizen more through his tubular cantilevered chair designs than through his buildings. His "Wassily" Kandinsky chair, too, is widely copied. At La Caude, France, stands what may be regarded as his most stunning building, the IBM Research Center. Breuer's Housing and Urban Development building in Washington, D. C., as well as his Whitney Museum in Manhattan are said to be too monumental. As a tribute to his achievement, the Metropolitan Museum of New York in 1972 staged the first one-man architecture show in its history for Marcel Breuer. *Time* paid similar compliments when it wrote: "his life is a road map of modern architecture. . . . He is a compleat designer — of everything from kitchen cabinets to entire cities."[25] *House and Garden* and other magazines feature his ideas on the place of design in modern living.[26]

Like Breuer, Ludwig Mies van der Rohe did his most significant work after coming to the United States. A schooled disciplinarian in a confused world, Mies van der Rohe is remembered for the phrase, "less is more." Born in Aachen, Germany, in 1886, he was associated with the Bauhaus almost from its inception, and after 1938 as head of the Armour Institute in Chicago — now renamed the Illinois Institue of Technology.[27] One of his favorite buildings was the Crown Hall on the I. I. T. campus. Another was his Chicago apartment complex at 860 Lakeshore Drive. Art critics have suggested that "the special climate and pace of Chicago helped him to create what he did."[28]

Mies also won acclaim for his Seagram Building in Manhattan and especially for his reasonable and clear design for the National Gallery in West Berlin. There were so many monuments to his creative genius by the time he died at the age of eighty-three that *Time* wrote, his "pure, honed elegance, as seen everywhere in his works, from his famous Barcelona chair (1929) to his glass-curtain walls, has transformed the appearance of every major city on earth. No modern architect has been more widely (or in most cases more clumsily) imitated."[29]

Walter Gropius also solidified his remarkable reputation after leaving Germany in disgust in 1934 to come to the United States. Beginning in 1938, he served for years as chairman of Harvard's Department of Architecture which provided him with the opportunity to influence some of America's now famous architects: Philip Johnson, Ulrich Franzen, John Johansen, and I. M. Pei. His pupil, Franzen, was himself born in Germany, but his major contributions, among them the Philip Morris Operations Center at Richmond, are all in the United States. Johansen, once a staunch Gropius disciple, is said to be rethinking some of the "architectural commandments handed down years ago by the late Mies van der Rohe and Walter Gropius."[30]

Gropius was a distinguished teacher and administrator and to these tasks he dedicated his time up to 1952. Not until he left Harvard did major, award-winning commissions come his way. Among them are some of the world's most admired buildings: the U. S. Embassy in Athens, which blends the Bauhaus style with the image of the Parthenon; the modern campus of the University of Baghdad, several academic buildings at Harvard and Brandeis, and the Pan Am Building in New York. He also won awards for the IBM World Trade Center in Teheran and was commissioned to design an entirely new city of Selb in Bavaria, the home of Rosenthal porcelain.[31]

Before abandoning the Bauhaus group, the German-American artist, Lyonel Feininger, ought to be mentioned. His father, Carl, came to America as a Forty-eighter and, like Carl Schurz, participated in the Civil War. Having settled in Charleston, Carl Feininger fought on the Confederate side, although his father-in-law, John Lutz, served in the Union army. After the war, the

Feiningers moved to New York where Lyonel was born in 1871. At the age of sixteen, the young Feininger was sent to study music in Germany, but his attention turned immediately to the visual arts. For the next fifty years, 1887 - 1937, Feininger lived continuously in Germany, spending his early years as an illustrator in Berlin.[32] In 1919 he became the first teacher of painting and graphic arts at the the newly formed Bauhaus. Several colleagues in the Expressionistic School — Paul Klee, Wassily Kandinsky and Oskar Schlemmer — were also engaged at the Bauhaus.

Not until 1928 did Feininger think of returning to the United States. American consular authorities allowed him to remain in Dessau but cautioned that he would eventually have to return to retain his American citizenship — a privilege he never considered resigning.[33] After 1933 Feininger became worried about his status as an American living in Germany, especially because of his sons. Andreas was an architect, later a famous photographer. Laurence was a distinguished musicologist. Theodore Lux, the youngest, had become a painter. The talents of the elder Feininger — architecture, optics, music, and painting — had found their reflection in his sons. Though uneasy about the forces of hate in Germany, the Feiningers did not leave Germany until 1937, when the prodigal son returned to America as a political refugee.

Feininger went to Mills College in California, where he taught for a summer because his associate, Oskar Kokoschka, had canceled his engagement. In 1938, Lyonel and his wife Julia settled into a Manhattan apartment not far from where he was born near Gramercy Park. Shortly before his death on January 13, 1956, he wrote to his son Lux: "The doctor gave me yesterday the green light, but under express warning that I am still to be very careful and that I avoid overexertion. This doesn't look too good to me at this moment, for there is little one can achieve without exertion."[34] This was the spirit in which Feininger had lived his long life.

Another distinguished German-American artist was George Grosz.[35] Unlike Feininger, Grosz was born, not in America, but in Berlin in 1893, and he had only honorary membership in the German Bauhaus. Trained at academies in Dresden and Berlin, Grosz served in the German infantry during World War I. In 1920 he cofounded the Berlin Dadaists and exhibited his satirical drawings and lithographs, *Gott Mit Uns*. These were caricatures of German military, social, and political types. The government countered by arresting and fining Grosz. In 1923 he was arrested and fined again, although this time he successfully appealed his case. Following a one-man show in the United States in 1931, Grosz settled permanently in New York City. In addition to teaching at the Art Students League, he conducted his own school at Bayside on Long Island. In 1937, examples of his art were shown at the Nazi exhibition of degenerate art in Munich and his works were burned. Also, Grosz was stripped of German citizenship in 1938, whereupon he immediately became a citizen of the United States.

Grosz' description of his experiences before and upon arriving in America offer insight into the typical German immigrant experience. From his childhood, he recounts:

As time went on there remained not a single German family who did not have a near or distant relative in America. How often did I hear: "Yes, that was the brother of your grandfather who went over there. He wrote a few letters but then we never heard from him again." That was typical.

Sometimes people returned from the United States, usually for just a short trip. Such visits always created a miniature sensation, since the visitors always gave parties and spent the bit of money they had saved and brought with them in the form of travellers' checks. We would admire the brand-new suitcases with their many ship tags, the new suits, patent-leather shoes, pipes and 'half-diamond' cuff links. I can still see Jim, whose name in Germany had been Fritz, pulling some coins out of his pocket and letting them roll on the table as he carelessly said, with pipe in mouth: "*Los! lass ma anfahren.*" ("All hands to the bar.") Long after such a miraculous "uncle" had disappeared we continued to talk about him and wished to be like him.

It is rare to have one's dreams realized and not feel some slight disappointment at the same time. The discrepancy between dreams and reality is ordinarily rather great. New York, however, completely lived up to my expectations. I found the city exactly as I had imagined it, and was filled with enthusiasm.[36]

Invited by the Congress of Cultural Freedom to return to West Berlin in 1950, Grosz refused and would not even visit Germany until 1953. After two weeks he was back in New York sounding like a typical American tourist — how he had been cheated changing dollars to marks, how awful the whisky and plumbing were, and how shocked he was at the sinful night life in Berlin and Munich. Finally, in May, 1959, he was persuaded for family reasons to return to Germany. Just before sailing he received a gold medal from the American Academy of Arts and Sciences. The following July 5 in Berlin, Grosz died, one of the greatest creative artists of our time.

The Bauhaus was not the only institution to be transplanted to the United States during the period of National Socialism. Soon after Lyonel Feininger arrived in New York, he wrote: "Julia and I were invited to a supper at the New School for Social Research in honor of the architect Erich Mendelsohn. . . . More than half the guests present were from many countries of Europe, and it was a great pleasure to find many people who knew me well for my former work in Germany."[37] Feininger was referring to the New School for Social Research, the German exile university in New York City. In 1973, the school celebrated its fortieth year of existence in the presence of its honored guest, Willy Brandt, the Chancellor of West Germany.

The New School began in 1919 as a strictly American institution designed by independent-minded scholars who wanted no part of the restrictions on academic freedom placed on them at other universities. In 1933 the University in Exile was established as an adjunct to the New School. To this center, refugee scholars who had been dismissed from their positions by the totalitarian governments of Europe, were invited. More than 250 came in all, among the first, Max Wertheimer, founder of Gestalt psychology; the economists Karl Brandt and Gerhard Colm, both later members of the President's Council of Economic Advisers; Max Ascoli, later publisher of the *Reporter;* Kurt Riezler, Rector of Frankfurt University; and the political theorist, Arnold Brecht. The University in Exile began with an announcement which appeared in the August 19, 1933, edition of the *New York Times* under a front-page headline EXILES' UNIVERSITY OPENS HERE OCT. 1; FACULTY GERMAN.

One year later in 1934 the University in Exile was converted into the Graduate Faculty of Political and Social Science, the first degree-granting unit of the New School. It was staffed almost entirely by European professors who guided master's and doctoral programs in economics, philosophy, political science, psychology, and sociology. Now in its fifth decade, the Graduate Faculty continues to build on the intellectual legacy of its emigré founders by expanding its essential and distinctive role in American education and international scholarship.

Besides the refugees in America who had been linked to Black

Mountain College, the Bauhaus, or the University in Exile, there were countless individual emigrés who settled temporarily in America during the Nazi period. Donald Fleming and Bernard Bailyn in *The Intellectual Migration* provide an appendix with short biographies of 300 notables. Many, like Bertolt Brecht, were dramatists; the brothers Thomas and Heinrich Mann were novelists; Herbert and Ludwig Marcuse were both philosophers. Above and beyond the list of emigrés who returned to Europe later, there were thousands, now distinguished, who came to America with their parents, received their higher education in the United States, and were assimilated into the American mainstream. Unfortunately, it is impossible to measure this gain to American society.

During the nineteenth century, every German-American was proud to claim ethnic kinship with the statesman Carl Schurz. His role as a general in the Civil War, as Secretary of the Interior, and as director of Indian affairs gave him a prominence not enjoyed by any other German-American, and his feats have been recounted often. His contribution as a pioneer in the conservation of America's forests, however, is rarely mentioned. As a member of the cabinet, Schurz pressed so vigorously for conservation that opponents of Schurz in the Senate attacked the Secretary, claiming that "a Native of the Kingdom of Prussia . . . was applying to the Territory of Montana the land laws of Prussia, not the land laws of the settled territories of the United States." In retrospect, Schurz disclaimed any great victory for forest protection: "What I did with regard to the public forests was simply to arrest devastation, in which I partially succeeded, and for which I was lustily denounced, and to strive from year to year to obtain from Congress legislation for the protection of forests in which I largely failed."[38]

What Schurz did for politics, John Augustus Roebling did for nineteenth-century bridge building. Born in 1806, Roebling was an engineer of the Prussian government when he decided to emigrate to the United States. He arrived in 1831 at a time when roads were being built west of the Alleghenies. Bridges were still being made of wood, mortised together by carpenters. Roebling dreamed of a technological breakthrough that would employ wire ropes for suspension. His first bridge over the Monongahela River in Pittsburgh was followed ten years later in 1855 by an audacious project over the Niagara Falls Whirlpools, built for the Great Western Railway of Canada. Then came the span over the Ohio River at Cincinnati in 1866 and finally the Brooklyn Bridge which, in July, 1869, claimed his life. Today the John A. Roebling Company in Trenton, New Jersey, is a major supplier for suspension bridges. It produced cable for the Golden Gate, the George Washington, and the Tacoma Narrows bridges.[39]

Less famous than either Schurz or Roebling but no less significant for the world was Ottmar Mergenthaler's printing machine. Born in Germany in 1854, Mergenthaler landed in Baltimore in 1872, where he worked first as a clock repairman. He then set out to build a mechanical device to advance the process of typesetting that dated from the days of Gutenberg. When he demonstrated his product in 1886 in the composing room of the *New York Tribune*, Whitelaw Reid, publisher of the *Tribune*, cried: "Ottmar, you have done it. A line of type!" And from that day, the invention had its name, Linotype.[40]

In medicine, too, the names of German-Americans come to mind. To mention just one, there was Abraham Jacobi, born on May 6, 1830, in the province of Westphalia. Jacobi was a physician, teacher, and social reformer. Like Carl Schurz, he believed in the revolution of 1848 and paid the price by being arrested for high treason and confined to prison until 1853. At the suggestion of Schurz, Jacobi settled in New York, where he founded the German Dispensary in 1857 for aiding the German immigrant poor. In 1866 he established German Hospital, now known as Lenox Hill Hospital, and the School for Nurses in 1887. A professor at New York Medical College, Jacobi acquired the name, "Father of American Pediatrics."[41] Jacobi was president of many medical organizations, received honorary degrees from five American universities, and in 1893, he declined a chair in medicine offered by the University of Berlin. At the age of seventy he was presented with a *Festschrift* of articles written by fifty-three specialists, and at eighty-two he was elected president of the American Medical Association. After a rich and full life, he died in 1919 at the age of eighty-nine.

More spectacular than Jacobi's gains in medicine was the wartime release of nuclear energy. Without question, the explosion of an atomic device in 1945 would have been impossible without the one hundred refugees from Fascist countries who joined the American scientific ranks between 1933 and 1941.[42] While a few of them, notably Albert Einstein, arrived before 1933, the majority came after the Nazis came to power. Four German scientists held Nobel prizes before they came: Einstein, James Franck, Otto Loewi, and Victor Hess, while others were awarded the coveted honor for work done in the United States, among them Felix Bloch (1952), Otto Stern (1943), Konrad Bloch (1964), and Hans Bethe (1967). Bethe, who was born in Strasbourg, taught at the Universities of Munich and Tübingen before coming to the United States. A citizen since 1941, Bethe served as Chief of theoretical physics at the Manhattan Project in Los Alamos, where the atomic bomb was built. Neither Edward Teller nor Leo Szilard were Germans by birth, but both studied and worked in Germany for years before coming to the united States. Together with Einstein, Teller and six others convinced President Franklin Roosevelt that the atom bomb project ought to be undertaken. Szilard, like Teller, was born in Hungary but took his Ph.D. in Berlin and taught there from 1925 - 1932. He, too, wrote to Roosevelt about the bomb, convinced Einstein to sign the letter, and worked on the project. Before his death in 1964 at La Jolla, California, Szilard turned to the study of biology.[43]

When the decision was reached to go ahead with the bomb, the man in charge, General Leslie Richard Groves, insisted on putting the controversial physicist, Dr. Julius Robert Oppenheimer in charge as the "indispensable man" for Los Alamos. Like Lyonel Feininger, Oppenheimer was born in New York City. He studied at Harvard, but took his Ph.D. at the University of Göttingen under the noted physicist, Max Born. Ten years after accepting the assignment at Los Alamos, Oppenheimer was declared untrustworthy by the United States Government, because he had written in July, 1953, in *Foreign Affairs:* "The very least we can conclude is that our twenty-thousandth bomb, useful as it may be in filling the vast munitions pipelines of a great war, will not in any deep strategic sense offset their two-thousandth." Such was Oppenheimer's prophetic warning about the American-Soviet arms race, and for this his security clearance was revoked.

On November 22, 1963, the newspapers reported that President John F. Kennedy, who had bestowed the Enrico Fermi award on Edward Teller, the father of the hydrogen bomb, and Hans Bethe, would personally hand it to the exonerated J. Robert Oppenheimer on December 2. (On December 2, 1942 Enrico Fermi, an Italian, had achieved the world's first nuclear chain reaction.) Less than twelve hours after the reports appeared, Kennedy was dead in

Dallas. In his place on December 2, stood President Lyndon Johnson, who conferred the prize as originally planned[44] Due to the parallel with Nazism — a citizen censured by his government for speaking out on what he believed to be morally right — Oppenheimer's trial inspired a popular stage play in Germany, translated into English as In the Matter of J. Robert Oppenheimer.[45]

Like Szilard, there were German-born scientists in the 1930s who shifted their interests in response to new stimuli encountered in their new homeland. Perhaps the most remarkable by-product of such a career switch was the discovery of deoxyribonucleic acid, or the carrier of heredity, known as the Crick-Watson model of DNA. Actually, four pioneers were involved — Erwin Schrödinger, Leo Szilard, Max Delbrück, and the Italian Salvador Luria.[46] Their precursors in the investigation were Ernst Haeckel and Jacques Loeb. Perhaps the most intensive work on the discovery was performed by Max Delbrück, a quantum mechanics expert, after he fled Germany and became a Rockefeller Fellow at Caltech in 1937. After long and intense study with Luria and Delbrück, Watson became the final synthesizer of the "secret of life."

In the field of space travel, too, the United States benefited from the influx of rocket experts who arrived from Germany after World War II. In this area, the key figure was Wernher von Braun, born on an estate near Posen in eastern Germany. His father was Secretary of Agriculture in one of the last cabinets of the Weimar Republic. Beginning in 1932, von Braun was a civilian expert for the German Army which provided him with proving grounds. His rockets first performed successfully in 1934, winning him prestige and in 1937, a 250-mile firing range at Peenemünde on the Baltic Sea. At this site during World War II, scientists developed the infamous V-2 (Vergeltungswaffe — "weapon of retribution"), which started hitting targets in England in 1944.[47]

After the German war effort collapsed, von Braun decided to flee toward the West in order to surrender to American Forces. "Operation Paperclip" was the code name for a program to round up scientific personnel and equipment. It attracted von Braun and at least 120 other scientists, chemists, aerodynamicists, and metallurgists, who signed contracts to come to the United States and work on rockets. At first the men and sixteen shiploads of captured equipment were "exiled" at Fort Bliss, Texas. After the Korean War, however, they moved to Huntsville, Alabama, to build today's space machines. Their first success came in 1953 with the firing of the Redstone Missile from Cape Canaveral.

The vehicles used to launch America's Explorer series were Redstone rockets, the direct descendants of the German V-2, but satellites were not orbited until 1958, a few months after the Russians had launched their sputnik. From the humiliating days of 1958, von Braun and his team went on to produce the Saturn 5, the huge powerhouse which flawlessly sent ten astronauts to the moon. Finally, at the age of sixty in 1972, von Braun, in the words of *Newsweek*, "The German-born engineering genius who made the U. S. space program possible, decided that the time had come for him to lift off. . . . In his new orbit, von Braun will serve as a vice president for engineering and development at Fairchild Industries."[48]

Earlier in the chapter, reference was made to the great German-born political scientist, Carl Schurz. In closing, mention should also be made of the German-born refugee from Hitler's Germany, Secretary of State Henry A. Kissinger. Born in the town of Fürth in 1923, Kissinger left home at the age of fifteen to take up life in the United States. He graduated summa cum laude from Harvard, where he took his Ph.D. in 1954 and stayed on as a professor in the International Seminar. By 1958 he was known for his writings on foreign affairs, and by 1965 he had won several distinguished prizes for his publications. During this time he also served as chief adviser to then Governor Nelson Rockefeller who in turn brought him to the attention of President Richard Nixon. Since 1968 he has been the chief architect of American foreign policy, although he was not appointed to the office of Secretary of State until late in 1973. His negotiations for peace in Vietnam in January, 1973, won him the Nobel Peace Prize.[49]

In this and in the preceding chapter we have been introduced to individuals who "spoke" to the world through the international "languages" of the arts and sciences. Some would have been great whether or not they emigrated to the United States. Others needed the elbow room which America provided to develop their talents fully. Music in the United States reaped benefits from a century of German immigration. American architecture might have developed differently without the Bauhaus associates in our midst. No one knows how different the world might be without the European emigrés who cooperated to build atomic weapons in the United States. Quite likely the space program would have been considerably retarded without the technology inherited from the German newcomers. All of the men described briefly in these two chapters rose high above the anonymous immigrants from Germany who are the primary heroes of this book.

CHAPTER 12

German-language Newspapers and Belles-lettres in the United States

BECAUSE THE STORY OF THE GERMAN-LANGUAGE PRESS HAS BEEN TOLD elsewhere,[1] this chapter shall concern itself with only the broad picture. The history of German belles-lettres has not been as well synthesized, but this category of writing, too, has been treated comprehensively in previous publications.[2]

Paradoxically, the German press in the United States failed, if anything, by fulfilling its purposes too well. To the extent that the columnists and editors succeeded in bridging the gap from Fatherland to new homeland, the need for the foreign-language vehicle of information had been fulfilled. Preservation of its audience was in the best interest of the German press and therefore editors fostered German-speaking communities to perpetuate the German culture in America. At the same time, the German immigrant press fulfilled its duty to introduce the German-speaking citizen to the political, social, and economic patterns of America. Publishers of German materials performed well in the latter capacity but not without fear for their financial futures.

The mortality rate of German-language papers and periodicals in the United States was high. Anyone with a little capital and a lot of ethnic pride could start a newspaper. Sustaining it was something else. If a community was steadily acquiring new immigration, it was easy for the paper to survive and even to thrive. But as soon as fresh immigration diminished, disaster for the German publisher loomed ahead. Older immigrants steadily acclimatized themselves to the English culture, and it was rare for second-generation German-Americans to lend support to a local German paper.

Some papers found their usefulness by feeding readers large doses of news from abroad. Their appeal lay in quieting the homesickness of those who had said goodbye to the Fatherland. Gradually, however, time and new experiences erased the vivid memories of home, and the German immigrant grew more interested in news about his land of adoption. This always cast the German editor into a schizophrenic position. Sooner or later, readers changed their attitudes toward Germany, but even as the interest of older German-Americans waned, the more recent arrivals required more European fare. Of necessity the editor had to cater constantly to both types. Perhaps, as Carl Wittke suggests, this dilemma explains why German papers of the twentieth century were so full of sentimental poetry and fiction. The first-generation Germans in America needed an emotional compensation for what they had left behind. Romantic novels and tear-dripping short stories cushioned the shock of transition by allowing the immigrant to identify with imaginary characters who spoke his native language.

The German in America was led gracefully into the culture of the New World by such foreign-language readings. He also found advice on how to speed the process of adjusting to new institutions. It is probably true that information about jobs, farmlands, and new opportunities somewhere in a growing America was best delivered to the German immigrant in his own language. The immigrant also trusted himself to venture into new regions as long as he could study the unknown beforehand in his own language.

Some German publications served special audiences. Many fostered the interests of religious groups. Others were opinionated organs which called for the destruction of religious organizations. Some publishers propounded wild political points of view to any audience that would listen, whereas others established papers to publicize their ideas on how to cure the world's ills. Most of the latter carried little news about current events, and they did not appeal to large numbers.

There is good sense in the contention of Herman Raster, editor of Chicago's *Illinois Staatszeitung*, that the German press in America was just as important for the Germans in America as were German churches and schools. Besides sustaining the German culture, the press also gave the immigrant a feeling of pride in the cultural achievements of his people on both sides of the Atlantic. Carl Schurz expanded on this point by defining the purposes of the German press as fourfold: (1) to explain America to the German immigrant, (2) to promote cooperation among the Germans in America, (3) to inform the Germans living in the United States about Germany, and

(4) to teach the German immigrant about the "open-handed generosity" of the United States.[3]

The German press in America was a viable enterprise in colonial times. But distinction came only with the arrival of the Forty-eighters. Wherever Forty-eighters settled they initiated literary and musical societies, freethinker movements, gymnastic organizations, and, not least, newspapers. Often the latter were an adjunct of one of the former. Repeatedly we find that one or more Forty-eighters followed the professions of doctor, lawyer, teacher, or politician, and edited a newspaper on the side. For example, Carl Schurz was active in many fields and published several newspapers. Gustav Körner was a politician, diplomat, and lawyer, but also a newspaperman. Over half of these publishers were rationalists and freethinkers who railed against established institutions in American society. In a tabulation of their professional activities it has been shown that fully half of the Forty-eighters were active in journalism.[4] At one time, a majority of all German newspapers in the United States were controlled by Forty-eighters.

Statistics illustrate these facts. In 1840 there were approximately forty German papers in the United States. During the year when the revolutions of 1848 erupted, the number was nearly twice that. Within four years, the total had increased to 133 and eight years later in 1860 there were approximately 266 German papers in America. Not only the number of papers, but the circulation statistics of the established organs also increased by leaps and bounds. The daily New York *Staatszeitung* tripled its subscriptions from 4,800 in 1851 to 15,300 by 1856. Other cities showed similar patterns of growth. In 1860, Pittsburgh supported five German dailies, and St. Louis had more.[5] Chicago and Milwaukee witnessed a doubling of both the German population and the circulation figures of the German papers. In Minnesota, Iowa, and in countless towns of Missouri, the first German newspapers were established by Forty-eighters. It was a period of impressive expansion in numbers which was accompanied by major improvements in tone, substance, quality of editing, and layout. In short, the period between 1848 and the outbreak of the Civil War can be referred to as the golden age of German-language newspapers in the United States.

Led by the liberal Forty-eighters, the German press in America prior to the Civil War was closely allied with the cause of abolition. Some of the older German papers, however, made no apologies for their opposition to abolition. At best, they conceded that gradual emancipation of the slaves might prove satisfactory. Often the older papers sided with English-language editors in opposing suffrage for the blacks. During the Civil War, many Forty-eighters continued their cry for emancipation while others turned critical of the North's leaders, especially of President Abraham Lincoln. A few German papers expressed their ethnic feelings in calling for the promotion of Civil War officers like German-born Franz Sigel. They also defended controversial German generals like Ludwig Blenker and Carl Schurz. During the electioneering of 1864, some German papers switched their support from Lincoln to the Democratic candidate, but the majority endorsed the President for a second term.

Later in the nineteenth century, German editors were seldom unanimous about any issue except the Franco-German War of 1870 - 1871. Having forgotten the suppression of liberals during the revolutions of 1848, and no longer apprehensive about Prussian power, German journalists in America became excited about Germany's victories in 1870. Echoing the German-American community, headlines cheered the prospects of a united Germany emerging in the heartland of Europe. Few editors criticized the methods employed to achieve unification. Discussions about reform, liberal revolution, and republicanism quickly faded as subscribers and advertisers ushered in a new heyday for German publishing in the United States.

Casting another glance at statistics, we note that in 1876 there were seventy-four German dailies which had a total circulation of just under 300,000. There were 374 weeklies, which had a combined list of subscribers in excess of one million. Thirty-one monthlies accounted for an additional 156,000 subscribers. In 1885, German papers represented 79 percent of all foreign-language publications in the United States. In 1890 the sum of German publications reached 727 — and this rose further to over 800 by 1894. This was the summit year for German journalism in the United States. Thereafter a decline set in, gradual at first, then more rapid. As the years passed, paper after paper disappeared due to vanishing interest of the readers. Nevertheless, just prior to World War I, the German press led all other foreign publications in the United States.[6]

It was World War I that put the capstone on the German press in the United States. Fear and hysteria triggered action by the government. Before the outbreak in Europe, the German press in America no longer covered German foreign policy or news. In most German-American communities, local problems and social activities commanded the full attention of the German editor. Prohibition was usually an issue, and it was allocated a fair share of the space as was women's suffrage. After the war broke out on the Continent, the run-of-the-mill German paper hardly differed from the average English-language paper. Most Americans, including those whose country of birth had been Germany, were undoubtedly anxious to remain isolated from the European struggle.

During World War I, before American involvement, there was little evidence that Germany influenced American opinion by way of the German press in America. What success the German government did achieve in the propaganda war was won by means of an agency in New York which issued press releases, interviews, lectures, movies, and other materials. Occasionally an average American was won over to the German cause. Mostly, the targets of these activities were the non-German people of America. The propaganda war between the British and the Germans raged regardless of efforts by the German press in the United States on behalf of American neutrality. In 1916, some Americans of German descent who wrote in the German press were guilty of indiscretions, but rarely of misdemeanors. Hermann Ridder of the New York *Staats-Zeitung* flew the German flag over his building, and when the mayor of New York ordered it removed, he hung it inside. Some editors blasted American manufacturers of war materials for providing the Allies with armaments. Until April 6, 1917, when war was declared, the vast majority of German-American publishers espoused neutrality and the cause of peace.

When a declaration of war was announced by the president, subscriptions to German papers plummeted. The following October, 1917, Congress enacted a law which, for the first time in American history, controlled the foreign-language press in the United States. Henceforth, all matters relating to the war had to be submitted to the local postmaster for censoring until such time as the government became convinced of the paper's loyalty and issued a permit exempting it from the time-consuming and, in particular, the expensive process of filing English translations.[7]

By 1918 German papers were closing or suspending operations indefinitely. A few converted to bilingual and then to English-language organs. In 1920, Ayer's *Newspaper Annual* indicated that there were only 278 German-language publications, many of which were house organs for lodges, churches, and social organizations. After the armistice, German newspapers waged a losing battle to regain their subscribers. That the struggle was in vain is illustrated by the 1930 statistics which show that German publications had declined to 172 — down over 100 from the 1920 mark — and down to a fraction of the high-tide publication year of 1894 when the total exceeded 800. World War II took a further toll, and by 1950 there were only sixty German papers left, including only seven dailies. At the beginning of World War II, New York led all other states in the number of German publications, followed by Illinois, Ohio, Minnesota, Pennsylvania, and Texas. As World War II ran its course, consolidation removed many titles from the newsstands and the shrinking process continued through the 1950s.

By 1975 there were just forty-four German-language publications in the United States and these included scholarly journals and fraternal publications. Only the Chicago *Abendpost*, the New York *Staats-Zeitung und Herold,* and the Milwaukee *Deutsche Zeitung* offered daily service. Weeklies still appeared in Los Angeles, San Francisco, Denver, Baltimore, Detroit, St. Louis, Omaha, Irvington (New Jersey), Buffalo, Cincinnati, Cleveland, Philadelphia, and Milwaukee.[8] These represented the battered survivors of a German-language press that once was the most proud and most numerous of all the foreign-language publications in the entire United States. The names of many descendants of German-language publications bestride the news world today — to mention just two of them — that of Joseph Pulitzer, who graduated from the St. Louis *Westliche Post* and that of the Ridder family, whose association with the New York *Staats-Zeitung und Herold* has grown into a news media empire that harbors within its borders numerous newspapers, radio, and television stations of the Midwest.

Also from the pens of German-American writers, originated German-language books, poetry, travelogues, reminiscences, accounts of pioneer life, autobiographies, and countless stories of the travail of immigrant life.[9] Some wrote in praise of democracy. Others denounced social evils and heaped commentary upon polemic about the new homeland. What they had to say attracted a contemporary audience but lacked the literary quality to command continued attention. No American of German birth or descent enjoys a reputation in Germany for the work he produced in the United States. The literary feats of Thomas Mann, Bertolt Brecht, and other political refugees whose work in the United States reveals literary merit have received world-wide acclaim, but none of them deals with German-American themes in works written while in residence in the United States.

The highest rated German literary works depicting the American scene are the ethnographical novels of Charles Sealsfield, the pen name of Karl Postl. Postl was born in 1793 near Prague, where he entered the monastery and was ordained to the priesthood. For political reasons, it appears, he fled to the United States in 1822 and stayed until 1826. After a visit to Germany he came back to America until 1832. Thereafter he made his domicile in Switzerland and visited the United States periodically until his death in 1864. During his travels in North America he lived for extended periods in Pennsylvania and in Arkansas. Some of his works were first published in Germany, others in America in English, and were subsequently translated into German. Sealsfield was a close observer of the New World and the American character.[10] Due to revived interest in Sealsfield both in Germany and in the United States, his collected works are being reissued.

Several poets who enjoyed a literary reputation in the German-speaking lands journeyed to the United States and expressed their American experiences to varying degrees in their writings. Such a man was Nikolaus Franz Niembsch, known popularly as Nikolaus Lenau. Born and educated in the Austrian Empire, Lenau came to the United States in 1832. Landing in Baltimore, he traveled across Pennsylvania, stopping at Bedford, Pittsburgh, and at the Harmonist colony in Economy. Later he bought a 400-acre farm in Crawford County near the present town of Bucyrus, Ohio. Neighbors remember him as a refined gentleman, elegantly dressed in a fur coat and white gloves. At first he dealt a few blows with the ax to a couple of primeval trees in a vain attempt to clear his Ohio land, but soon gave up and abandoned the undertaking. On his return trip, Lenau paid brief visits to prominent sites in America and then boarded a ship for Bremen from New York.[11] Embittered by his life in the wilds, Lenau wrote later of the United States as the *verschweinte* ("piggish") instead of the *Vereinte Staaten* ("United States") and perpetuated the misinformation that in the New World, birds do not sing nor do flowers have fragrance.

Another writer in this category was the Austrian Anastasius Grün, a nom de plume for Anton Alexander Graf von Auersperg. Grün never visited the United States. In spite of that, he excelled in describing the New World in his poetry. He sends greetings to the Susquehanna, to Washington's Monument, to the American forest, the Red Man, and the Ohio, and includes a glorious description of an imagined Fourth of July celebration in Pittsburgh.

The most prolific writer to describe America was Karl May. The son of a poor weaver, May was born in 1842, and worked as an elementary teacher. He was apprehended for stealing and served time in prison before he turned to writing stories, many of which bulged with adventurous escapades from the American West. Although he had never viewed the scenes of his novels, he excelled in depicting the American Indian and the white settlers as they enacted the drama of winning the West. May wrote more than seventy novels of which his best known is *Winnetou*; his most popular hero was the "noble savage," Old Shatterhand. After finishing his opus and selling millions of copies, May toured the United States shortly before his death in 1912. To this day, May is Germany's best-selling author.[12]

Several writers in Germany dealt with the theme of emigration to America. Gottfried Duden, for example, wrote of his western journey with an eye toward luring German immigrants to the New World. In addition to the handbooks, guides, and travelers' tips which were published in Germany as factual material, there was also fiction such as the novel *Streif- und Jagdzüge durch die Vereinigten Staaten Nord Americas* published in Bremen in 1844 by Friedrich Gerstäcker. The novelist spent six years in the United States and loved to tell about his experiences. He extolled the American system of government and ridiculed German factionalism. Typical of educated Germans in America at that time, Gerstäcker was not impressed by the average German immigrant he knew in Cincinnati and New York.[13] Cynical in some respects, Gerstäcker nevertheless lauded American pioneer virtues.

There were other authors of fiction who typified the characteristics of Gerstäcker. Heinrich Zschokke wrote a novel about the founding of Maryland. Theodore Griesinger produced novelettes about German immigrants in the United States. Friedrich Spielhagen wrote books with settings among the German settlements in the Mohawk Valley.[14]

Most previously mentioned works were published in Germany. Other writers composed their material in the German language and printed it in the United States. One such writer was Emil Klauprecht, who published the novel, *Cincinnati oder die Geheimnisse des Westerns*, at Cincinnati in 1854. Friedrich Hassaurek also wrote about, and published in, Cincinnati as did Samuel Ludvigh, known for his ultraliberal journal, *Die Fackel*. Adolph Douai and Heinrich Börnstein used the setting of St. Louis for their contributions, while Reinhold Solger's novel, *Anton in America, Novelle aus dem deutsch-amerikanischen Leben*, was published in New York in 1872. According to some, this was the best known of all German prose pieces published in the United States in the nineteenth century.[15]

As the nineteenth century wore to a close, more and more German-Americans were American-born citizens whose mother tongue happened to be German. This group, too, had its quota of authors. Usually if an American of German descent expressed his thoughts in German, it meant that he had been reared in a German-speaking community in the United States. Such communities preserved German culture only because certain favorable circumstances prevailed. Heinz Kloss has pointed out that German immigrants to the United States fell into two large camps. One was the liberal camp, whose members gravitated to the urban centers where they were soon assimilated. The other was the religious camp in which members tended to become farmers. They homesteaded lands adjacent to each other to create a German-speaking countryside. The religious camp also incorporated urban dwellers who formed tightly knit German-speaking wards and precincts in the larger cities.[16] The liberals were individualists who did not blend well with any other cohesive group. The religious immigrants, however, enjoyed the solidarity which emanated from their churches, and thus it was this latter group which preserved a German literary heritage in America.

From the German religious immigrants — Catholic, Lutheran, and other Protestants — came a considerable body of German literature during the 1880s and 1890s. Much of it was intended to counteract the brugeoning secular literature which adversely influenced German-American communities. Religious publishers directed didactic literature replete wth role models for Christian virtues at the young via the German mother tongue. Saving the faith and saving the language were almost synonymous. Pastor Carl H. Rohe of Syracuse and Clara Rieger Berens of St. Louis exemplify Lutheran writers who appealed to the German-speaking youth market. Others were Frank Frether of the Reformed Church and J. J. Messmer whose cause was not only propagation of the faith but propagation of reform, prohibition, and the rights of laborers to strike against industrial robber barons.[17]

There were also nonreligious writers who crusaded for socialist causes within the German-American communities. The Freidenker Publishing House of Milwaukee printed the works of several authors who called for social reconstruction and, in a few cases, for a dictatorship of the proletariat. Many writers in this category were Forty-eighters or heirs of the Forty-eighters. Late in the nineteenth century the radical brand of socialists faded. In the twentieth century several German-born authors revived the socialist theme, for example, Franz Kafka in his novel *Amerika* and Bertolt Brecht in his play *St. Joan of the Stockyards*. These authors made use of the American scene to illustrate the plight of the underdog in the materialistic system of capitalism.

Taking the whole of belles-lettres, several conclusions can be drawn. (1) There were no movements or schools of German-language literature in America, although there were themes and categories such as the religiodidactic group, recurrence of the emigration theme, the ethnographic novel, and the motif of materialism. (2) The vast majority of these writers were German-born. American-born authors did not appear until the 1880s, and the few who did were associated with religious communities and church-affiliated schools. (3) A dichotomy existed between urban-based liberal writers and churchgoing conservatives, although neither group formed a homogeneous school in opposition to the other. Both were antagonistic toward each other and undoubtedly injured the chances of German publishing in America by decimating the potential readership. (4) Most of the writing which was not polemic or proselytizing in nature was intended as entertainment. Couched between the lines, however, was light satire against the Irish, against temperance, against Anglo-American prejudice toward foreigners, and against corruption in politics, slaveholding, land acquisition, and zealous town booming. (5) Some of the prose and much of the poetry expressed nostalgia for the homeland, known as the *Heimweh* motif. (6) Finally, there have been and continue to be prose and poetry writers in America who use the German language to express themselves on a wide variety of topics. Their works have found respectable outlets, and it appears that the market for such material is growing.[18] Several societies that promote German-language literature in America are the *Verband deutschsprachiger Autoren in Amerika* (Cincinnati), Society for German-American Studies (Cleveland), *Die literarische Gesellschaft von Chicago,* and the *Literarischer Verein* of New York.

On the whole, publications in German provided the German element in the United States with the means by which their immigrant experiences could be shared and a sense of identity maintained. In one respect, such writings helped consolidate the German heritage in America. In another, the German press grew closer to American attitudes and, by that token, advanced the German element in accommodating itself to American society.

Late in the 1920s the American journalist, H. L. Mencken, the son of German-Americans of Baltimore, wrote a description of the Germans in America in which he decried their loss of cultural influence and political power. He remarked that there were no longer any German-language newspapers of substance and he argued that even the German bookstores would have passed from the scene except for the patronage of Anglo-Americans whose talent and good taste for literature prompted them to buy German publications. Americans of German ancestry, he noted, no longer were able to cope with the German language.[19] With the World War I experience to hasten the process, the German-American community in the United States had spun itself into oblivion within the American mainstream. The German-language presses had no alternative but to disband.

CHAPTER 13

The Russian-Germans in the United States

RUSSIAN-GERMANS — EMIGRANTS FROM THE VARIOUS GERMAN STATES who had lived in Russia for several generations — first began to migrate to America from the Black Sea and Volga regions of Russia in 1873. Between 1763 and 1859 it had been the policy of the Russian government to invite colonists from Germany to settle in Russia. Largely, the Russians wanted western colonists to bring vast uninhabited steppe land under cultivation and to wrest it from nomadic bands. Thus, in 1763, the German-born Empress, Catherine II of Russia, issued a manifesto offering German immigrants inducements to settle in her country. Colonists and their descendants were guaranteed (a) financing and free land, (b) exemption from military service, (c) control over their churches and schools, and (d) local self-government.[1]

The manifesto coincided with years of famine and oppression in southwestern Germany. As a result, large numbers headed for Russia, while lesser numbers departed for the American colonies. About this time, the leader of the American Harmony Society, George Rapp, contacted President Thomas Jefferson urging him to facilitate emigration from Baden-Württemberg to the United States. The bill which the President proposed in response to Rapp's appeal passed the Senate, but failed in the House, when the speaker broke a tie negatively. Consequently, thousands of Germans who were anticipating the Millennium calculated to begin in 1836 found their haven, not with Rapp in America, but with the Russian Czar, Alexander of Holy Alliance fame.[2]

The first colonists to arrive in Russia settled along the Volga River where, between 1764 and 1786 some 23,000 Germans established 104 separate colonies. Beginning in 1789, Mennonites (who originated in Switzerland but tarried for decades in North Germany and Holland as well as Prussia) settled in the Black Sea region. Between the years 1854 and 1859, Mennonites also colonized the Volga region.[3]

Non-Mennonite Germans migrated to the Black Sea region during the reign of Catherine's grandson, Alexander I (1801 - 1825), who issued a proclamation in 1804 inviting more German immigrants to Russia, now with new stipulations: "Our aim must not be so much the settlement of those lands by foreigners but the settlement of them by a limited number of such immigrants as can serve as models for agricultural occupations and handicrafts; it is necessary to limit them to the most essential: to good, well-to-do farmers. . . ."[4] Alexander's invitation was reminiscent of Catherine's because once again the German states were being ravaged — formerly by the Seven Years' War, now by the Napoleonic Wars. Now, however, the German immigrants had to bring along goods and cash in addition to agricultural and mechanical skills. Like Catherine's immigrants, they, too, could leave Russia any time, providing they advanced taxes. The result of the two manifestos was that both rulers received immigrants, Catherine obtaining them in quantity, whereas Alexander's were more conspicuous for quality.

By the time colonization was terminated in 1859, thousands of Germans had settled in the Ukraine, the Crimea, Transcaucasia, and Bessarabia. Due to high birth rates, the German population grew from the original 100,000 immigrants to 1.7 million. In 1914 there were 300 mother colonies and some 3,000 daughter colonies. Until 1871, when the Russian Government began abrogating their special privileges, the Germans in Russia chose to remain segregated from their Russian neighbors. They had German-language schools, churches, and village administration. There was neither intermarriage with Russians nor cultural interchange. An 1871 decree called on them to integrate. When a second one in 1874 instituted military conscription, thousands of the Russian-Germans availed themselves of the ten-year grace period to leave Russia.[5]

Between 1872 and 1920, nearly 120,000 Russian-Germans emigrated to the United States. The peak year was 1912. When World War I broke out in 1914, the tidal wave fell to a trickle. According to the 1920 census, the Russian-German stock living in the United States (first and second generation Russian-Germans) amounted to 301,214. North Dakota had 69,985, Kansas 31,512, South Dakota 30,937, Nebraska 22,421 and there were lesser numbers in other states. It was estimated in 1940 that there were as many as 400,000 Americans of Russian-German stock in the United States.[6]

The Russian-Germans are to this day an identifiable group in the United States. They are strongly religious — almost clannish in their loyalty to the Lutheran, Reformed, or Catholic denominations and include several Mennonites sects whose faith admonishes separatism. Their settlements in Russia conditioned them for a tradition of colony existence, and when they settled on lands in America they selected adjacent tracts so that social isolation from other ethnic neighbors was possible on the Great Plains. Just as in Russia, they tended to follow a pattern of religious homogeneity when they homesteaded in the United States. As a result, the church, the school, and social contact reinforced the Russian-Germans in their group-conscious identity.[7]

The Russian-Germans who settled in the Dakotas were primarily from the Black Sea region of Russia. Protestant in religious affiliation, these were the first to arrive in 1873. A short time later, Germans from the Volga River began settling in the central Great Plains states. As a rule, the Volga Germans were Catholic. The centers of the Catholic Russian-Germans are Ellis and Rush Counties, Kansas, south and east of the town of Hays.[8] Protestant Volga Germans frequently settled in Lincoln or Sutton, Nebraska and later found work in the sugar beet fields of Colorado.[9]

The Russian-German settlements in the United States can be divided into two groups — one according to geographic area of origin in Russia and the other according to religious denomination. Geographically, there were two sources: the Black Sea and the Volga River. Smaller numbers came from Bessarabia, Volhynia, the Caucasus, and elsewhere. Religiously, they were Catholic, Protestant (Reformed or Lutheran), and Mennonite (meaning also the Hutterites).

When the Russian-Germans first arrived in America, they sought to retain their life-in-isolation both as to geographic origin and religious distinction. At first this seemed feasible, for the Russian-Germans came at a time when the Great Plains were being opened to agriculture. Vast tracts of land were available for homesteading and group settlement by Black Sea German Protestants, Volga German Catholics, and other ethnic subgroups. To earlier European immigrants, the Great Plains represented an environment that was unfamiliar. Up to 1875, it had been alleged that the region was a great American desert laced with nomads. Travel across the Great Plains was fraught with hardship and danger. Humid-climate farming did not work on semiarid lands. Recent studies indicate that agrarian utilization of the Great Plains was delayed until the arrival of the Russian-Germans whose field of experience was suitable to the conditions of Great Plains farming.[10]

On the one hand, then, the Russian-Gemans were experientially equipped to cope with the climate and soil conditions of the Great Plains. On the other, their arrival coincided with the roll-back of the Indian civilizations and the construction of transcontinental railroads. The last outposts to be claimed from the Indians and opened up by the railroads for settlement were the Dakotas. Therefore, it is no accident that North and South Dakota, along with western Kansas, were the three states in the Union which received the largest numbers of Russian-Germans. True to their habits of agriculture on the Russian steppes, these immigrants became the backbone of America's wheat farming, having brought with them in 1874 the hardy strains of Turkey red hard wheat. Fifty years later, agents of Soviet Russia came to Kansas to buy back wheat which the Russian-Germans had taken with them.[11] In 1973 and subsequently the Russians were back again to purchase millions of bushels of the wheat itself. In 1974, the U.S. Postal Department issued a ten cent commemorative stamp in its rural America series to recognize the contribution made by the Russian-Germans in bringing Turkey red hard wheat to the Great Plains.

To get established on the Great Plains, the Russian-Germans used base camps in Sutton and Lincoln, Nebraska, and in Yankton, South Dakota, then the territorial capital for both Dakotas. Soon they expanded into Hutchinson and Bon Homme Counties, South Dakota, which served as centers for expansion north and westward in the Dakotas and Canada. For the most part, these were Mennonites and Protestant Black Sea Germans.[12] During the 1880s, McPherson and Campbell Counties, especially the town of Eureka, South Dakota, represented the heart of Black Sea German settlement in America. Eureka was the spur end of the Chicago, Milwaukee, and St. Paul Railroad. By 1892, with Russian-German farmers raising wheat all over the landscape, Eureka was the largest primary wheat-shipping point in the world. Thirty-two commission houses had agents there to buy grain and forty-two elevators handled the more than four million bushels shipped each year. From the date of its establishment, Eureka took just three years to become the Milwaukee Road's most profitable shipping station with earnings in the range of $100,-000 monthly.[13]

Funneling through the distribution center of Eureka, Russian-

Germans pushed into the North Dakota counties of McIntosh, Emmons, and Logan. Later they followed the railroad construction lines into the geographic center of North Dakota. A high percentage of the population in the counties of Morton, Stark, Sheridan, Grand, Mercer, McLean, Stutsman and others was Russian-German.[14] Although eventually nearly every state in the Union had Russian-Germans, the state of North Dakota had by far the largest number, 70,000 in 1920.

With over 31,000 Russian-Germans in 1920, Kansas was second to North Dakota in providing homes for them. Here the Volga Germans clearly were in the majority, although there were Black Sea Mennonites at Hillsboro.[15] The Volga Germans settled most densely in Russell and, in particular, Ellis Counties, Kansas. By 1940, reports said, an observer could walk twenty or thirty miles in any direction without ever stepping off Volga German owned soil. In Ellis County, as in North and South Dakota, Russian-Germans named towns and settlements after the German colonies in Russia from whence they came. Thus, Herzog, Schoenchen, Munjor, Catherine, Pfeifer, Liebenthal, and others commemorate their former homes in Russia.[16]

The Ellis County area of Kansas is of special interest to American geographers because it was one of the few places in the United States where Europeans established a village pattern of settlement similar to the south German style. Accordingly, all the farmers lived and slept in town, but went out to work their scattered fields during the daytime. The Homestead Act prescribed that each farmer must dwell on his land and improve it over a five-year period. In effect, therefore, the immigrant farmers were precluded from following their German tradition of farm villages, but the basic pattern of a village did take hold in Ellis County. Houses and barns were built on village lots and farmers owned nonadjacent fields on various tracts within the township. Aerial photographs of the villages of Herzog, Catherine, Victoria, Pfeifer, and Munjor illustrate the long, narrow village garden plots. Also, atlases and platbooks from 1900 - 1910 depict the quilt-patched land ownership as well as such European farming styles as the common grazing lands.[17]

By 1920, large groups of Russian-Germans, exceeding 10,000 people were noted in the states of Nebraska and Colorado (over 20,000 each), and in Michigan, Washington, Wisconsin, California, and Oklahoma (over 10,000 each).[18]

The Russian-Germans in the United States have held more rigidly to their Germanic traditions than did the Germans who emigrated to America directly from the *Reich*. Their experience in Russia had conditioned them to live in isolation from the local population and to retain their Old World life-styles. One of these was the European village, which they established near Sutton, Nebraska, Yankton, South Dakota and Russell, Kansas, in addition to Ellis County. American journalists at the time made pleas for just such villages on the prairie.

The isolated farmhouse must be abandoned, and the people must draw together in villages. . . . Titles to homestead claims are now nearly all perfected by the required five years' occupancy of the land. Thus, there is no longer the necessity that the farmers should live upon the particular tracts which they cultivate. . . . Let us suppose that the owners of sixteen quarter-section farms. . . . should agree to remove their homes to the center of the tract. . . . The homes of the sixteen families would surround a village green, where the schoolhouse would stand. This could be used for church services on Sunday and for various social purposes on week-day evenings. . . . And there would probably be a store and a post office.[19]

While the case for *Dorf* living on the prairie never received a fair trial in America, Old World building styles have been noted in Russian-German communities. Settlers constructed the house and barn under one roof so that the occupants walked from the living room into the adjacent barn. Some houses had a "Russian kitchen." The inner core of the house consisted of a small room, ten or twelve feet square, in which there was a cook stove. This cubicle was made of earthen bricks which rose like a pyramid through the second floor of the house into a central chimney at the peak. Smoke was channeled through a recess in the earthen walls to heat a built-in oven, then rose freely through the pyramid in which hams and sausages could be hung for curing. Earthen brick walls extended through the living room so that heat was conducted to the whole house from this central system.[20]

Arriving on the treeless Great Plains, the Russian-Germans at first built sod houses. Later their experience on the Russian steppes served them well. Unlike their North European neighbors who demanded wood, the Russian-Germans manufactured their own building blocks from black prairie earth by wetting it, adding straw to bind it, forming it in boxes and drying it in the sun. Walls of these houses were usually two feet thick. Outside and inside they were whitewashed. In more recent years the outsides have been coated with regular siding, rendering the earthen house invisible to the untrained eye. However, the house remains practical, for it answers the problem of permanent construction with little lumber, holds warmth in winter and remains cool in summer.[21]

Churches in the Catholic Volga German settlements of Kansas resemble those of the old homeland in Russia. Examples are visible in Hays and Loretta, Kansas, Scottsbluff, Nebraska, Lincoln and Fresno, California, and Windsor, Colorado.[22] Also visible on Russian-German homesteads are the freestanding underground root cellars and summer kitchens. The summer kitchen allowed housewives an alternative to firing the heating centers in their earthen houses during the hot summer. Instead they cooked in a nearby shelter and took their food into the cool earthen houses to serve at meals.

Generally, the Russian-Germans followed religious traditions and even superstitions that are unknown outside these communities in the United States. The Volga Germans of Kansas seem to have been especially laden with such traditions. Fear of the dark, of cemeteries, and of storms evoked specific rituals. At Christmas, housewives sometimes baked an extra loaf of bread for the cat or dog to ward off hunger for the balance of the year. If someone died in the house, a clock would be stopped until after the burial. Rain on the first Friday of a month indicated that plenty of rain would fall for the balance of the month. "Mixed marriages" were not marriages between a Catholic and a non-Catholic but between individuals from different settlements of Russian-Germans. Even the marriage of a Russian-German with a German from the *Reich* was considered unthinkable until about 1900.[23]

By tradition, the Black Sea Germans were wheat farmers. The Volga Germans were more accustomed to other employment. For example, a Volga settlement in Pine Island, New York, had exclusive control of the onion industry. Another in southwest Michigan grew only peppermint. In Chicago, the Volga Germans were employed in construction and in Portland, Oregon, in the street maintenance department.[24]

Russian-Germans maintained German papers for each splinter group. There were Black Sea German newspapers and Volga German newspapers. Some were known as Catholic and others as Protestant among the two basic groups. The only one that functioned as *the* Russian-German organ was the *Dakota Freie Presse.* For generations this paper circulated not only in the 1,600 settlements of Russian-Germans in the United States but also in the colonies on the Volga and the Black Sea. American politicians conferred on it the title "Bible of the Russian-Germans." Among the people themselves, it was the one communications link with their people anywhere in the world.[25]

Assimilation of the Russian-Germans has not been a unidimensional process. "It would be wrong to say simply that their Americanization was slower or faster than their non-German neighbors. There was a natural selectivity at work; here and there, on various levels, the process was speeded up, here and there it was retarded. In the main it did, in fact, take a much longer period than the customary three generation Americanization process."[26]

Back in Russia, the Black Sea and Volga German colonies have all but disappeared. Laws passed in 1915 called for their annihilation. This order was stayed by the Bolshevik Revolution of 1917 which permitted them to form an "Autonomous Socialist Soviet Republic of the Volga Germans" with some 500,000 German-speaking citizens in 1924. But in 1941 when Hitler invaded Russia, Stalin ordered all German-speaking colonists deported to Soviet Asia. Twenty-three years later in 1964, Khrushchev rescinded Stalin's deportation order, but the Germans in Russia have not been permitted to return to their former homes. The 1970 census of the USSR lists 1,846,000 Soviet Germans living in various parts of Soviet Russia, the highest concentration being in the Middle Asian Republic of Kazakhstan.[27] The major new homes of the Black Sea and Volga Germans are, therefore, in Kazakhstan and on the American Great Plains.

CHAPTER 14

German-Americans in the Early Twentieth Century and in World War I

WHILE THE FIRST WORLD WAR WAS THE CATALYST FOR TOTAL assimilation of the Germans in America, the amalgamating process was well underway before the American declaration of war in 1917. After the turn of the century, the German language came to be used less and less in spite of efforts to halt its erosion. In fact, the German-born in the United States continued to show a conspicuous tendency toward naturalization. By 1910, more than 90 percent of the German-born had taken out first papers. Their closest rivals were the Scandinavians with some 80 percent, whereas less than 20 percent of the Balkan peoples had yet applied. Centrifugal forces would have caused the German element to disappear as swiftly and less noticeably if the martyr mentality of 1914 - 1918 had not provided a rallying issue.[1]

The war generated an outside force for revitalization. Its inner momentum came from the German-American Alliance, a national organization known officially as *Der Deutsch-Amerikanische Nationalbund*. The alliance came into existence two years after the Pan-German Union was founded in Berlin, suggesting to some that it was an extension of the union or some other arm of German imperialism. Officially constituted in October, 1901, the alliance grew out of a federation of the German societies in Pennsylvania. Under the able leadership of Dr. Charles J. Hexamer, the American-born son of a Forty-eighter and a prosperous engineer in Philadelphia, the alliance was established when representatives came together from Maryland, Ohio, New Jersey, Missouri, Wisconsin, and Minnesota.

According to its constitution, the alliance existed to promote the common good of German-Americans. A thirteen-point program ruled out overt political involvement, forbade religious activities, and proscribed nationalistic goals. German was to be fostered in the schools, but so was physical training in conjunction with the Turner philosophy. As was to be expected, the alliance opposed any limits on immigration. It called for conservation of America's forests and urged all German immigrants to acquire American citizenship and exercise their civic duties at the ballot box.[2]

Within ten years the German-American National Alliance had become the largest organization of any ethnic group in American history. Shortly before World War I, Louis Viereck addressed the Prussian Diet in Berlin, claiming the alliance would soon enjoy "the distinction of being the most widespread German body the world has ever seen."[3] At the time he spoke, the membership was reported at two million, concentrated in the strongly German states. A total of forty states had at least one chapter of the alliance. At its peak in 1916, the alliance claimed over three million members. The active membership was perhaps one tenth of that number.

Despite a triumph of numbers, the alliance's effectiveness was illusory. Its success rested on several supporting coincidences. For one, the German press promoted it as a means to sustain its own readership. More significantly, the brewing industry — exclusively in the hands of German-Americans — lavishly supported the alliance as a means of counterattacking prohibition which threatened the brewers with financial disaster. Thus the Anti-Saloon League did more to build the alliance than did German politicians in the *Reich* or the lovers of German culture in America. The alliance grew in proportion to the Prohibition party and in opposition to it. In 1908, this party aimed at the Germans by calling for "legislation basing suffrage only upon intelligence and ability to read and write the English language."[4] In the prewar twentieth century, many German-Americans were incapable of English-language usage.

With many southern states already "dry," the alliance prepared lists of "suitable" candidates for the 1914 elections, urging members to forget party loyalty if a candidate favored prohibition. As one German paper put it, "In this election campaign, it is as much a matter of 'to be or not to be' as it is over there for the Germans and Austro-Hungarians on the battlefields of Belgium, France and Russia."[5] Pamphlets were issued for citizenship training, as were German editions of state constitutions and public documents. Also, the alliance spread its umbrella to include aloof organizations like the Catholic *Central-Verein*, the American Truth Society, and the Irish-German Leagues.

Once the war broke out in Europe, the effect on the Germans in America was like the prohibition issue — it drew them together. During the initial stages, the Germans joined pacifist groups and advocated strict neutrality. They tried to counter British propaganda, opposed loans to the Allies, and promoted legislation to embargo the shipment of arms.[6] Dr. Charles Hexamer appealed personally to Congress in favor of a bill prohibiting the export of war materiel. The bill's chief spokesman was German-born Richard Bartholdt from Missouri's tenth district, who warned that Germany and Austria claimed the kinship of twenty-five million Americans who cast at least five million votes.

Embargo legislation was coordinated by Bartholdt and Representative Henry Vollmer of Davenport, Iowa. The German press and churches throughout America championed the embargo and bundles of two million supporting signatures arrived at the Capitol, triggering charges of a German lobby, a pro-German plot, and "a close resemblance to treason." But, with the assistance of President Wilson, the embargo bill was pigeonholed. The embargo storm broke anew on May 7, 1915, when the *Lusitania*, its hold allegedly stuffed with cargoes of arms which the bill would have forbidden, was torpedoed by German submarines.

Later in 1915 the Allies petitioned Washington for a billion-dollar loan. Dr. Hexamer spoke for the alliance in denouncing the application and warned that German-American depositors would create a run on participating banks. Rumors spread that German-Americans would divert their money into a separate banking system and alarmed bankers refused any association with the loan. As a result, the Allies had to send over money to keep the bond prices at par. Unaware of the inherent contradiction, it appears, German-American leaders continued to promote the sale of imperial German loans in the United States; at least ten million dollars worth were subscribed by the end of 1915.[7]

As the shouting escalated, the German-Americans gave up on legislation and turned to the elections of 1916 to redress grievances. Populists and Irish-Americans lined up with the Germans, prompting President Wilson to reject as unpatriotic those Americans who needed hyphens in their names. In the course of the campaign, the Allies operated their propaganda machines in America and the Germans, with less subtlety, were close behind.[8] Abandoning plans to establish an English-language paper of their own, the German government instead cooperated with George Sylvester Viereck in publishing the *Fatherland,* an organ of the German-American Alliance. Columnists for the weekly saw little difference between Germany's violation of Belgian neutrality and the United States' seizure of Texas or California. They pointed out that George Washington had fought the same enemy against whom Germany now waged war.

Exactly what subsidies came to the *Fatherland* from the German treasury is unclear. Nor is it apparent how American public opinion was changed by the publication. It is known that German-Americans sympathized with the German side while neutrality continued. During the 1916 campaign, therefore, Wilson opted for a "definite and unequivocal repudiation of the hyphen vote."[9] At its convention in St. Louis in 1916, the Democratic party adopted a plank which singled out the German-American Alliance. "We condemn all alliances and combinations of individuals in this country, of whatever nationality or descent, who agree and conspire together for the purpose of embarrassing or weakening our government or of improperly influencing or coercing our public representatives in dealing or in negotiating with any foreign power."[10]

Led by virtually every German paper in the nation, the German-Americans bolted the Democratic party in wholesale numbers and flocked to Republican candidate, Charles Evans Hughes. German-Irish leagues were born, and in some cities there were joint celebrations of St. Patrick's Day and Bismarck's birthday. That the Irish and Germans joined hands is not as absurd as it might appear. The Irish were Catholic. England was Protestant. On a number of occasions just prior to World War I, nominally Catholic France failed to support the Catholic Church. Austria and Hungary were staunch defenders of Catholic policy in Europe. The German Catholic *Central-Verein* in the early days of the war pledged full sympathy with the Central Powers. Although few Irish prelates among the American hierarchy took sides, Irish laymen were candidly pro-German because the defeat of England offered the best hope for Irish independence from Great Britain.[11]

Late in the campaign, Hughes acknowledged the support of his Irish-German coalition. Soon hostile cartoonists depicted him wearing a German spike helmet and as a mercenary trudging in the shadow of the Kaiser. Sensing expediency, Wilson repudiated the hyphenate vote at every opportunity: "I am the candidate of a party, but I am above all things an American citizen. I neither seek the favor nor fear the displeasure of that small alien element which puts loyalty to any foreign power before loyalty to the United States."[12] When the pro-German Jeremiah O'Leary sent Wilson a telegram denouncing his pro-British stance, Wilson again begged: "I would feel deeply mortified to have you or anybody like you vote for me. Since you have access to many disloyal Americans and I have not, I will ask you to convey this message to them."[13] Even Johann von Bernstorff, the German ambassador in Washington, sensed that the German effort to defeat Wilson was boomeranging.

The Germans and their Irish consorts resorted to questionable tactics. It appears that the explosion of July 30, 1916, which rocked New York harbor destroying seven million dollars worth of explosives destined for the Allies, was their deed. Viereck's *Fatherland* saw the hand of God in it, noting that the explosion shattered every window in the "bomb-proof" office of J. P. Morgan.[14] The real culprits have never been identified, but the job was credited to German socialists, Irish revolutionaries, and their sympathizers. Rather than winning votes, the incidents tipped cautious supporters in favor of Wilson.

When the returns came in, Wilson had won reelection handily. Evidence suggests that many Germans held for the Democratic candidate, Wilson, perhaps because they were ashamed of the blatant efforts of imperial German propagandists.[15] On the heels of the election, the German-American Alliance went into a sudden tailspin. The defeat of Hughes was an implicit defeat of the alliance. In a number of states, the German-Americans also lost the battle against prohibition. The case for woman suffrage gained ground, and it was no comfort to the Germans when prohibition triumphed without female votes. Worst of all, defeats in these issues did nothing to frighten President Wilson into a more neutral position toward the Central Powers.[16]

After the election, America veered toward deeper involvement with the Allies. In January, 1917, came the Zimmermann telegram which stipulated that unrestricted submarine warfare would soon begin and that if the United States did not remain neutral, Germany would conclude an alliance with Mexico and Japan to cause trouble at the back door. Initially it was thought the telegram was a hoax. But the following March, Foreign Minister Arthur Zimmermann in a Berlin press conference acknowledged its authenticity. Suddenly Americans imagined Mexicans swarming across the Rio Grande led by German officers.

In a frantic effort to salvage the peace, German-language papers carried pleas in English, claiming that the real threat to American security lay with joining the bankrupt Allies. It was of no avail. The Zimmermann telegram discredited the German press and the alliance. Public opinion tilted in favor of the President and on April 2, 1917, he asked Congress to declare war on the Central Powers. In the wink of an eye, Germans threw away their *Deutschtum* as an embarrassing possession.

With things German under suspicion, it is not surprising that an American who was not of German descent emerged as the political leader of the German element in the United States. His name was Robert Marion La Follette, the senator from Wisconsin. The Germans did not elect a descendant of their people to national office until Dwight Eisenhower, but in La Follette they acquired in action what they lacked in name. A hero of liberal Germans in Wisconsin, La Follette had fought hard against American involvement through his speeches and his paper, *La Follette's Magazine*. When the resolution for declaration of war against Germany came to a vote in the Senate on April 4, 1917, Senator La Follette (followed by George Norris of Nebraska and William Stone of Missouri) voted against it and spoke out bitterly as no American with a German name could have done without being arrested.[17] It passed the Senate eighty-two to six, and the House, 373 to forty-four.

La Follette's leadership was of little avail against the unbridled emotionalism unleashed against the Germans. Organizations such as the *Nord-Amerikanischer Turnerbund* called on their members "to silence the tender voice of the heart," but the hysteria did not abate. German-language newspaper editors professed "we have not the least sympathy with the German government as it is constituted today and we have devoted all we have to the cause of the United States."[18] Societies sprang up among German-Americans to promote "Americanism." However, with the tacit endorsement of the Wilson cabinet, Attorney General Thomas Gregory organized 200,000 untrained, volunteer detectives to feed the Justice Department with information about suspected aliens and disloyal citizens. Named the American Protective League, the members took oaths, carried badges, and conducted hundreds of thousands of investigations. The APL failed to catch a single *bona fide* spy but succeeded in creating an awful climate of suspicion and alarm.[19]

Charges and arrests resulted in convictions on flimsy evidence. A German-speaking minister in Ohio was indicted for violating the Espionage Act by remarks made while burying a soldier. In St.

Louis, a German Methodist pastor was arrested for returning a Liberty bond circular with a criticism of Wilson written on it. In a Texas town, the mayor and ten citizens were arrested for displaying a German flag over the Germania Club house. A seventeen-year-old school girl was dismissed for refusing to sing "America." Allegedly, Germans posing as Bible salesmen tried to stir up the Negroes in the South. In Dayton, the militia guarded the water works against feared acts of German sabotage. German-speaking Red Cross workers in Denver supposedly put glass in bandages and bacteria in medical supplies. Cincinnati's meat packers were rumored to be grinding glass into sausages and in South Dakota, a Mennonite flour-mill was closed when a customer reported finding glass chips in the flour. On the name plate of the Bismarck railroad station, patriots painted "To hell with this stupid Hun. What did he ever do for us?" Across the nation, hamburger became salisbury steak and sauerkraut turned to liberty cabbage. German fried potatoes disappeared, Brooklyn's Hamburg Avenue became Wilson Avenue; German-town, Nebraska, turned to Garland; Berlin, Iowa, became Lincoln, pinochle was retitled liberty, and pacifists were rechristened "spiritual aliens." In the early morning hours of April 5, 1918, German-born Robert P. Prager was seized by a mob of 200 and hanged as a lesson in patriotism.[20]

German shepherd dogs became Alsatian shepherds and dachshunds were stoned. Boy Scouts burned German-language papers on the streets of Columbus, Ohio, and the National Guard burned German books in Baraboo, Wisconsin, and other cities. Musical organizations purged Wagner, Schubert, Schumann, and Beethoven, and Italian opera experienced its finest hour. German-language schools were closed, and strict control was exercised over the German-language press. To speed the assimilation of Germans (and other nationality groups), the Council of National Defense, created by Congress in 1916, was extended to each state. Some governors gave the councils no authority, but in the Midwest several legislatures enacted statutes granting the state, county, and local councils of defense sweeping legal powers, including that of sub-poena and punishment for contempt. Added to this structure was a broad array of committees on Americanization. As one writer put it, "The war has taught us the need of a more united people, speaking one language, thinking one tradition, and holding allegiance to one patriotism — America."[21] The "Hun" language, judged to be the major block to assimilation, stimulated the worst hysteria. German was forbidden by state councils of defense not only in schools but in churches, over the telephone, and in semipublic places. The secretary of Iowa's council of defense typified the sentiment: "If their language is disloyal, they should be imprisoned. If their acts are disloyal, they should be shot."[22]

Before America's entry, it is true, the German-Americans had contributed much to war victims in the Fatherland. Austria and Hungary also received support through the German and the Austro-Hungarian Red Cross units operating in the United States. Generally the initiative for such societies came from the German-American Alliance which originally appealed for $2,000,000 over the signature of Dr. Charles Hexamer. Funds were channeled through the German, Austrian, and Hungarian Consulates in the United States.[23] But this activity should not have made the Germans suspect, because the British, French, Polish, and Italian Red Cross units functioned in America in exactly the same fashion. German-American churches also collected funds for war victims and channeled them via sister church bodies in Germany. The Missouri Synod, for example, sent some $61,000 to its counterpart in Saxony.[24]

After the United States declared war, the Germans in America ceased aiding war-torn countries and donated generously to the American war chest. If an isolated slacker was identified, local councils of defense quickly brought him into line. Advertisements for Liberty bonds appeared in all German-language papers, although there was little editorial enthusiasm for the project. But, when the first loan drive was over, Treasury Secretary William G. McAdoo sent a letter to all foreign-language editors praising "those of foreign birth" for their undoubted loyalty.[25]

In most cases, the Germans easily subscribed their Liberty loan quotas. In Milwaukee they substantially exceeded their suggested sum of fourteen million dollars by purchasing eighteen million.[26] Often, however, selling campaigns were accompanied by odious publicity stunts: Kaiser Wilhelm would be depicted as the "beast of Berlin" and posters showed babies being tortured by Huns. To prove their loyalty, German-American leaders and editors spearheaded loan drives, frequently as door-to-door bond salesmen. German societies staged parades and rallies to open the purses, and many a German pastor elicited subscriptions from the pulpit. The

Missouri Synod proclaimed June 3, 1917, "Liberty Loan Sunday."
The Teutonic Society of Sedalia, Missouri put all its funds into
bonds, and in New York, the *Liederkranz* Singing Society subscribed to $150,000 on a single evening.[27] The St. Louis *Liederkranz*
bought $525,000 in Liberty bonds and 101 of its members served in
the armed forces.

On the battlefields, too, the response of German-Americans was
overwhelmingly positive. General of the Armies, John J. Pershing
and Captain Eddie Rickenbacker were among the heroes to achieve
stardom for their wartime achievements. By the thousands, un-
heralded others lived out what Carl Schurz eloquently prophesied at
the October 6, 1904, celebration of German Day in St. Louis: "We
German-Americans are the hyphen between Germany and America;
we present the living demonstration of the fact that a large population may be transplanted from one to another country and may be
devoted to the new fatherland for life and death. . . ."[28]

Rickenbacker, originally spelled Richenbacher, and Pershing,
whose name was anglicized from Pfoerschin, were never questioned
about their loyalty. But a few were, among them, Joseph Wehner,
whose father was born in Germany. After being hounded by surveillance teams, he arrived overseas in time to participate in the
most dramatic air battles of World War I. Wehner fought
superhumanly against German fighters and observation balloons until he was finally knocked out of the skies to his death by four German fokkers.[29] A few whole units like the Wisconsin Thirty-Second
were suspect until hand-to-hand combat in the Vosges Mountains
and on the Marne River removed the doubts.

For the most part, the German-Americans cooperated with conscription. Initiated by a law that went into effect on May 18, 1917,
the draft made all men between the ages of twenty-one and twenty-
six liable for military service. No one was permitted to furnish substitutes as in Civil War days. Few German-Americans were in a
mood to oppose the draft. However, the Mennonites, Friends
(Quakers), and especially the Hutterites were conscientious objectors. They refused to serve in active units or to buy Liberty bonds.
Instead, they made substantial donations to the Red Cross and for
relief work, but their eleemosynary activities did not buy leniency
from the draft boards. Economic reprisals came almost immediately
and law enforcement was not far behind. On occasion "legal action"
took the form of mock courts-martial — a conscientious objector

standing face to a stone wall, the minutes being counted down, and the command "Fire!" But no bullets were triggered and a reprieve was ordered instead.[30]

Most conscientious objectors were confined at Alcatraz, Fort Leavenworth, or other federal prisons, where they were maltreated. Some were forced to stand for hours in the cold, others were manacled to bars inside their cells without clothing. After four months of this treatment, two Hutterites from South Dakota died of pneumonia and overexposure. Early in 1918, therefore, the Hutterites appealed to President Wilson to allow alternate service for their draft-aged males. They pointed out that not a single conscientious objector had yet changed his mind as a result of a prison sentence. But Wilson was unwilling to accord them special privileges. Thus, their leaders made provisions for all men of military age to leave the United States clandestinely for Canada, and in time a general exodus occurred.[31]

Belligerent, though not very widespread resistance to the war and the draft, came also from non-Mennonites, for example, in New Ulm, Minnesota. One month before America's entry in April, 1917, New Ulm held a referendum to answer the question whether the United States should participate in the war. By a vote of more than twenty to one, the citizens opposed the declaration and delivered their results to government officials.

Three months later on July 25, 1917, more than ten thousand citizens gathered in the New Ulm public park to protest sending drafted men to the front.[32] As Mayor Dr. Louis A. Fritsche presided, City Attorney Albert Pfaender, County Auditor Louis Vogel, and local editor Albert Steinhäuser participated in the demonstration. The state's Public Safety Commission investigated the matter and reported to the governor that the people of New Ulm had remained within the letter of the law while outraging its spirit. The report said local draftees were encouraged to believe that a way existed for them to evade the draft. For depicting draftees as "martyrs, dragged to an unjust fate by a tyrannical and cruel government," the commission recommended that the three officials be removed from office.

Governor Joseph A. A. Burnquist suspended them and they responded by offering their resignations. These were tabled until autumn, 1917, when the commission took 500 pages of testimony from witnesses and the officials. Vogel said he had simply led a parade in honor of the drafted men. Pfaender and Fritsche testified that Brown County citizens were dissatisfied with the law and that a meeting was called to explain the legality of conscription. After Burnquist had read the testimony, he ruled that the officials had been "unpatriotic and un-American" and concluded that Fritsche and Pfaender should be removed from office. Vogel, however, was reinstated.

While public safety commissions found lesser disaffection in other areas of the German belt, evidence of genuine disloyalty to the United States has been open to various interpretations. In the views of many, displeasure with the draft did not spell treason, nor did support of the war necessarily indicate patriotism. Missouri Synod leaders noted that "pro-American" meant being explicity "anti-German." One of their arguments was "Why must American Germans be held accountable and persecuted for the sins of a government they have long past forsaken?" Why indeed, condemn Americans of German descent who fled Germany precisely because they disagreed with the character of German government? [33]

If the constitutional rights of some German-Americans were abridged, the maligned usually restrained their anger in public. In the privacy of voting booths, however, they often struck back. During the off-year elections of 1918, German-Americans intensified the trend started in 1916 to bolt the Democratic party which they had axiomatically supported for a century. Democratic losses were particularly evident in counties where the Germans held a substantial number of votes. Deficits for Democratic candidates in 1918 did not automatically result in gains for the Republicans, however. Often voters gravitated away from both parties in favor of the Socialists, as seen in Wisconsin.[34] Complicating the balloting that year was the popularity of the isolationist Nonpartisan League, particularly among rural German-Americans.[35]

By the time the 1918 campaigns got underway, the Germans no longer were guided by the German-American Alliance. In the face of hysterical public opinion, numerous state chapters had voluntarily dissolved or adopted new names. Toledo's alliance suspended itself indefinitely. Kansas City's chapter changed its title to "American Citizenship Association." Nebraska's died quietly.[36] Virtually all of them refrained from holding meetings.

Nationally the picture was even more severe. The once-mighty

Deutsch-Amerikanisher Nationalbund came under siege in January, 1918, when Senator William Henry King of Utah introduced a bill in Congress to repeal its charter. Theodore Roosevelt attacked: "Organizations like the German-American Alliance have served Germany against America. Hereafter we must see that the melting pot really does melt. There should be but one language in this country — the English."[37] Between February 23 and April 13, 1918, the Senate held hearings with the cooperation of the alliance's new president, Siegmund Georg von Bosse. Von Bosse welcomed the opportunity to testify in hopes of clearing the organization from charges of disloyalty.

But the investigators did not differentiate between evidence based on activities carried out by the alliance before, and those which occurred after the United States had entered the war. Quotations from alliance publications were taken out of context and some evidence was presented in German, which the committee members did not understand. The main witness against the alliance was Gustavus Ohlinger, who charged that it was identical with the Pan-German Union, an arm of the Berlin government. A second witness, Henry C. Campbell, an editor of the *Milwaukee Journal*, also charged the alliance with Pan-German Unionism, which he substantiated with the ridiculous claim that the alliance attempted to control the politics of Wisconsin. Action came on July 2, 1918, when the King Bill passed handily, abrogating the 1907 charter of the German-American Alliance, which Congress had authorized.

Thus ended the struggle of the alliance against prohibition, feminism, Puritanism, and "all follies which threaten personal liberty." The $30,000 in its treasury were paid to the American Red Cross. Accused of being an extension of the kaiser's tentacles in the United States, its real nature was more accurately characterized by a disillusioned member:

Behind the German-American Alliance, the keg and the barrel of those patriotic pan-Germans, the United States Brewers' Association, always found a safe and strong refuge. In the councils of the Alliance I never heard of the *Drang nach Osten*, of the Germanic people's mission to kulturize the world, or of the German empire's need of more sun, but rather an appeal to rally round the keg and present an unbroken front to the white-ribbon hordes.[38]

In the course of 1919, the armistice held in Europe, but in

America committees on Americanization waged war to eradicate hyphenism at all levels. States, municipalities, school boards, and industry joined hands to "reeducate" the citizens, sometimes through University Extension divisions.[39] To fill the vacuum left by the alliance, the German element organized the Steuben Society headed by former Missouri Congressman Richard Bartholdt to "guide our citizens through the intricacies of public policies, to warn them against political intrigues and to oppose alien-influenced government." The new organization carefully segregated itself from imperial Germany by noting that the German-Americans emigrated not only from the post-1871 German Empire, but also from the German-speaking states of Austria, Switzerland, the Baltic, Hungary, Bohemia, and South Russia. Although the Steuben Society held national conferences throughout the 1920s, its membership never exceeded 20,000 and its effectiveness was minimal.[40]

New developments on the American political horizon also deflected suspicion from the German element. One was the Red Scare, a catch name for Socialists, Marxists, Bolsheviks — by whatever name they were known. In a few instances, however, the Red Scare was personified by a German-speaking representative, such as Victor Berger, whose family origins were in the Austro-Hungarian Empire. Active in Milwaukee municipal government, Berger, a Socialist, went to Washington as a result of the Socialist party victory in the First Wisconsin District in 1910. Berger was reelected in 1918, but his colleagues refused to seat him on charges that he had opposed America's entry into the war. The Supreme Court later acquitted him, but Berger was not readmitted to the House until 1923.[41]

In the election of 1920, Ohio's Governor James M. Cox of Dayton became the Democratic standard bearer against Republican Senator Warren Harding of Marion, Ohio. Neither held much appeal for the German-Americans. On principle they rejected the Wilsonian Democrats, while Cox enjoyed a "wet" image which should have helped. His advantage was canceled, however, by his opposition to German-language education. In a special message to the Ohio Legislature in 1919, Cox had urged passage of a law to abolish the use of German in Ohio's elementary schools, calling German-language education "a distinct menace to Americanism and part of a plot formed by the German government to make school children loyal to it."[42] His statement, editorialized widely during the 1920 presidential campaign, proved to be a major liability to his candidacy. The Steuben Society and the German-language press strongly supported Harding, with the result that he won by a landslide. Not all the Germans who rejected Cox at the polls, did so by voting for Harding. Many marked their ballots for the Nonpartisan League, especially in the upper midwestern farm states, and for La Follette's Progressives in Wisconsin.

Although German-American political power had dissipated, humanitarian concern for ethnic brothers in the Old World burned brightly after hostilities ceased. Expressing dismay that the blockade of Germany continued until July, 1919, when the new German government ratified the Versailles treaty, many Americans of German descent called for the shipment of relief food to Germany. At first, Congress was opposed. About the only supporter was Senator Robert La Follette — at the time under censure for his pro-German and antiwar activities in the Senate. At the outset, therefore, church groups, singing societies, and individuals in the German-American communities worked independently. Beginning in 1919, however, a variety of programs were coordinated under Herbert Hoover and the American Friends Service Committee.

Although all Americans joined the relief effort in the 1920s, aid for Germany in the years immediately following the war came from the German-Americans, and it was generous. As soon as the blockade and postal ban were lifted in July, 1919, Milwaukee's post office reported handling over 100,000 packages of butter, sausage, and flour in the subsequent eighteen months. There are estimates of $120,000,000 in personal donations sent by the Germans in America to their former homeland between 1919 and 1921,[43] and of 300 German-American societies launched to raise money and provide food. Some used personal contacts, such as the editor of the *Dakota Freie Presse* who channeled relief to hungry children in East Prussia by way of a brother who lived there. With money collected from its readers, the paper maintained a health resort on the Baltic, where one hundred children per month were brought to be nourished back to health.[44]

More dramatic efforts were made by German-American farmers in Kansas, Texas, South Dakota, North Dakota, Iowa, and Wisconsin, who donated cows to relieve the tight supply of milk available to German children. A central office, the American Dairy Cattle Company of Chicago, handled the cow collection. German-American businessmen, churches, and banks cooperated. At least four shiploads of cows reached Germany, where the animals were distributed to various cities, usually where there were orphanages without adequate milk supplies.[45]

On one occasion native Americans tried to interrupt a shipment of cows. After the cows, solicited near Freeman, Tripp, and Scotland, South Dakota, had been corralled for entrainment, lynch-law patriots stampeded them, killing several. When the cows were rounded up, anti-German agitators attempted to storm the herd during the night, but were deterred by a posse of 200 farmers armed with shotguns. Later when the cows moved by train through Sioux City, Iowa, the American Legion tried to halt the shipment by legal action — but failed. When the cows reached Baltimore for embarkation, another attempt was made by the Legion to prevent delivery but again without success. All cow consignments were effected by a single vessel, the *West Arrow*, which carried some 740 cows per trip.

More conventional donations reached Germany by way of the Quakers and their American Friends Service Committee, though not without opposition from American columnists and the U. S. State Department. However, Herbert Hoover refused to bow to public opinion. With little government support he established the quasi-private American Relief Administration. Hoover eventually won a modicum of support by unloading huge agricultural surpluses, which boosted farm prices in the United States. At first Hoover extracted substantial contributions mainly from German-American financiers. Later he appealed to all Americans through his new organization, the European Relief Council. This organization set its goal at $33,000,000 in food and medical care. In February, 1921, it announced that Americans had contributed $29,000,000, a sum larger than any previous peacetime overseas aid effort.[46]

Response to Hoover's ERC campaign by the six million Germans in America was not good. On the average they gave less than fifteen cents each, whereas other Americans contributed an average of more than twenty-seven cents each. Consequently the European Relief Council ceased its program of aid to German children, and shifted its emphasis to Eastern Europe. Hoover's action infuriated the Germans in America, but they soon quieted down and continued their relief work privately. No figures are available to indicate how great this aid was.

When all is said, the larger fact emerges as a credit to all Americans: that Europe's descendants in America did not forget their ancestral homelands in the hour of greatest need. Moreover, the massive relief was accepted not so much as aid from a specific nationality group but from all the assimilated peoples of the United States.

CHAPTER 15

The Relationship of Nazi Germany to America's German Element

WHEN THE FIRST WORLD WAR ENDED, A NEW PHOBIA EMERGED — THE suspicion of everything foreign. In response, political isolationism spread across the country before coming to rest in the Midwest. By the Midwest can be understood the states of Iowa, Minnesota, Missouri, the Dakotas, Kansas, and Nebraska on the western side, and the states of Wisconsin, Illinois, Indiana, Michigan, and Ohio on the eastern side. Political scientists acknowledge that in the 1920s and 1930s these were the states most heavily populated by Germans. They have shown that isolationist voting was strongest in this region between the years 1933 and 1950.[1] Of all states in the nation, North Dakota was considered the most isolationist. This led analysts to the conclusion that isolationism thrived among Americans of German descent, for, they argued, North Dakota, among all the states in the Union, had the largest percentage of German descendants in its total population.

Political scientists also point to the correlation between isolationism in a locality and the percentage of foreign stock living in the area. In the states of Wisconsin, Minnesota, North Dakota, and Iowa, it appears, the Germanic populations tended to be more isolationist than peoples of different national origins.[2] They conclude that the Germans were so bitterly disillusioned after the close of World War I that they tended to turn inward, preferring that the nation follow its own independent direction.

This sentiment was strengthened by another American phobia — the fear of continuing immigration. While efforts to limit the influx of foreigners were by no means initiated only during the post-World War I period, the isolationist, anti-immigration mood provided the final spur for the passage of such laws. The first anti-immigrant sentiment in America became evident during the Know-Nothing demonstrations of the 1850s. The major objective of the Know-Nothings, however, was not so much to curtail immigration as to limit the political power of new arrivals. That was only one of the reasons, and there were others. During the nineteenth century much prejudice was directed against the Catholic Church by Protestants who viewed it as a foreign element controlled by an alien power. After World War I, however, the target of anti-immigrant opinion was broadened to encompass all of the foreign-born.

Made uneasy by continued heavy immigration, Congress passed a law on February 20, 1907, creating and defining the duties of a new Immigration Commission. Three years later the commission filed its enormous report — forty-two volumes in all.[3] It was not conspicuous for its objectivity. The average American easily became convinced that the country's ills stemmed from the inferior quality of the newcomers. The remedy, it was felt, lay in a reduction of immigrants admitted and with stringent restrictions on certain nationalities.

Slowly the proposition to restrain immigration gained momentum. At first there were literacy tests. On three occasions, 1896, 1913, and 1915 Congress passed bills, but each time the president vetoed them. With the European war as an incentive in 1917, the literacy test was enacted over President Wilson's veto. At first the law seemed to have its desired effect of halting immigration, but when the war ended it turned out that immigrants could read after all and immigration accelerated.

The end of the war brought the ghost of isolationism, the Red Scare, and other xenophobic tendencies. Three laws, passed successfully in 1921, 1924, and 1929, set an absolute limit of 150,000 immigrants annually for peoples arriving from any country other than those in the Western Hemisphere. Each nationality group in America was determined by the percentage of a particular national stock already living in the United States. Thus England, Germany, and Ireland received relatively large quotas while countries like Italy, Poland, and Greece were severely limited.[4]

Coupled with the enactment of a quota system was the improvement in postwar economic conditions in Europe, which limited emigration. The population of some countries had been decimated by war and every available body was needed at home. Russia and Italy, among others, forbade the departure of citizens, whether for purposes of emigration or for temporary visits. Immigration to the United States thus slowed to a trickle and even reversed itself during the 1930s when more people left than entered the United States. Immigration from Germany, well under the quota in the 1920s, was radically interrupted when Adolph Hitler's National Socialist German Workers' Party seized power in 1933.

Shortly after solidifying his control over the German people at home, Hitler declared that Germans all over the world owed allegiance to the German *Reich,* and allowed that he would make only superficial distinctions for Germans holding foreign citizenship. Outlining a program for the millions of Germans living overseas, Nazi propagandists defined Germans as "those of German descent and German blood who live abroad . . . , German people on this side of the border, and German people on the other side of the border! These borders exist on the maps, but not in our hearts!"[5]

Few of the Germans in America responded positively to the Führer's dictates. If anything, the blatant propaganda caused them to sever whatever loyalty they still felt for the Fatherland. Two thirds of the 1,600,000 German-born living in the United States in 1930 had arrived prior to World War I. There were nearly seven million persons of German stock in the States, but over 75 percent of these were born in America. The mere 600,000 more recent immigrants from Germany represented a tiny minority in a total U.S. population of 124 million.[6] Yet it was not they but a handpicked core of German citizens who were designated to carry the swastika to American shores.

As early as 1924, even as Hitler was serving a prison sentence for his beerhall putsch of 1923, the Nazi party was making a beachhead in the United States. It was led by one of the Führer's lieutenants, Kurt Georg Wilhelm Ludecke, who fled to America and recruited members. Operating independently and without financial support from Germany, Ludecke worked on the Germans in America but opposed the formation of Nazi cells in this country.

Somewhat later, under the leadership of Fritz Gissibl, German immigrants in Chicago organized a *Sturm Abteilung* (cell of storm troopers) incorporated as "Teutonia" under the laws of the State of Illinois. This unit won the sanction of the German Nazi party and eventually became the Nazi party, U. S. A. It had locals in New York, Detroit, Milwaukee, Boston, Philadelphia, and other cities. In June, 1932, Ludecke was appointed official representative of the party in the United States, but when Hitler was made chancellor on January 30, 1933, sharp resistance arose against the Nazi party in

America. In March, 1933, Berlin ordered all Nazi cells in the United States dissolved, and shortly thereafter Heinz Spanknoebel, former head of the Nazi group in Detroit, was empowered to plan a new organization to succeed the Nazi party in the United States. It came to be known as the "Society of the Friends of New Germany."[7]

Known officially as the *Bund der Freunde des neuen Deutschlands,* the organization received assurances from Rudolf Hess that it would be the official Nazi unit in North America. American public opinion had to be soothed, however, and for this task, Goebbles designated German Consul General, Dr. Otto Kiep (executed by Hitler in 1944), to engage a public relations firm to disseminate pro-German information. Due to quarreling among the agencies in Germany, Kiep received only $31,000 initially but on September 1, 1933, the Friends of New Germany were, despite hardships, able to commence publication of their new organ, *Das neue Deutschland,* a small weekly distributed from New York. It included a special section in English called the "German Outlook."

Because Heinz Spanknoebel revealed his connections to the Third Reich, American leaders grew suspicious. Reports circulated that Goebbels had sent 300 propagandists with millions of dollars to subvert public opinion in the United States. In October, therefore, Congressman Samuel Dickstein of New York, Chairman of the House Committee on Immigration and Naturalization, announced plans to scrutinize the matter of Nazi agents in the United States. A warrant went out for Spanknoebel's arrest but before he could be apprehended, he fled the country. Simultaneously, the Committee announced that it would investigate the Friends of the New Germany organization. In response, the German Government ordered Germans in the United States to cease all political activity and specified that only German citizens would be permitted in the Nazi party. The Friends of New Germany were ordered by the *Auslandsorganisation* to assume a more American image. Dr. Otto Kiep was recalled and activities in the United States slowed considerably. During most of 1934, the House Committee scrutinized the Friends and, in February, 1935, it reported that there were indeed budding activities of the Nazis in the United States.[8]

In 1936 there existed seventy-four official and unofficial agencies in Germany that were concerned in one way or another with the German people living beyond the borders. Officially they were subject to the Foreign Office *(das auswärtige Amt).* The party office was not a government agency, although the party's *Auslandsorganisation* participated in policy-making because the Hitler party was scarcely distinguishable from the Hitler government. Most of the agencies carried out routine missions: exchange students, religious conferences, tourist services, and the like. There was one which predated Hitler and which functioned during the Nazi period not as a policy-making body but as a clearing house for activities and contacts, some of which directly involved the ruling government. This was the *Deutsche Ausland-Institut*. It still exists, although after World War II it was reorganized and retitled the *Institut für Auslandsbeziehungen*.[9] Known publicly as the DAI, the institute was created in 1917 to put forward Germany's best image in the neutral trading areas during World War I. It was headquartered in Stuttgart, because this "City of Foreign Germans" was the center of the Swabian district, which had furnished the highest percentage of emigrating Germans over the centuries.[10]

The objectives had been laid down for the institute after imperial Germany collapsed in 1918. They were to provide a central reference for the German peoples living all over the world. The institute also provided a depository for materials on aspects of German life in foreign countries. In short, it familiarized the *Reichsdeutschen* with the *Volksdeutschen*. At its best, the institute was a research center for information on German settlements outside Germany. By 1933, it had assembled some 40,000 volumes, an impressive photo and newspaper file, and subscriptions to 1,700 newspapers and periodicals from all countries of the world in which Germans were living.[11]

It was in 1935 that the Nazi Government recognized the importance of the *Deutsche Ausland-Institut*. Thereafter expansion of the library was readily accomplished. In 1939, it contained over 100,000 volumes and files of German newspapers from most German settlements abroad. There was also a registry of over 40,000 German groups and a steadily mounting accumulation of 30,000 photos received monthly regarding Germans living outside Germany. Between 500 and 600 pieces of reading material arrived daily, and each day from 1,100 to 1,500 personal letters inundated the institute. If a German was planning to emigrate to, for example, Chicago, he could depart with considerable information about the city as well as the addresses of a few social contact persons and of several mutual aid societies to ease his transition. With Hitler in power, however, there was little demand for these services because emigration was virtually prohibited. Nevertheless, the institute stepped up its activities not only in its archival organization but also in such areas as foreign press opinion, map making, family research, and film lending. The *Amerikaabteilung* ("department on America") was especially vigorous.[12]

For the brief period of perhaps one year, the Germans in America were torn between a sense of pride in the new political success accruing to the old Fatherland under the leadership of Hitler, and a sense of shame at the crimes he and the Nazi party were perpetrating. By the middle of 1934, however, verified newspaper reports and fleeing victims of Nazi terror had reached the United States. As a result, German-Americans flocked to join the Jewish instigated boycott which various American groups had organized to halt the purchase of anything from Germany. When the boycott first started in 1933, agents of the German government established the *Deutschamerikanischen Wirtschaftsausschuss* ("German-American Economic Commitee") to counter the effectiveness of the boycott, and individual German-Americans and organizations such as the Steuben Society publicly protested against the idea. In 1934, however, individuals and groups all fell into line behind the American viewpoint.

The Carl Schurz Memorial Foundation also took steps in 1934 to insure that its organization would not engage in propaganda work in America. Established in 1930 for the purpose of strengthening cultural relations between Germany and America, the foundation at first was embarrassed by the Nazi rise to power. But in 1934 after its executive secretary, Dr. Wilbur K. Thomas, returned from Germany, the mood at headquarters changed. The foundation's magazine, *Germany Today, An American Magazine of Goodwill*, which had been subsidized by the German Government, was phased out and a new journal — the *American-German Review* — was substituted. Later, in 1936 -1937, Dr. Heinz Kloss, a top scholar for the DAI on America, was hired by the Schurz Foundation to make a feasibility study on establishing a research seminar to be called the American-German Institute. It never came to fruition, though not because Kloss did not recommend it. At the time he commented that there were perhaps twenty million people of German origin living in the United States and of these, about two million spoke fluent German.

It should be noted, parenthetically, that the Carl Schurz Foundation had nothing to do with the *Vereinigung Carl Schurz* which was based in Berlin during the 1920s and 1930s for the purpose of aiding Americans who wanted to visit Germany to see for themselves how conditions really were under the Weimar and Nazi governments. Likewise, we should observe here that the Carl Schurz Memorial Foundation is today the National Carl Schurz Association, which is dedicated to the teaching of German in America.

While the Carl Schurz Foundation chose a pathway separate from the Nazi Government, the Nazi rulers never lacked spokesmen for their cause in the United States. Their most unabashed supporter was George Sylvester Viereck, who had served Germany so effectively as the propagandist editor of the *Fatherland*, later called the *American Monthly*, during the dark days of World War I. In 1934, Viereck testified to the House Committee that he had been on Consul Kiep's payroll and that he had edited a series of pamphlets entitled *Speaking of Hitler*.

The Munich-born Viereck was kept on the payroll of the newspaper *Münchner Neuste Nachrichten* as a foreign correspondent, partly for news transcriptions, partly to funnel cash to him for his American publications. Soon American newspaper editors became aware of Viereck's purposes, and they attacked him bitterly. In spite of opposition, Viereck, by means of his Flanders Hall Press, kept on publishing books, advertisements, and magazines, some under the tutelage of bogus organizations like the "Mothers of America." His most important organ was *Facts in Review*, which was distributed by the German Library of Information. Initially, the weekly was sent to a select group of 20,000 influential citizens, Congressmen, educators, and journalists.[13] In May, 1940, *Facts in Review* was expanded to a press run of 75,000 and special numbers were printed with as many of 220,000 copies. The German Library of Information supplied copies to influential circles of American life: libraries, radio stations, newspapers, YMCA's, college newspapers, some 12,000 Protestant and 10,000 Catholic pastors, and others. When, in June, 1941, the American Government halted publication of the *Facts*, the journal was removed from libraries.

Facts was a successful venture, skillfully prepared and widely distributed. For example, on December 23, 1940, it presented a low-key piece of propaganda with its title story "Christmas in the Bavarian Alps." Readers encountered peaceful peasants of Alpine

Germany. Here was a people at war on the Eastern front, it is true, but a people that had contributed significantly to 400 years of Christmas art which the issue also depicted in commemoration of the 400th anniversary that year of the Dresden choir. The last edition of the *Facts* appeared on June 7, 1941. It was a publication that has been evaluated as an outstanding example "of German propaganda, which was attempting to convey a juxtaposition of military triumph, intellectual and spiritual enlightenment, and social dynamism."[14]

As a footnote to Viereck's propaganda involvement, it should be noted that he was the son of the author Louis Viereck, who immigrated to the United States in 1896 when Georg Sylvester was only thirteen. Louis' name appeared in this book in the chapter on the German-language schools. Georg attended New York schools and studied at New York University. From 1943 - 1947 he spent time in prison for seditious activities after Germany declared war on the United States. After being sentenced, Viereck declared candidly:

America is the only country to which I owe allegiance. But I am no hater of Germany. I deplore the cruel war between the land of my birth and the land of my choice. . . . I shall never foreswear my German ancestry, betray my convictions, or spit on the graves of my forefathers. Like Luther at Wittenberg and Woodrow Wilson in Washington: Here I stand; I can do no other."[15]

By the time of his death on March 19, 1962 in Holyoke, Massachusetts, Viereck had made a respectable contribution to German-American culture by writing poetry and history before and after the two world wars. Among his American-born children was Peter Viereck, a prolific writer and American educator, who served loyally and patriotically with the American army in Africa and Italy during World War II. A younger son, George Sylvester, Jr., was killed in battle at Anzio in 1944 during his father's prison term.

Returning to the year 1935, we note that the "Friends of New Germany" had looked for rescue to the Fatherland but received little help. In the glare of publicity surrounding the House investigation, the German government in October, 1935, prohibited German citizens from holding membership in the Friends society. In an effort to save itself, the organization passed through a transition which resulted in new leadership and a new name. The new name was the

Deutschamerikanische Volksbund ("German-American People's League") and the new leader, or *Führer* as he was popularly known, was Fritz Julius Kuhn. Both were ratified at a convention held in 1936 in Buffalo. For short, the name was D.A.V.B., but popularly it was seldom captioned in any other form than simply "the Bund." Its leader, Kuhn, was German-born, but he had been in the United States since 1924, and he was an American citizen.[16]

In retrospect, the Bund was more vociferous than effective. Nevertheless, during 1938 and 1939 it organized service centers throughout the United States and claimed a sympathetic following in excess of 200,000.[17] The Bund appealed to a large number of remnants of the Ku Klux Klan, the Black Legion, the Gold Shirts, the Pan-Aryan Alliance, and similar organizations. At one time it operated camps where children were drilled in German military tactics using sticks and wooden guns under the guise of sport. On the economic front, it issued business directories showing German-Americans where to buy. Financial support for the Bund was raised by the German-American Business League which obtained tribute from merchants, consumers, and the general membership. Annual income for the Bund has been estimated in the millions, of which a cut was allegedly forwarded periodically to the Nazi organization in Germany.[18]

In 1937, some forty Americans of German descent and of Nazi sympathy traveled to the Fifth Congress of Germans Abroad in Stuttgart. Eyewitnesses found the Americans outfitted in uniforms of the Bund, saluting with "Heil Hitler," and giving speeches punctuated by "Sieg Heil."[19] On various occasions during their trip they reiterated their intentions — to struggle in the United States against Communism, the C.I.O., Jewish influences, and boycotts against Germany. As a result the Federal Bureau of Investigation released a thousand-page report on the Bund.

In May, 1938, Fritz Kuhn returned from Germany, where he claimed to have been received with open arms by the top *Führer*. In reality, Kuhn had a meeting with Hitler only once — in August, 1936.[20] Immediately the Bund became the subject of a new Congressional investigation led by the House Un-American Activities Committee, chaired this time by Martin Dies. Undaunted, Kuhn preached that German-Americans would soon form a voting bloc grounded on race-conscious principles which would explicitly reject the country-wide notion of an American melting pot.[21]

Across the nation, anti-Nazi organizations sprang up and German-Americans, rather than flocking to the support of the Bund's *Führer*, hastened to shed their German identities. As the Committee of Martin Dies opened hearings, a shock wave of adverse publicity for the Bund swept the nation.[22] The man who had chaired the earlier probe into Nazi actions in the United States, Congressman Samuel Dickstein, warned his colleagues in the Congress that there were perhaps 450,000 Bundists in America. Fritz Kuhn was somewhat more modest, claiming a membership of 230,000. Martin Dies in his book, *The Trojan Horse*, pegged the figure at 100,000 members. Both the Justice Department and the F.B.I. held to an estimated membership in the Bund of about 6,500 — the same figure which the German Ambassador, Dr. Hans Heinrich Dieckhoff, had reported secretly in 1938 to the German Foreign Office. During his testimony before the Committee, Kuhn denied any connection with the German *Ausland-Institut*.

Exact figures on the Bund's membership shall probably never be known, because Kuhn saw to it that the files were destroyed before the hearings were begun, in order to guarantee immunity for former members. Kuhn did admit that 40 percent of the active participants were not Germans nor even Americans of German descent but disgruntled cast-offs from various right-wing groups of the general American population. During the investigation, Ambassador Dieckhoff also reported to the Foreign Office in Berlin that the German element in the United States was much weaker numerically than commonly assumed in Hitler's Germany. Using Chicago as an example, he noted there had been 700,000 Germans living there, of whom 40,000 were members of German clubs and of these, only 450 belonged to the Bund. He concluded that there was no possibility at all that the Germans in America would use political power for the benefit of the Third Reich.[23]

A spectacular event in the Bund's life took place in 1936 when an estimated 20,000 Bund members gathered in Madison Square Garden in New York City to hear Avery Brundage, Chairman of the American Olympic Committee, address them on the subject of the 1936 Olympic games in Germany. German Ambassador Hans Luther also spoke.[24] This episode was only a prelude to the much more raucous rally staged at Madison Square Garden on February 20, 1939, under the guise of celebrating Washington's birthday. More than 22,000 people attended, but crowd analyzers subsequently concluded that many were curiosity seekers. During the activities, anti-Nazis began heckling the speakers and protesting with such vigor that sporadic brawls escalated into a full-scale riot.[25] Public opinion was singularly inflamed by the meeting, and the Bund's decline accelerated rapidly thereafter. The German Nazi party backed farther away from the American Bund, while the German-American press and organizations, particularly in the midwestern German strongholds, took up the torch to purge the Bund from American soil.

Suddenly in May, 1939, the Nazi movement in the United States received a fatal blow when Fritz Kuhn was indicted for the embezzlement of Bund funds and sped off ignominiously to prison.[26] In 1943 he was released from New York's Clinton Prison, denaturalized, and confined for extradition on Ellis Island.[27]

At the Nuremberg Trials after the war, Ernst Wilhelm Bohle, head of the *Auslandsorganisation*, maintained that the American Bund never received any financial support from Germany. Captured documents also make clear that the Bund was indeed a noisy, militant offshoot. Upon the request of the U.S. State Department, Berlin had severed all contact with the Bund in 1935. Again in 1937 both the German *Auslandsorganisation* and the *Volksdeutsche Mittelstelle*, the central party agency for activities of "the racial Germans abroad," were approached by U.S. officials, and both promised to keep their hands off the German-Americans. In March, 1938, the German Foreign Office informed Washington that the Bund was no longer allowed to wear German emblems and that all authorities in the Reich had been reminded of the ban against communicating with the Bund. Except for a few isolated violations, German officials abided fully by these agreements.[28] By the time Fritz Kuhn died in his native Munich in 1951, he was a completely forgotten man in his adopted Yorkville section of New York.[29]

When the United States entered World War II and declared war on Germany late in 1941, Germans in America no longer expressed sympathy with the leadership in their land of origin. Unlike the situation in World War I, the cases of terror and aggression by Germany's Nazi rulers underlined the issues of right and wrong in the minds of German-Americans. Consequently, it was easier for them to maintain their inner sense of loyalty to the old homeland while rejecting the practices of its Fascist dictatorship.[30]

Not that American politicians were without anxiety about the

German-Americans. In September, 1942, after the American industrial machine was beginning to roll, *Fortune* magazine published a special issue containing two articles dealing with America as a "Nation of Nations" and the danger of exploding "Steam from the Melting Pot."[31] Clearly, Americans were disturbed by the prospect of a Nazi fifth column developing and springing into action in the United States.[32] For the most part the fears were unfounded. The only overt enemy infiltration of the United States occurred in 1942 when nine saboteurs were put ashore on America's East Coast by German submarines. One group landed on Long Island, the other in Florida. But an informant among the group blew the whistle, and after only two weeks all were in prison. Two were sentenced to lengthy imprisonment; the remainder lost their lives in the electric chair.[33]

An interesting, bizarre, and little-known incident in the history of Germans in America during World War II was a plan formulated by the Nazi Government to recruit German-speaking people in the United States. In the main, the proposal was directed at those emigrants who had left the Weimar Republic between 1918 and 1933. They were to be resettled in the territory Germany expected to conquer beyond its eastern borders. The Germans in America were considered especially attractive for this purpose because, it was reasoned, they had proven their mettle as industrial workers and agricultural pioneers in the United States. Thus, they were deemed ideal for the sophisticated industry and agriculture that were to be developed in the Warthegau (a district of western Poland) and in Upper Silesia.

Out of the correspondence between the *Deutsches Ausland-Institut* and members of the German-American Bund, there came into existence a society known as the *Kameradschaft USA*. The purpose of the *Kameradschaft* was to solicit Germans in America who were willing to return to Germany. The structure of the *Kameradschaft* was loose and it functioned under the authority of the *Auslandsorganisation*, usually known simply as the AO, with Gauleiter Ernst Wilhelm Bohle at the helm. Bohle was himself a *Rückwanderer* who had been born a British subject in Africa, and who retained dual German-English citizenship. He claimed English nationality because of his birth and German nationality from his father, a German professor in Cape Town who had been naturalized in England with the stipulation that he could exercise German

citizenship whenever he happened to be in Germany.[34] Begun in
1938, the *Kameradschaft USA* grew steadily and soon boasted of
societies for returned Americans in Munich, Berlin, Hamburg,
Hanover, Düsseldorf, Leipzig, Braunschweig, and Frankfurt.[35]

Just how many German-Americans returned to Germany under
the plan is difficult to ascertain. One report indicates there were
over 800 *Rückwanderer* present at a meeting of the Berlin
Kameradschaft in 1942. Other documents list the number of all
returning emigrants from the United States at 6,860 persons.[36] The
total eligible for repatriation was no doubt limited because the main
thrust of the campaign was not directed at the older, established
German-Americans in the United States. For instance, the estimated
400,000 German-Americans living in Pennsylvania were judged unlikely to return to Europe. Nor was much effort expended on the
Germans in Texas and the Midwest. German-American Catholics
were judged to be anti - Third Reich. However, the older German
Lutherans in America were believed to be steadfastly pro-German.
Nevertheless, all immigrants who had departed from Germany prior
to 1914 were excluded from the scope of the *Kameradschaft USA*.

The people who merited the highest interest were those who had
come to America following the First World War — some 400,000 as
of 1930 — and in particular those 250,000 *Reichsdeutsche* who in
1940 had not yet applied for first citizenship papers. More than half
of them were thought to be living in New York and the surrounding
areas and were presumed to be dissatisfied with life in the United
States. Nazi schemers further theorized that most of the
Rückwanderer would come from the larger cities and that they
would make their chief contribution to Germany, not as soldiers, but
as skilled workers — exactly what was needed for the Warthegau
and Upper Silesia (formerly part of Germany but today part of
western Poland). As for settlement in the agricultural districts of
Poland, the Russian-Germans in the United States were singled out
for special attention to husband the farmlands along the Russian
frontier.[37]

In general it appears that returnees from America were most un-
happy with the situation they discovered upon arrival in Germany.
Many experienced difficulties securing German citizenship, and
others had no living accommodations and no jobs. All of those who
settled in the Polish terrritories were, by 1944, cast into the plight of
war refugees. In the face of an advancing enemy battlefront, the

Reich Germans received priority of evacuation over the American returnee (the *Volksdeutsche* as they were known). Even the Black Sea Germans from Russia received preferential treatment during the abandonment of German holdings in Poland. Thus, what began as a settler's dream for repatriated Germans from America ended in a nightmare.[38]

It has not been determined how many German-born individuals departed from the United States in the weeks and months that followed the outbreak of hostilities between America and Germany late in 1941. A number — journalists, for example — were ordered to leave, whereas others were exchanged for Americans who found themselves caught behind the borders of Germany when the war started. The vast majority chose to stay in the United States and to acquire citizenship as early as possible. Because their number was so large, anxieties welled up as to what might happen if the German-Americans turned sympathetic toward the German cause.

Such fears are understandable if we realize that, according to the 1940 census, the German-born living in America when World War II started totaled more than 1,237,000. The Germans were easily the largest foreign-born population in the United States except for the Italians, who numbered 1,523,000. But this fact offered little comfort since Italy's Fascist dictator, Mussolini, was at that time Germany's staunchest ally. If, in 1940, one also added to the total foreign-born population the children born in America of families in which both parents were of the same foreign-born nationality, then the Germans in America amounted to nearly 5,000,000 while the closest competitors were the Italians with less than 4,000,000. Add to the five million figure the children having at least one German-born parent and the 1940 German stock rises to 6,500,000.

Nor were the anxieties of some native Americans put to rest by leaders of German-American societies who, during the 1930s, had taken pronounced anti-Nazi positions. The head of the Steuben Society, Theodor H. Hoffmann, for example, had discussed with Hitler in 1934 the waning influence of the German element in the United States. Hoffmann laid the primary blame for this loss at the feet of the Friends of the New Germany, the American Bund.[39] On April 30, 1941, however, Theodor Hoffmann spoke over a radio station in Milwaukee alleging that a majority of the 32,000,000 Americans of German descent wanted to keep the United States out of any war: "Americans of German extraction do not want Com-

munism, Fascism or Nazism, and they do not want British im-
perialism. They want Americanism."[40] Subsequently, Senator
Gerald P. Nye of North Dakota inserted Hoffmann's speech into the
Congressional Record.

However, there were organizations to counter the general
American view that German-Americans were automatically sym-
pathetic to nazism. The Loyal Americans of German Descent, led by
Dr. George N. Shuster, the German-American Congress for
Democracy, the German-American Democratic Society of Greater
New York City, the Wisconsin Federation of German-American
Societies,[41] the German-American Anti-Nazi League, and others
worked with German elements in the labor unions and other sectors
of American society to promote loyalty to the United States' war effort.

During World War II, according to one writer, approximately one
third of the eleven million Americans in the Armed Forces were of
German stock. All three branches had leaders of German ancestry.
General Eisenhower descended from German sectarians in Pennsylvania. General Carl Spaatz, also of Pennsylvania Dutch origin,
served as a chief advisor to Eisenhower. He planned the air war on
Germany and later commanded the bomber force over Japan. Ad-
miral Chester W. Nimitz, commander of the Pacific fleet, was of
German background and General Walter Krueger, commander of
the war in the Pacific, was born in Germany. Americans crossed the
Rhine River on amphibious tanks perfected by Donald Roebling, a
great-grandson of bridge-building John Roebling. Henry J. Kaiser, a
leading American industrialist during the war, was the son of a German Forty-eighter. Thousands of German-born Americans distinguished themselves for bravery on the front lines.[42]

When native American mistrust of German-stock Americans was
proved wrong by the full participation of the Germans in the war,
German-Americans at home breathed a sigh of relief. But they did
not forget that Franklin Roosevelt was the president who declared
war on Germany. In contrast to World War I, German-Americans
during World War II were sophisticated in restraining their
emotions in public.[43] But in the privacy of the ballot box they freely
vented their frustrations. Samuel Lubell discovered that in counties
where citizens of German stock were in the majority, the balloting
turned strongly against Roosevelt: "By far the strongest common
characteristic of the isolationist-voting counties is the residence

there of ethnic groups with a pro-German or anti-British bias."[44] Whereas Franklin Roosevelt's majority vote decreased on a nationwide basis by only 7 percent in 1940 as compared to 1936, there were twenty counties in the United States where his loss exceeded 35 percent. Nineteen of these twenty counties were characterized as German-speaking. In thirty-five other counties where Roosevelt's loss was between 25 and 34 percent, the Germans represented the strongest or second strongest ethnic group in residence there. The same results were evident in counties where Roosevelt had lesser percentage losses.

It has been pointed out that Roosevelt adopted an anti-German foreign policy between the 1936 and 1940 elections. This policy shift triggered the defection of Germans from the Democratic party, not only on the national level, but also in state and local elections.[45] In the South, where few Germans had settled, there was substantially more enthusiasm for the support of Great Britain than in the Midwest. In the Yankee East, descendants of English stock repeatedly increased their percentage of votes for Roosevelt and for the Democratic party through four consecutive elections. But in states of the Midwest where the German element was strongest — Kansas, Iowa, Nebraska, North and South Dakota — whole states swung from the Democratic to the Republican party. In other states — Texas, Ohio, Wisconsin, Minnesota, Missouri — it was only the heavily German counties that voted Republican. In 1944, the Roosevelt pluralities were further eroded along the pattern established in 1940. The point to be remembered, then, is that the German-Americans, like most other nationality groups in America, loyally supported the United States at war and willingly sent their sons to prove it. But in the secrecy of the ballot booth, a tugging at the heart strings determined how German-Americans voted.

Perhaps the best evidence of a German-American backlash at the polls was demonstrated by the Truman upset in 1948. Numerous experts were confounded by the unpredictable strength Harry S. Truman was able to muster in Republican strongholds of the Midwest. Early in 1949, in an effort to uncover what lay at the root of the election upset, Samuel Lubell made several swings around the country ringing doorbells and comparing results of the 1948 voting returns. His most astounding discovery was that German voters had been held in the Republican party until 1948 by a dislike of Roosevelt's foreign policy.

According to Lubell, it was one of the great ironies of history that, by virtue of his death, Roosevelt removed the roadblock to a successful Democratic party assault on the staunch Republican citadels in the Midwest.[46] Missouri, Ohio, Minnesota, Wisconsin, and Iowa — the principal states Lubell visited — illustrated the sensational voter switches which created the Truman miracle. German precincts in St. Louis that went heavily for Dewey in 1944 fell handily to Truman in 1948. In Wisconsin, it was the small-town merchants and farmers of German descent who abandoned the Republican party in 1948 to cast ballots with Milwaukee voters who had remained loyal to the Democrats. Over a dozen rural counties in Wisconsin that were lost by Roosevelt both in 1940 and 1944, came back to the Democratic fold in 1948.

Apparently there were two features about Truman's foreign policy that removed vestigial German-American antagonism toward the Truman administration. One was the Marshall Plan and the other was the Berlin Airlift.[47] Both were initiated almost single-handedly by the Truman White House in the election year of 1948. During the same year, St. Louisans, to take just one example, were reported to be sending $30,000 monthly in aid to relatives in Germany. To them, the fact that the Federal Government for once was helping their ethnic brothers — from which the British-Americans had benefited during two World Wars — could only boost Truman's chances at the polls. The crowning irony of the 1948 election, then, was that the Republican party, rather than the Democratic, suffered a loss from the death of President Roosevelt.

The year 1948 and the reelection of President Truman marks a turning point in the history of the Germans in America, and therefore serves as a convenient conclusion for this chapter. Worsening relations with the Soviet Union and with China induced the United States and her Allies to reconstitute their relationship with Germany in order to build a defense against the spread of communism in central Europe. In 1948, the people of West Germany wrote a new constitution and founded the German Federal Republic with the approval of the occupying Allies. This action brought a new legal status and occasioned the currency reform which started the country on its road to postwar recovery. A few months later the Soviets countered the Allied measures by allowing the East Germans to establish a semiautonomous communist regime, called the German Democratic Republic, in their half of the former German Reich.

While all these developments were taking place, no German-American wanted to admit that the World War II period in history had ended and that a new era was dawning, one which would resolve the German question by a permanent division of the Fatherland. Nazism had been purged from the land by war in 1945. But its vestiges dragged on via the Nuremberg War Crimes Trials until March, 1949. At that time the Allied Control Council, dubious of its authority on an international level, forsook the endeavor to bring Nazi criminals to justice and turned over its records to the new West German Government. The period of deep shame for people of German descent receded from consciousness. Gradually it was possible once again to be proud of the new homeland — proud that is of West Germany, for East Germany became the new villain in American public opinion. German-Americans, except for the new immigrants during the years immediately following World War II, emerged from the debacle more Americanized than ever.

CHAPTER 16

The German-Americans Today

FOR SEVERAL YEARS AFTER WORLD WAR II, AMERICANS OF GERMAN descent found it a handicap to admit to German background, although it was not due to anti-German hostility the way it was during World War I. Ethnic pride in being German was gone. New immigrants from Germany and from the German-speaking areas of Eastern Europe were welcomed in America, but they arrived with a mark of Cain — the designation "displaced person." The DP was treated fairly, but he was a third-class citizen, not much better off than the blacks and other minorities. Quickly, the DP perceived that acceptance was hindered rather than helped by joining whatever vestiges were left of *Deutschtum* in the united States. Success was to be found in abandoning the immigrant image to join the mainstream of American professional and labor careers at the earliest possible opportunity. At any rate, the new immigrants did not identify with the romantic, nostalgic Old World culture which was characteristic of the older German-Americans.

American politicians, however, were not so quick in abandoning their faith in ethnic politics as they prepared for elections in the early 1950s. Having learned their lesson in 1948, the Republicans formulated strategy for 1952. A chief salient of their organization was the Ethnic Origins Division of the Republican National Committee. By June, 1952, the committee had made available detailed studies of the distribution of Americans of foreign origin, broken down by politically strategic states, cities, and Congressional districts. It also gathered data on foreign-language publications, ethnic churches, and organizations, and cut phonograph records in the respective foreign languages. Each edition featured a political talk tract, the *Star Spangled Banner*, and the national anthem of the country of origin.[1] The plan worked successfully on German-

Americans, in part because in Dwight Eisenhower they recognized one of their own descendants, if only faintly. Eisenhower was, however, not entirely without liabilities among German voters, some of whom felt that he was at least partly responsible for the Carthaginian peace that had been imposed upon Germany. Some also charged that Eisenhower had to share responsibility for the half-implemented Morgenthau Plan, which aimed at reducing the industrial might of the Fatherland to zero. Inevitably, critics also saddled the general with the heartless exiling of some 200,000 German prisoners of war who were turned over to Russia for slave labor after the conclusion of hostilities. The plan, known as "Operation Keelhaul," was particularly harsh toward the Russian-Germans, for they were Soviet citizens who had fled from their native land and joined the German Army as a means to escape communism.[2]

As the 1952 campaign went into its home stretch, the Democrats sensed that they had neglected to concentrate enough energy on the ethnic vote. On the stump for Adlai E. Stevenson, Truman complained bitterly that the Republicans were playing a game of gutter politics by stirring up "our citizens who have ties of blood" with the peoples of Europe. In spite of Truman's lament, Eisenhower was swept into office on November 4, 1952, with a spectacular plurality of the votes. Virtually all of the one-time isolationist German ethnic vote of the Midwest cascaded into the Eisenhower victory column. Eight years later these same areas held solidly for Republican candidate Nixon, though they were highly fragmented by the Goldwater debacle in 1964. Seemingly, then, the Republican National Committee's Ethnic Origins Division had done for Eisenhower in 1952 what a less conscious, but similar plan, had done for Truman in 1948.

Successful as the Eisenhower strategy proved to be, it should not be concluded that the German vote alone elected Eisenhower. In fact, it may have been one of the least significant German bloc votes because of Eisenhower's liabilities — the defeat of Germany and the prisoner issue — among German-Americans. Whatever its significance, the German vote has been catered to less and less since 1952. This is phenomenal because as late as the 1950 census, the Germans of foreign birth, or of German-born and mixed parentage living in the United States, still represented the largest foreign white stock in the nation. In 1950 they amounted to 14 percent of the total U. S. population. The only similarly large bloc of foreign stock was the Italians with 13.5 percent. The Polish were a distant third with but 8.3 percent. When looking at the foreign-born only, the Germans in 1950 totaled 984,000, a figure which is second only to the Italians who numbered 1,427,000.[3] Also in 1950 there were 5,000,-000 persons in the United States whose mother tongue was German, well over a million more than the Italian speakers, the other large non-English speaking group in America at that time. Whatever the explanation, the German element grew ever more invisible during the 1950s.

Several journalists have tried to assess what happened to the German-American community during those years. One, Berlin-born Gerard H. Wilk, an emigré New Yorker since 1946, recorded the words of a German immigrant worker whom he interviewed in New York in 1954: "Those *Vereinsmeier* [club enthusiasts], they keep wishing for a Germany that doesn't exist any more. I can't understand all that gush of theirs. Forever singing about the Rhine, the Main, the Neckar — they live in a vacuum, Herr Wilk; it's neither fish nor fowl, as the saying goes, it's neither Germany nor America. . . . My sons are married, my grandchildren don't know a word of German except for the Christmas songs. I'm satisfied, no regrets."[4]

In Wilk's view, the four or five hundred German clubs in the metropolitan New York area were recruiting their members among the sons and daughters of post - World War I German immigrants. The emphasis was on entertainment, but each organization had its *Herr Präsident* who took his duties seriously and easily developed a consensus in his constituency if he stuck to the standard, well-known festivals and celebrations. Wilk theorized that in one respect, a separatist German-American culture had developed in the United States when the Germans were threatened by Nativism during the 1850s. A century before his time, Wilk contended, the Germans had cut themselves off, founded their own societies, churches, schools, and newspapers and built a wall around their brand of American individualism which slowed their assimilation. Dying a peaceful death after the turn of the century, the feelings of being under siege were rekindled during World War I, but assimilation was hastened, Wilk believed, by Hitler and his propaganda. The Germans in America in the 1950s, according to Wilk, wanted no part of politics — any politics, German or American.

Although this explanation may be incomplete, the fact remains that the German vote largely disappeared during the 1950s. There are no longer any German political candidates, no German component in the ethnic structure of any American city's political machine, and seemingly there was no German-American backlash to the desegregation movement during the 1960s. When Nathan Glazer, Andrew Greeley, Michael Novak and others write about American ethnics, they rarely include references to the German element. Today there is only the Anglo-Teutonic white stock, which makes up a segment of America's silent majority. Undoubtedly the German-American voter could be aroused again with a volatile issue, but none is apparent on the horizon.

Due, perhaps, to the economic miracle in West Germany, the political restructuring, and the high degree of military and economic cooperation between the United States and Germany, the peoples of both nations feel particularly at ease in communication together. Exchange students in high schools and colleges, marriage partners, and German professionals on temporary assignments in the United States are welcomed in even the smallest, most conservative American community. German-born scientists hold top positions in the American space program and in government and industry. Perhaps it is significant that the German element did not take particular pride in seeing the Nixon White House and the original Nixon Cabinet packed with men whose names were German — Kleindienst, Haldeman, Ehrlichman, Ziegler, and others — nor were they disillusioned in the slightest when some of these men were convicted for their Watergate crimes. For that matter, while Americans generally laud German-born Secretary of State Henry Kissinger, one seldom hears German-Americans express ethnic pride or a sense of cultural identity with him. In Kissinger's native Germany, however, nearly every citizen hastens to remind one that Kissinger is German-born.

In the 1960 and 1970 census reports, the Germans continued to stand second only to the Italians in the percentages which they represent in the total U. S. population. With 14 percent in 1950, the German stock population in America dropped to 12.7 percent in 1960, and further to 10.8 percent in 1970. Since Italian immigration to America was more recent than that of the Germans, the Italian stock percentages of the total U. S. population declined less rapidly, from 13.5 percent (second to the German) in 1950 to 13.3 percent in 1960 and down to 12.6 percent in 1970. However, the censuses indicate that by far the largest number of citizens living in the United States who spoke a foreign language as their mother tongue in 1950 and again in 1960 were the Germans. In 1970, there were still 4,891,-000 persons whose native tongue was reported to be German. Even in 1970, the sum total of German-speaking people was not exceeded by any other non-English language spoken in the United States, except, for the first time in American history, Spanish. In 1970, Spanish was spoken by 6,127,000 persons living within the United States. Native speakers of Italian, the only other numerically significant foreign tongue of persons in the United States, according to the 1970 census, totaled 3,118,000.[5]

As noted, the Italians in 1950 represented the one group of foreign stock that surpassed the Germans in percentage of total United States population. What is not generally known is the fact that the Italians were particularly prone to returning to their mother country. This tendency to return accounts for the relatively small number of Americans whose mother tongue was Italian in 1950 and 1960. During the fifteen years prior to World War I, the Italians comprised the largest immigrant group entering America. But in the same period, at least 1,500,000 Italians left the United States for their homeland. During the two decades following World War I, fully 40 percent of the immigrants who came from Italy also returned after a few years.[6]

Germans also returned to the Fatherland after World War I, but in far fewer numbers. Between 1831 and 1850, fewer than 7 percent of the German immigrants migrated back to Germany. In the decades from 1850 - 1870, the percentage of new immigrants from Germany who were repatriated increased to 17 percent. Between 1870 and 1890, there was an economic depression in the United States which seems to have caused German repatriates to increase to approximately 28 percent. After the turn of the century, emigration back to Germany continued at a rate of over 25 percent until World War I, when repatriation dropped radically. Statistics for the years 1930 - 1940 are also low. For the post - World War II period, the year 1947 can be considered typical. During 1947, the ratio of German immigrants to repatriates was 19,368 to 134.[7]

In studying American immigration, it becomes clear that the Italians and the nationality groups of the Austro-Hungarian Empire were those most inclined toward remigration. The German element ranks fourth in "staying tendency," behind the Jews, the Irish, and the Scotch. Temporary repatriation was attractive to the Germans during the period from 1916 - 1924 because the returnee's dollar possessed extraordinarily high buying power in the Weimar Republic. In 1941, the percentage of repatriates leaving America for Germany reached 43 percent, indicating that some Germans in America at that time chose to cast their future with the Third Reich by departing on the last boats that left after the bombing of Pearl Harbor. Immigration from Germany was extremely low in 1941, however, and therefore the 43 percent rate of repatriates over immigrants is not significant.

Most returnees were unmarried males. Families that immigrated tended to remain in the United States. During the years between 1895 and 1914, the majority of German immigrants were trained industrial workers, engineers, and tradespeople who sought employment outside Germany but never intended to remain abroad for life. Consequently, repatriates typically were people who had retired from the professions, business, and family farms. Although these facts are important, it is worth repeating that both the Germans and the Irish — the two largest immigrant groups in America — were among those most likely to remain in America. As has been said, the Germans and the Irish are the foreign-born Americans who sing the most nostalgic songs but are also the most careful not to transform their yearnings into reality.[8]

Viewed against the statistics of heavy German immigration and light repatriation, it is understandable why certain Americans from time to time had xenophobic reactions toward the German element in America. Even the casual student of ethnic groups in America knows that the Germans were the largest and the most visible foreign element in the United States for over a century. To the observer of ethnic groups in the 1970s, however, the Germans seem to be largely assimilated.

No one can say precisely how many Germans have traveled across the Atlantic to settle in the United States. It is clear, however, that they have been immigrating from early colonial times right up to the present. The peaks of German immigration occurred in three sequential crests which rose sharply above the steady annual immigration between the years 1840 and 1890. For purposes of comparison, we must study the immigration totals for all nationalities, between the years 1820 and 1970. We note that the number of Germans who emigrated to the United States during that period exceeds the total for any other country, including Great Britain. There were 6,800,000 immigrants from Germany. Germany's closest rival, Italy, contributed 5,100,000, whereas Great Britain supplied 4,760,000, Ireland, 4,700,000. Immediately below Ireland on the roster is the Austro-Hungarian Empire with 4,200,000. Switzerland gave the United States 340,000 immigrants, and there were 3,300,000 from the Soviet Union.[9]

Three observations emanate from these data. First, it can be assumed that a significant percentage of the immigrants from Austria-Hungary were German-speaking and that in America these people identified with those born in the German states. The Germman nation did not exist prior to 1870; Austria-Hungary did not come into formal existence until 1867; the only bond of cohesion between the central Europeans who emigrated to America was the German language. Let us group one third of the immigrants from Austria-Hungary as German-speaking, namely, 1,400,000. Second, approximately 74 percent of the population of Switzerland is German-speaking. Therefore it would not be excessive to include two thirds of the Swiss immigrants in the German-speaking total in the United States, that is, 224,000. Finally, the U. S. Census in 1920 reported that there were 116,000 Germans from Russia living in the United States as of that date. Let us include these Black Sea and Volga Germans in the German-speaking immigration to the United States.

It would not be an exaggeration, then, to conclude that at least 8,540,000 German-speaking people migrated to the United States between 1820 and 1970. Census data for the period prior to 1820 are not available. The composite 8.54 million figure significantly surpasses the total number of immigrants from all of Great Britain and it approaches the combined total from both Great Britain and Ireland. We should note, of course, that English-speaking immigrants from the British Isles who arrived prior to the revolutionary war undoubtedly surpassed numerically those from any other nation. However, we must not forget that there were many German-speaking religious dissenters in colonial America as well. It is hoped that these statistics will demonstrate the numerical impact made on the American way of life by German-American churches, schools, the press, and other institutions.

Today there is a plethora of German-American organizations, but few of them have broad influence. The Steuben Society, successor of the German-American Alliance, is largely confined to the eastern United States. Only the *Deutsch-Amerikanischer National-Kongress*, known by its abbreviation DANK, has seminational status. Founded in 1958, the congress held its first assembly and was chartered by Illinois in 1959. DANK's goals are unification of German-Americans, friendship between the United States and Germany, preservation of the German language and customs, and the distribution of accurate information to counter-balance false information about the Germans. Its greatest strength is in the Chicago area, but it has affiliates in Wisconsin, Indiana, Ohio, Iowa, Michigan, Minnesota, New Jersey, Arkansas, Pennsylvania, and Washington, D. C. Youth activities, a monthly called *Der Deutsch-Amerikaner*, and travel opportunities round out the program of DANK.[10]

Many cities in the United States continue their German singing clubs, variously named *Männerchöre* and *Damenchöre*, but the German mutual aid and gymnastic societies have dwindled to a handful. German-language newspapers, too, have declined. The 140-year-old *New Yorker Staats-Zeitung und Herold* (which publishes regional papers in German) continues its proud tradition, and there are others: The *Amerika Herold* and regional papers published by the Tribune Company of Omaha, the *Chicago Abendpost*, the New York *Aufbau*, the Cincinnati *Kurier*, the Buffalo *Volksfreund* the *Detroiter Abendpost*, the St. Louis *Deutsche Wochenschrift*, the Milwaukee *Herold* (printed by Tribune in Omaha), the Cleveland *Wächter und Anzeiger*, the *California Staats-Zeitung* of Los Angeles, the *Plattdütsche Post* of Staten Island, and the New Jersey *Freie Zeitung*. The German, Austrian, and Hungarian societies of Chicago publish the weekly fifteen-page *Eintracht* for the German-language clubs in that city — an indication of the lively German-American community in Chicago.

To the question "What about the German-Americans today?" we might refer to the anecdote of a European who journeyed to the New World in the eighteenth century. Asked what kind of people the Americans were, the traveler replied, "There are no foreigners. Everybody is an American." His answer was both a definition and a prophecy. And yet, curiosity is awakening in younger Americans of German descent.

Perhaps the crux of the revived interest was expressed by a fourth-generation German-American pastor who told me, "We are a strange and rootless bunch. Whatever we are, whether it is Germans trying to be Americans or Americans trying to be Germans, we are all searching for identity." A descendant of Forty-eighters, the man gives Sunday sermons in German — although he has never visited Germany. But he knows history and explains that German-Americans are worse off than other hyphenates in America because their ethnic roots are so fragmented.

The German immigrant until 1870 had no nation, only many German states. Austria-Hungary was a hybrid of many peoples. Those from Luxembourg, Switzerland, Poland, Czechoslovakia, and Russia might be German-speaking, if not German by nationality, and they identified with the German element in the United States. But, according to the youthful pastor, the Germans suffer from one additional identity-shattering bit of history: of all the immigrant groups in the United States, the Germans alone were splintered along religious lines. They were Protestant or Catholic. But Protestant meant Lutheran or Reformed — plus the many sects. Add to the complexity the indigenous regionalism that afflicts Germans everywhere (Prussian vs. Rhinelander, Hamburger vs. Bavarian) and the puzzle becomes insoluble.

German historians in the 1930s expressed sarcasm when they referred to the United States as that "grave of *Deutschtum*." Implied in the phrase was the truism that German nationalism in the United States is dead and buried. Nationalism has been welcomed in our time as a bulwark against the loss of identity. Charles De Gaulle turned his perception of this fact into political advantage. But not even the wildest dreamer would think of wooing the Germans in America the way De Gaulle courted the French-speaking people of Quebec. The German-Americans who still pursue the German culture in America remind the observer of a great Gatsby. They are marvelous courtly lovers who seek the affection of their lady *Deutschtum* with a passion that is old, less than ardent, and quite out of date. And besides, the ladylove has already passed away.

Notes and References

Chapter One

1. Robert-Hermann Tenbrock, *A History of Germany*, trans. Paul J. Dine (Munich: Max Hueber, 1968), p. 75.
2. Christopher Dawson, *Understanding Europe* (New York: Sheed Ward, 1952), pp. 71 ff.
3. C. V. Wedgwood, *The Thirty Years War* (New York: Doubleday, 1938), p. 496.

Chapter Two

1. See Albert B. Faust, *The German Element in the United States*, vol. I (New York: Steuben Society, 1927), pp. 6 - 7. This book remains the authoritative statement concerning the Germans in America, particularly for the early period. Faust's information is included in many other more recent books on the Germans in America, including a few such as Theodore Huebener, *The Germans in America* (New York: Chilton, 1962), Victor W. von Hagen, *Der Ruf der neuen Welt* (Munich: Droemer Knaur, 1970), and Richard O'Connor, *The German-Americans* (New York: Little, Brown and Co., 1968).
2. See Faust, pp. 4 - 5 and von Hagen, pp. 16 - 20.
3. Paul H. Baginsky, "Early German Interest in the New World (1494 - 1618)," *American-German Review* 5 (August, 1939), 8 - 13.
4. Klaus Wust, *The Virginia Germans* (Charlottesville: Univ. of Virginia Press, 1969), p. 9. See also Klaus Wust, "German Craftsmen in Jamestown," *American-German Review* 23 (April - May, 1957), 10 - 11.
5. Milton Rubincam, "On the Use of the Term 'Palatine,'" *American-German Review* 10 (October, 1943), 15.
6. Wust, pp. 10 - 14.
7. Dieter Cunz, *The Maryland Germans* (Princeton: Princeton University Press, 1948), pp. 19 ff. and p. 41.
8. Faust, I, 30 ff. See also Harold Jantz, "Pastorius, Intangible Values," *American-German Review* 25 (1958), 4 - 7.

9. See "1683 - Krefelder gründen Germantown," in A. H. Gläser, *600 Jahre Stadt Krefeld* (Krefeld: Joh. van Acken, 1968), pp. 61 ff., and William Hubben, "Pilgrims from Krefeld," *American-German Review* 25 (1958), 8 - 17.

10. Hildegard Binder Johnson, "The Germantown Protest of 1688 Against Negro Slavery," *Pennsylvania Magazine of History and Biography*, April, 1941, pp. 145 - 56.

11. Faust, I, 115. See Andrew Steinmetz, "Kelpius: The Hermit of the Wissahickon," *American-German Review* 7 (August, 1941), 7 - 11, and Felix Reichmann and Eugene E. Doll, "Ephrata as Seen by Contemporaries," *Pennsylvania German Folklore Society*, 17 (1953).

12. For more information about the count, see Johm R. Weinlick, *Count Zinzendorf* (Nashville: Abingdon, 1956). See also, Elizabeth H. Zorb, "Zinzendorf and Bethlehem, Pa." *American-German Review* 11 (August, 1945), 9 ff.

13. See Julius Friedrich Sachse, ed. and tr., *Daniel Falckner's Curieuse Nachricht from Pennsylvania: The Book That Stimulated the Great German Immigration to Pennsylvania in the Early Years of the XVIII Century* (Lancaster, Pennsylvania German Society, 1905), pp. 13 - 206.

14. Elmer Schultz Gerhard, "What Conrad Weiser Wrote About Count von Zinzendorf and the Indians," *American-German Review* 12 (February, 1946), 14 ff. See also Thomas McHugh, "The Moravian Missions to the American Indian: An Early American Peace Corps," *Pennsylvania History* 33 (1966), 412 - 31.

15. P. A. Strobel, *The Salzburgers and Their Descendants* (Baltimore, 1885), p. 63.

16. See George F. Jones, ed., *Detailed Reports on the Salzburger Emigrants who Settled in America* ... (Athens: Univ. of Georgia Press, 1968), pp. 25 - 115.

17. See Faust, I, 235.

18. Jones, *Detailed Reports*, p. 177.

19. Jones, p. 122. See also Hildegard Binder Johnson, "Die Haltung der Salzburger in Georgia zur Sklaverei," *Mitteilungen der Gesellschaft für Salzburger Landeskunde* 78 (1936), 183 - 96.

20. Joseph Schafer, "The Yankee and the Teuton in Wisconsin," *The Wisconsin Magazine of History* 6 (1922), 130.

21. Lucy F. Bittinger, *The Germans in Colonial Times* (New York: Russell & Russell, 1901; reissued 1968).

22. Robert Henry Billigmeier, *Americans From Germany: A Study in Cultural Diversity* (Belmont, Calif.: Wadsworth Publishing, 1974), pp. 19 ff.

23. See Faust, I, 271.

24. Faust quotes Francis Parkman, *Montcalm and Wolfe*, 6th ed. (Boston, 1855) II, pp. 144 - 50 to illustrate Indian attitudes and loyalties. See also Arthur D. Graeff, "The Pennsylvania Germans as Soldiers," in Ralph Wood,

ed., *The Pennsylvania Germans* (Princeton: Princeton University Press, 1942), pp. 227 ff.

25. Faust, I, p. 285.

26. Ludwig Beutin, *Bremen und Amerika* (Bremen: Carl Schunemann, 1953), pp. 27, ff. See Mary Cable, "Damned Plague Ships and Swimming Coffins," *American Heritage* 11 (August, 1960), 74 ff.

27. Wilhelm Mönckmeier, *Die deutsche überseeische Auswanderung* (Jena: 1912), p. 474.

28. Cunz, *Maryland Germans*, p. 92, and Wust, *Virginia Germans*, p. 51.

29. Richard Shyrock, "British versus German Traditions in Colonial Agriculture," *The Mississippi Valley Historical Review*, 26 (1939 - 1940), 39 - 54.

30. Benjamin Rush, "An Account of the Manners of the German Inhabitants of Pennsylvania," *Proceedings of the Pennsylvania German Society*, 19 (Lancaster, Pa., 1910), 40 ff.

31. Andreas Dorpalen, "The Political Influence of the German Element in Colonial America," *Pennsylvania History* 6 (1939), 147 - 58 and 221 - 39.

32. Cunz, *Maryland Germans*, p. 114. See also, William Beidelman, *The Story of the Pennsylvania Germans* (Easton, Pa., Express Book Print, 1898), pp. 48 ff. and Walter Allen Knittle, *The Early Eighteenth Century Palatine Emigration, A British Government Redemptioner Project to Manufacture Naval Stores* (Philadelphia, Dorrance, 1937).

33. O'Connor, *The German-Americans*, p. 24.

Chapter Three

1. Faust, I, 291.

2. Cunz, *The Maryland Germans*, p. 131 and Lucy Bittinger, *The Germans in Colonial Times*, pp. 235 - 76.

3. O'Connor, *The German-Americans*, p. 36.

4. George von Skal, *History of German Immigration in the United States* (New York: Frederick T. Smiley, no date), p. 18.

5. Henry A. Muhlenberg, *The Life of Major-General Peter Muhlenberg of the Revoutionary Army* (Philadelphia: Carey and Hart, 1849), pp. 28 - 33. See also Paul A. W. Wallace, *The Muhlenbergs of Pennsylvania* (Philadelphia, 1950) and Felix Reichmann, *The Muhlenberg Family, A Bibliography* (Philadelphia, 1943).

6. Freeman, H. Hart, *The Valley of Virginia in the American Revolution* (Chapel Hill: University of North Carolina Press, 1942), p. 85 footnote 3. See also Wust, *Virginia Germans*, p. 78.

7. Wust, p. 80.

8. Henry Muhlenberg, p. 53.

9. von Skal, p. 21. See also Faust, I, 306 ff.

10. Faust, I, 321 and Friedrich Kapp, *The Life of Frederick William von Steuben* (New York: Mason Brothers, 1859).

11. John McAuley Palmer, *General von Steuben* (New Haven: Yale University Press, 1937), pp. 49 ff. See also Edgar Erskine Hume, "Steuben and the Society of the Cincinnati," *American-German Review* 1 (March, 1935), 17 - 19.

12. Palmer, p. 113.

13. O'Connor, p. 50.

14. Morgan H. Pritchett and Edith von Semensky, "The Three Wills of Baron von Steuben," *The Report: A Journal of German-American History, Society for the History of the Germans in Maryland*, hereafter cited as *The Report*, SHGM, 35 (1972), 19 - 26 and Theodore H. Hoffmann, "Steuben Day - September Seventeenth, 1936," *American-German Review* 3 (March, 1937), 24 - 26.

15. *Der Deutsche Pionier*, 7, 217.

16. Friedrich Kapp, *The Life of John Kalb, Major-General in the Revolutionary Army* (New York: Holt & Company, 1884) and A. E. Zucker, *General De Kalb, Lafayette's Mentor* (Chapel Hill: Univ. of North Carolina, 1966).

17. J. G. Rosengaten, *The German Soldier in the Wars of the United States* (Philadelphia: J. B. Lippincott, 1890), p. 58 ff. See also, Max von Eelking, *Die Deutschen Hülfstruppen in Nordamerika im Befreiungskriege, 1776 - 1783*, 2 vols. (Hanover, 1863).

18. See Friedrich Kapp, *Der Soldatenhandel deutscher Fürsten nach Amerika: Ein Beitrag zur Kulturgeschichte des achtzehnten Jahrhunderts*. 2nd rev. ed. (Berlin: Julius Springer, 1874).

19. J. G. Rosengarten, "American History from German Archives with Reference to the German Soldiers in the Revolution and Franklin's Visit to Germany," *The Pennsylvania-German Society* 13 (Lancaster, Pa. 1904), 1 - 49. See also Clifford Neal Smith, "Some British and German Deserters During the American Revolution," *National Genealogical Society Quarterly* 60 (December, 1972), 267 - 75.

20. Frederick A. Klemm, "American-Prussian Diplomatic Relations During the Revolutionary War," *American-German Review* 13 (February, 1947), 12 - 16.

21. Robert-Hermann Tenbrock, *A History of Germany*, p. 159.

22. See Frank G. Ryder, "An American View of Germany — 1817," *American-German Review* 25 (February - March, 1959), pp. 16 - 19.

23. See, for example, *Maryland State Proceedings*, March 25 and August 15, 1779.

24. See Mack Walker, *Germany and the Emigration 1816 - 1885* (Cambridge: Harvard Univ. Pres, 1964), pp. 1 ff., & Von Skal, p. 25.

25. Marcus L. Hansen, *The Atlantic Migration of 1607 - 1860* (Cambridge, Mass.: Harvard University Press, 1940), p. 24.

26. Among others, Faust, I, pp. 374 ff.

27. La Vern J. Rippley, "The Chillicothe Germans," *Ohio History* 75 (1966), 212 ff.

Chapter Four

1. See William G. Bek, "Gottfried Duden's *Report*, 1824 - 1827," *Missouri Historical Review* 12, 13, 14 (1917 - 1919), 1 - 21, 44 - 281, 29 - 73. See also E. D. Kargau, "Missouri's German Immigration," *Missouri Historical Quarterly* 2 (1900), 23.

2. J. Hanno Deiler, *The Settlement of the German Coast of Louisiana* and *The Creoles of German Descent* (San Francisco: R & E Associates Reprint, 1968), Karl J. Arndt, "The Life and Mission of Count Leon," *American-German Review* 6 (June, 1940), 5 ff., and Arthur Moehlenbrock, "J. Hanno Deiler: Cultural Pioneer of the South," *American-German Review* 8 (February, 1942), 25 - 27.

3. Max Hannemann, *Das Deutschtum in den Vereinigten Staaten, Seine Verbreitung und Entwicklung seit der Mitte des 19. Jahrhunderts* in *Petermanns Mitteilungen*, supplement 224 (Gotha: Justus Perthus, 1936), pp. 19 ff.

4. J. A. Wagener, "Die Deutschen in Süd Carolina," *Der Deutsche Pionier* 3 (1871 - 1872), 234 ff.

5. Max Hannemann, pp. 63 ff. See also Dr. G. Engelmann, "Zur Geschichte der ersten deutschen Ansiedlungen in Illinois," *Deutsch-Amerikanische Geschichtsblätter* 16 (1916), 248 - 79.

6. Terry G. Jordan, *German Seed in Texas Soil: Immigrant Farmers in Nineteenth-Century Texas* (Austin: University of Texas Press, 1966). See also Gilbert Giddings Benjamin, *The Germans in Texas* (San Francisco: R & E Associates, originally published 1909, reprinted 1970).

7. Rudolph von Biesele, *The History of German Settlements in Texas 1831 - 1861* (Austin: Von Boeckmann-Jones, 1930), pp. 66 - 110, and Leopold Biesele, "Prince Solms's Trip to Texas, 1844 - 1845," *The Southwestern Historical Quarterly* 40 (1936), 1 - 25. See also Wolf-Heino Struck, *Die Auswanderung aus dem Herzogtum Nassau 1806 - 1966* (Wiesbaden: Franz Steiner Verlag, 1966), chapter 3, pp. 50 - 71, and Marcus L. Hansen, *The Atlantic Migration 1706 - 1860*, pp. 232 ff.

8. Jordan, p. 50, Faust, I, p. 490, Florence Dombey Shreve, "Fredericksburg, Texas, an Old German Settlement," *American-German Review* 7 (February, 1941), 9 - 12 and Selma Metaenthin-Raunick, "New Braunfels 1845 - 1945," ibid. 11 (June, 1945), 5 ff. and (August, 1945), 23 ff.

9. Art Kowert, "LBJ's Boyhood Among the German-Americans in Texas," *American-German Review* 34 (August - September, 1968), 2 - 6.

10. Earl W. Fornell, "The German Pioneers of Galveston Island," *American-German Review* 22 (February - March, 1956), 15.

11. Faust, I, p. 508 and O'Connor, p. 189.

12. Erwin G. Gudde, *German Pioneers in Early California* (San Francisco: R & E Associates, 1970), p. 6 ff. and idem, "Anaheim - The Mother Colony of Southern California," *American-German Review* 7 (August, 1941), 4 ff.

13. George Peter Hammond, *German Interest in California before 1850*,

(M.A. thesis, University of California, Berkeley, 1921; reprinted by R & E Associates, 1971), pp. 24 - 25.

14. Ibid., p. 31. The publishers acknowledged that "the foregoing was written about a year ago, with a truly prophetic spirit, and it shows how much the advantages of California were already then appreciated by the Germans. . . ."

15. Hermann Hoffmann, *Californien, Nevada und Mexico* (Basel: Schweighauser, 1871).

16. See "The Idea of Founding a New Germany in North America," in John A. Hawgood, *The Tragedy of German-America* (New York: Arno Press, 1970), pp. 93 ff.

17. A. E. Zucker, ed., *The Forty-Eighters: Political Refugees of the German Revolution of 1848* (New York: Columbia University Press, 1950), Carl Wittke, *Refugees of Revolution: The German Forty-Eighters in America* (Philadelphia: University of Pennsylvania Press, 1952), and Irmgard Erhorn, *Die deutsche Einwanderung der Dreissiger und Achtundvierziger in die Vereinigten Staaten und ihre Stellung zur nordamerikanischen Politik* (Hamburg: Hans Christian, 1937). See also Don Heinrich Tolzmann, *German-Americana: A Bibliography* (Metuchen, N. J.: Scarecrow Press, 1975), pp. 305 - 8.

18. Karl J. R. Arndt, "American Incitement to Revolution on the Eve of the Frankfurt Parliament," *American-German Review* 11 (April, 1945), 24 - 25 and Alice Reynolds, "Friedrich Hecker," *American-German Review* 12 (April, 1946), 4 - 7.

19. Arndt, "American Incitement . . . ," 25.

20. Ernest Bruncken, "German Political Refugees in the United States During the Period from 1815 - 1860," *Deutsch-Amerikanische Geschichtsblätter* 3 (1903), 33.

21. Ibid., p. 35. See also Hildegard Binder Johnson, "Adjustment to the United States," in Zucker, *The Forty-Eighters*, p. 47.

22. Hermann Rothfuss, "Plays for Pioneers: German Drama in Rural Minnesota," *Minnesota History* 35 (Summer, 1955), 239 - 42. See also Esther M. Olson, "The German Theater in Chicago," *Jahrbuch der deutschamerikanischen Geschichtsblätter* 33 (1937), 71 - 123, and Ralph Wood, "Geschichte des deutschen Theaters von Cincinnati," ibid. 32 (1932), 415 - 522.

23. Ernest Bruncken, "The Political Activity of Wisconsin Germans, 1854 - 60," *Wisconsin State Hisorical Society Proceedings* 69 (1901), 190 - 211, and Frederick C. Luebke, *Immigrants and Politics: The Germans of Nebraska, 1880 - 1900* (Lincoln: University of Nebraska Press, 1969).

24. Far into the twentieth century, however, Wisconsin's Germans voted for governors with German names: Fred Zimmerman in 1927, Walter Kohler in 1929. Albert Schmedeman in 1933, Julius P. Heil in 1939, and Walter J.

Kohler Jr. in 1951. Between 1927 and 1957 the only governor without a German name was Philip F. La Follette (1931 - 1933), and this was due to the patriarchial, pro-German name of Robert M. La Follette.

25. Bruncken, "The Political Activity . . . ," p. 209.

26. Quoted in Bruncken, ibid., pp. 196 - 97.

27. Robert E. Dickinson, *The Regions of Germany* (New York: Oxford University Press, 1945).

28. J. D. Angell, quoted in O'Connor, p. 113.

29. Faust, II, 126. See also Hildegard Binder Johnson, "The Germantown Protest of 1688 Against Negro Slavery," pp. 145 - 56.

30. Carl Wittke, *We Who Built America: The Saga of the Immigrant* (Cleveland: Case Western Reserve University Press, 1964), pp. 200 ff.

31. Heinrich H. Maurer, "The Earlier German Nationalism in America," *American Journal of Sociology* 22 (1917), 532.

32. Andreas Dorpalen, "The German Element and the Issues of the Civil War," in Frederick C. Luebke, ed., *Ethnic Voters and the Election of Lincoln* (Lincoln: University of Nebraska Press, 1971), pp. 68 ff.

33. Quoted in Reinhard H. Luthin, "Lincoln Appeals to German-American Voters," *American-German Review* 25 (June - July, 1959), 6.

34. George H. Daniels, "Immigrant Vote in the 1860 Election: The Case of Iowa," in Luebke, *Ethnic Voters*, pp. 110 - 25.

35. Hildegard Binder Johnson, "The Election of 1860 and the Germans in Minnesota," in Luebke, *Ethnic Voters*, pp. 92 - 109.

36. Joseph Schafer, "Who Elected Lincoln?" *The American Historical Review* 47 (October, 1941), 51 - 63.

37. Dora Edinger, "A Feminist Forty-Eighter," *American-German Review* 8 (June, 1942), 19 and Albert B. Faust, "Mathilde Franziska Giesler-Anneke: *Memoiren einer Frau aus dem Badisch-Pfälzischen Feldzug* and a Sketch of Her Career," *German American Annals* 16 (1918), 73 - 140.

38. L. V. Baumbach, *Neue Briefe aus den Vereinigten Staaten von Nordamerika* (Cassel, 1856), quoted in Billigmeier, p. 67.

39. Eitel W. Dobert, "The Radicals," in Zucker, *The Forty-Eighters*, p. 179 and Cecyle S. Neidle, *Great Immigrants* (New York: Twayne, 1973), pp. 107 ff.

40. Nicolaus Mohr, *Excursion Through America*, tr. La Vern J. Rippley (Chicago: R. R. Donnelley, 1973), pp. 134 ff. and p. 230. See also Newell Searle, "Minnesota State Forestry Association: Seedbed of Forest Conservation," *Minnesota History* 44 (1974), 23.

Chapter Five

1. See Marcus L. Hansen, "The Revolution of 1848 and German Emigration," *Journal of Economic and Business History* 2 (August, 1930), 657.

2. A. E. Parkins, *The South: Its Economic-Geographic Development* (New York: Wiley and Sons, 1949), p. 206.

3. See "Dr. Adalbert J. Volck" of Baltimore who adhered actively to the Southern cause — *Dictionary of American Biography*, 19, 288. As a cartoonist, Volck counteracted the North's German Forty-eighter cartoonist, Thomas Nast. See also Dieter Cunz, "The Maryland Germans in the Civil War," *Maryland Historical Magazine* 36 (1941), 416 - 17.

4. Ella Lonn, *Foreigners in the Confederacy* (Chapel Hill: University of North Carolina Press, 1940), pp. 417 ff. and Dieter Cunz, pp. 394 - 419.

5. Lonn, p. 46.

6. Quoted in *The Pennsylvania German* 5 (1904), 44.

7. Faust, I, pp. 530 ff., O'Connor, p. 137 ff., and Bruce Catton, *This Hallowed Ground* (New York: Doubleday, 1955), pp. 30 - 35 and 49 - 51. See also Audrey L. Olson, C.S.J., "St. Louis Germans, 1850 - 1920: The Nature of an Immigrant Community and its Relation to the Assimilation Process," (unpubl. Ph. D. diss., University of Kansas, 1970), pp. 172 - 73.

8. Quoted in Faust, I, 533.

9. See Galusha Anderson, *The Story of a Border City During the Civil War* (Boston: Little, Brown & Co., 1908), Francis Grierson, *The Valley of Shadows* (New York: Harper & Row, 1948), pp. 229 - 31, and Alexander C. Niven, "The Role of German Volunteers in St. Louis, 1861," *American-German Review* 28 (February - March, 1962), 29 - 30.

10. Faust, I, pp. 522 ff.

11. Faust, I, 526. See also Ella Lonn, *Desertion During the Civil War* (New York: The Century Co., 1928). It should be mentioned that other scholars put the totals of Germans who fought in the Civil War considerably higher than does Gould. Georg von Bosse, *Das Deutsche Element in den Vereinigten Staaten* (New York: Steiger, 1908), p. 258 lists the figure at 235,000 without adequately explaining how he arrived at his total. Wilhelm Kaufmann, *Die Deutschen im amerikanischen Bürgerkriege* (Munich: R. Oldenbourg, 1911) pp. 118 ff. offers the figures of 216,000 German-born soldiers, 300,000 first generation Germans and 234,000 Germans of second and later generations.

12. Wittke, *We Who Built America*, p. 238.

13. Frederick Frankiin Schrader, *The Germans in the Making of America* (Boston: Stratford Co., 1924), p. 201.

14. Faust, I, pp. 527 - 28. See also Kaufmann, pp. 181 - 90.

15. Henry Metzner, *A Brief History of the American Turnerbund*, tr. Theodore Stempfel, Jr. (Pittsburgh: Turnerbund Committee, 1924), pp. 18 - 24.

16. See Dieter Cunz, ed., "Civil War Letters of a German Immigrant," *American-German Review* 11 (October, 1944), 30 - 33.

17. Wittke, *We Who Built America*, p. 242. A mass-meeting of the Chicago Germans was held on November 10, 1861. Here, too, radical anti-Lincoln sentiments were expressed. Fremont was hailed as the surest means to end

the war and the crowd agreed with the *Illinois Staatszeitung* which came out in favor of Fremont for President stating editorially that "through proclaiming him as future·President, the people will protest in the most vigorous manner against the weak-hearted and weak-sighted acts of the present government." See Andrew J. Townsend, "The Germans of Chicago," *Deutsch-Amerikanische Geschichtsblätter* 32 (1932), 27 - 28.

18. Harry H. Anderson, ed., Margaret Wolff, tr., *German-American Pioneers in Wisconsin and Michigan: The Frank-Kerler Letters, 1849 - 1864* (Milwaukee: Milwaukee Co. Historical Society, 1971), p. 528.

19. Ibid., p. 552.

20. Kaufmann, p. 133.

21. Bruce Catton, *The Glory Road* (New York: Doubleday, 1952), p. 193.

22. Kaufmann, pp. 137 ff. See also Ralph H. Lutz, *Die Beziehungen zwischen Deutschland und den Vereinigten Staaten während des Sezessionskrieges* (Heidelberg: Carl Winter, 1911).

23. Kaufmann, p. 238. United States bonds sold at 67 in 1863, fell to 37 during 1864 and climbed to 96 in 1870 when Germany cashed in her sizable war loan to finance the war against Napoleon III and the struggle for unification. See Edwin F. Eckert, "Lincoln and Bismark," *American German Review* 19 (February, 1953), 32.

24. Kaufmann, pp. 154 ff. See also Frank H. Smyrl, "Unionism in Texas, 1856 - 1861, "*Southwestern Historical Quarterly* 68 (1964 - 1965), 172 - 95.

25. Jordan, *German Seed in Texas Soil*, p. 183.

26. Ibid.

27. See Kaufmann, p. 159 and Robert W. Shook, "The Battle of the Neuces, August 10, 1862," *Southwestern Historical Quarterly* 66 (1962 - 1963), 31 ff.

28. Colman J. Barry, O.S.B., "New Prospects in Immigration Studies," in Henry S. Commager, ed., *Immigration and American History: Essays in Honor of Theodore C. Blegen* (Minneapolis: University of Minnesota Press, 1961), p. 135.

29. Wust, *The Virginia Germans*, pp. 218 - 30. See also Kaufmann, pp. 140 - 42.

30. Wust, *Virginia Germans*, p. 219.

31. Wust, p. 224.

32. Ella Lonn, *Foreigners in the Confederacy*, pp. 111 - 12 and Joseph G. Rosengarten, *The German Soldier in the Wars of the United States* (Philadelphia: Lippincott, 1886), pp. 84 - 85.

33. Quoted in Lonn, p. 121.

34. Alexander C. Niven, "German Military Literature and the Confederacy," *American-German Review* 25 (February - March, 1959), 31 - 33.

35. Georg von Bosse, *Das Deutsche Element in den Vereinigten Staaten*, pp. 259 - 70 and Faust, I, pp. 556 ff. See Jacob Picar, "The General on the

Black Horse," *American-German Review* 10 (August, 1944), 32 - 34 and Alfred C. Raphelson, "The Unheroic General," *American-German Review* 29 (October - November, 1962), 26 - 29.

36. Kaufmann, p. 368.

Chapter Six

1. Marcus Lee Hansen, *The Immigrant in American History*, p. 148.

2. O'Connor, *The German-Americans*, p. 184.

3. Mack Walker, *Germany and the Emigration 1816 - 1885* (Cambridge: Harvard University Press, 1964), pp. 44 and 176. For the earlier period see William J. Bromwell, *History of Immigration to the United States* (New York: Arno Press, 1969), originally published in 1856.

4. Faust, I, pp. 585 - 87 and Peter Marschalck, *Deutsche Überseewanderung im 19. Jahrhundert: Ein Beitrag zur soziologischen Theorie der Bevölkerung, Industrielle Welt*, 14 (Stuttgart: Klett, 1973).

5. Walker, p. 154. See also Philip A. M. Taylor, *The Distant Magnet: European Emigration to the U. S. A.* (New York: Harper & Row, 1971), pp. 37 ff.

6. Walker, p. 157. See also Lowell C. Bennion, "Flight from the Reich: A Geographic Exposition of Southwest German Emigration, 1683 - 1815" (unpubl. Ph.D. diss. Syracuse University, 1971).

7. Carl Wittke, *Refugees of Revolution*, p. 43.

8. See Marschalck, *Deutsche Überseewanderung*, pp. 79 - 82 for statistical tables showing the breakdown by profession of emigrants from the various German states between 1871 and 1898.

9. See for example Traugott Bromme, *Handbuch für Auswanderer und Reisende nach Nord-, Mittel- und Süd Amerika*, 7th edition (Bamberg, Buchnersch Verlag, 1954). For official German government policies on emigration, see Eugen von Philoppovich, ed., *Auswanderung und Auswanderungspolitik* (Leipzig: Duncker & Humbolt, 1892).

10. Wittke, *Refugees*, p. 45. See also Rolf Engelsing, *Bremen als Auswanderhafen 1683 - 1880* (Bremen: Carl Schünemann, 1961), p. 142.

11. For a list of all the twenty-seven emigration societies that existed between 1833 and 1850 as well as sources for information about each, see Peter Marschalck, *Deutsche Überseewanderung*, p. 21.

12. Wolf-Heino Struck, *Die Auswanderung aus dem Herzogtum Nassau*, pp. 61 ff. See also Ministerialsekretär Fey, "Die Entwicklung des Auswanderungswesens und Auswanderungsrechtes im Grossherzogtum Hessen," in von Philippovich, *Auswanderung*, pp. 216 ff.

13. For a breakdown on the numbers of Germans emigrating from the French and German ports by year, see Walter F. Willcox, ed., *International Migrations*, vol. I: *Statistics, Demographic Monographs* 7 (New York: Gordon and Breach, 1969), pp. 686 - 709.

14. For a description of the activities of immigrant aid societies in a variety of American cities, Baltimore, Chicago, Philadelphia, St. Louis, see Wittke, *Refugees of Revolution*, p. 55. For pictures of such institutions, see also Oscar Handlin, *A Pictorial History of Immigration* (New York: Crown, 1972), p. 137.

15. The popular handbook by C. L. Fleischmann, *Der Nordamerikanische Landwirth: Ein Handbuch für Ansiedler in den Vereinigten Staaten* (Frankfurt a. M.: G. F. Heyer, 1852) is an example of the productivity of German Emigration Societies.

16. Frank Thistlethwaite, "Migration From Europe Overseas in the 19th and 20th Centuries," *Rapports of the Eleventh International Congress of Historical Science*, 5 (1960), pp. 46 ff. See also Maldwyn Jones, "The Role of the United Kingdom in the Transatlantic Emigrant Trade" (unpubl. Ph.D. diss. Oxford University, 1956).

17. Marcus L. Hansen, *The Immigrant in American History*, pp. 192 - 93.

18. Thistlethwaite, in *Rapports*, especially p. 53. See also in a general way, Carlton C. Qualey, "Emmigration as a World Phenomenon," in Henry S. Commager, ed., *Immigration and American History*, pp. 96 - 106.

19. Walker, p. 177.

20. Dr. Leidig, "Die preussische Auswanderungspolitik," in von Philippovich, *Auswanderung*, pp. 448 - 49.

21. Walker, p. 183.

22. Marschalck, *Deutsche Überseewanderung*, pp. 72 - 76.

23. Wittke, *We Who Built America*, pp. 204 - 5. See also Elfrieda Lang, "Some Characteristics of German Immigrants in Dubois County, Indiana," *Indiana Magazine of History* 42 (1946), 29 - 46.

24. Friedrich Kapp, *Aus und Über Amerika: Thatsachen und Erlebnisse*, vol. I & II (Berlin: Julius Springer, 1876), especially vol. I, chapter 2, "Zur Auswanderungsfrage," pp. 159 - 222.

25. La Vern J. Rippley, "A New Life for Ellis Island," *Coronet* (April, 1967), p. 137, and Ann Novotny, *Strangers at the Door: Ellis Island, Castle Garden and the Great Migration to America* (Riverside, Conn.: Chatham Press, 1971), pp. 44 ff.

26. Quoted in Walker, p. 193. See also Rolf Engelsing, *Bremen als Auswandererhafen*, p. 171.

27. Walker, p. 197.

28. Wittke, *Refugees of Revolution*, pp. 357 ff. and La Vern J. Rippley, "The Columbus Germans," *A Journal of German-American History, The Report SHGM*, 33 (1968), 40.

29. Marschalck, *Deutsche Überseewanderung*, pp. 48 - 50.

30. Marschalck, pp. 24 - 27. In 1902 the German Colonial Society in Berlin established the Zentral-Auskunftstelle für Auswanderer (Center for Emigration Information) under tutelage of the Imperial German Foreign Office. Marschalck, p. 46.

Chapter Seven

1. Wittke, *Refugees*, p. 359.

2. Rippley, "The Columbus Germans," pp. 40 - 41.

3. *Wächter am Erie*, June 17, 1872.

4. Hildegard Binder Johnson, "German Forty-eighters in Davenport," *Iowa Journal of History and Politics* 44 (January, 1946), 8.

5. Wittke, *Refugees*, p. 360.

6. George C. Schoolfield, "The Great Cincinnati Novel," *Bulletin of the Historical and Philosophical Society of Ohio* 20 (1962), 58.

7. Wittke, *Refugees*, p. 368.

8. Kapp, *Aus und Über Amerika*, I, p. 187.

9. Rolf Engelsing, *Bremen als Auswandererhafen 1683 - 1880*, pp. 48, 122 - 23, 172.

10. Francis P. Epstein, "The Leopoldine Association — the German 'Propagation of the Faith' Society," *Illinois Catholic Historical Review* 3 (1920), 88 ff.; Benjamin J. Blied, *Austrian Aid to American Catholics, 1830 - 1860* (Milwaukee: no publisher listed, 1944); Theodore Roemer, O. F. M. Cap., "The Leopoldine Foundation and the Church in the United States," *Monograph Series*, 13 (New York: USCHS, 1933); especially, Theodore Roemer, O. F. M. Cap., *The Ludwigsmissionverein and the Catholic Church in the United States 1838 - 1913* (Washington, D. C.: The Catholic University Press, 1933), and Roemer, "Munich and Milwaukee, *Salesianum* 35 (April, 1934), 14 - 22.

11. Rev. Matthew Anthony Pekari, "The German Catholics in the United States of America," *Records of the American Catholic Historical Society* 36 (December, 1925), 345.

12. Peter Paul Cahensly, "Der St. Raphaelsverein zum Schutze katholischer deutscher Auswanderer," *Caritas-Schriften*, 5 (Freiburg in Breisgau, 1900). Breisgau, 1900).

13. Barry, *The Catholic Church and the German-Americans*, p. 30.

14. Pekari, "The German Catholics," p. 348.

15. Gottfried Mai, "Die Bemühungen der evangelischen Kirche um die deutschen Auswanderer nach Amerika 1815 - 1914" (Ph.D. dissertation, University of Hamburg, 1971; Bremen: microfilm print, 1972), pp. 43 - 191. A list of the Lutheran societies (twenty-nine in all) in the German-speaking countries to aid and assist German emigrants appears on pp. 191 - 93.

16. Wolf-Heino Struck, *Die Auswanderung aus dem Herzogtum Nassau*, pp. 110 - 11. For statistics showing the sums of money taken out of Nassau, see pp. 127 - 29.

17. Carl B. Schmidt, "Reminiscences of Foreign Immigration Work for Kansas," *Transactions and Collections of the Kansas State Historical Society* 9 (1905 - 1906), 490.

18. Ibid., p. 495. For further discussion of the cash flow to America by way

of German immigrants, see Friedrich Kapp, *Immigration and the Commissioners of Emigration*, chapter 8 "Capital Value of Immigration To This Country — Its Influence on the Population and the Nation's Wealth — Is Immigration a Matter of State or National Concern?" (New York: Arno Press, 1969), pp. 142 - 61. Claims that Russian-German immigrants brought over $1,000,000 to the destitute state of Kansas during the last half of 1874 and that they kept the Santa Fe Railroad from going bankrupt, seem exaggerated. For details, see Norman E. Saul, "The Migration of the Russian-Germans to Kansas," *Kansas Historical Quarterly* 40 (1974), 38 - 62.

19. See the footnotes in Rolf Engelsing, *Bremen als Auswandererhafen*, pp. 141 - 50 and Frederick P. Kenkel, "Germans on the Land," *Central-Blatt and Social Justice Review* (St. Louis) 28 (July - August, 1935), 137.

20. American companies bought equipment from German firms; see William Manchester, *The Arms of Krupp* (Boston: Little, Brown and Company, 1968), p. 141.

21. See Nicolaus Mohr, *Excursion Through America*, tr. La Vern J. Rippley, and Eugene V. Smalley, *History of the Northern Pacific Railroad* (New York: Putnam, 1883).

22. William L. Jenks, "Michigan Immigration," *Michigan History* 28 (1944), 75 - 76.

23. Theodore C. Blegen, "The Competition of the Northwestern States for Immigrants," *Wisconsin Magazine of History* 3 (1919 - 1920), 5.

24. Livia Appel and Theodore C. Blegen, "Official Encouragement of Immigration to Minnesota During the Territorial Period," *Minnesota History* 5 (1923), 170 - 71.

25. See the *First Biennial Report of the Board of Immigration* (Iowa), January 1, 1872.

26. Marcus L. Hansen, "Official Encouragement of Immigration to Iowa," *Iowa Journal of History and Politics* 19 (1921), 167. For a typical example of German immigrants who took their money to Wisconsin, see John Eiselmeier, "St. Nazianz, a German Settlement," *American-German Review* 8 (June, 1942), 22 ff.

27. Herbert S. Schell, "Official Immigration Activities of Dakota Territory," *North Dakota History* 7 (1932 - 1933), 5 - 24. See also Blegen, "The Competition," and Harold E. Briggs, "The Great Dakota Boom," *North Dakota Historical Quarterly* 4 (1929 - 1930), 105.

28. Bert J. Loewenberg, "Efforts of the South to Encourage Immigration, 1865 - 1900," *South Atlantic Quarterly* 33 (1934), 363 - 85.

29. Robert H. Woody, "The Labor and Immigration Problem of South Carolina During Reconstruction," *Mississippi Valley Historical Review* 18 (1931), 195 - 212, especially 196, 202, and 211.

30. John F. Sprague, "Maine as a District and as a State Has Had Two Successful Immigration Enterprises," *Sprague's Journal of Maine History* 7 (1920), 39 - 41.

31. Merle Curti and Kendall Birr, "The Immigrant and the American Image in Europe, 1860 - 1914," *Mississippi Valley Historical Review* 37 (1950 - 1951), 204.

32. Theodore C. Blegen, "Minnesota's Campaign for Immigrants," *Yearbook of the Swedish Historical Society* 11 (1926), 13.

33. The report is in the Governor's files, 608 A. L. S. It is reproduced in the *Yearbook of the Swedish Historical Society* 11 (1926), 55 - 64.

34. Rolf Engelsing, *Bremen als Auswandererhafen*, p. 145.

35. See Kate Asaphine Everest, "How Wisconsin Came By its Large German Element," *Collections of the State Historical Society of Wisconsin* 12 (1892), 329. See also Kate Everest Levi, "Geographical Origin of German Immigration to Wisconsin," ibid., 14 (1898), 341 - 93.

36. Richard C. Overton, *Burlington West: A Colonization History of the Burlington Railroad* (Cambridge, Mass.: Harvard University Press, 1941), p. 368.

37. Ibid., p. 369.

38. Harold F. Peterson, "Early Minnesota Railroads and the Quest for Settlers," *Minnesota History* 13 (1932), 27.

39. Richard M. Lunde, "Why Bismarck?" *The American-German Review* 27 (June - July, 1961), 28.

40. Peterson, "Early Minnesota Railroads . . . ," p. 36.

41. Harold F. Peterson, "Some Colonization Projects of the Northern Pacific Railroad,"*Minnesota History* 10 (1929), 127 - 44, James B. Hedges, "The Colonization Work of the Northern Pacific Railroad," *The Mississippi Valley Historical Review* 13 (1926), 311 - 41, and Siegfried Mickelson, "Promotional Activities of the Northern Pacific Railroad's Land and Immigration Departments, 1870 - 1902" (unpubl. M.A. thesis, University of Minnesota, 1940).

42. Hedges, "The Colonization Work . . . ," pp. 331 - 38.

43. Hildegard Binder Johnson, "Eduard Pelz and German Emigration," *Minnesota History* 31 (1950), 227.

44. Rolf Engelsing, *Bremen als Auswandererhafen*, pp. 27 - 49, 98 ff. and 131. See also, Philip Taylor, *The Distant Magnet*, chapter 7, "The Journey Under Sail," pp. 131 - 44 and chapter 8, "The Journey By Steam," pp. 145 - 66.

45. Charlotte Erickson, *American Industry and the European Immigrant, 1860 - 1885* (Cambridge: Harvard University Press, 1957), especially chapter 1, "Organized Efforts to Promote Immigration."

46. Curti and Birr, "The Immigrant and the American Image," 210.

47. Erickson, p. 25.

48. See the details for each German state in von Philippovich, *Auswanderung und Auswanderungspolitik*, e.g. for Württemberg, p. 283.

49. Erickson, pp. 29, and 148 ff.

50. Ibid., p. 39.

51. Wisconsin Commissioners of Immigration, *Annual Report* (1881), pp. 12 - 13.

52. Erickson, p. 88 and Marschalck, *Deutsche Überseewanderung*, p. 17.

53. Erickson, chapter 5, "The Distribution of Unskilled Immigrants to Industry," pp. 88 ff. See also Richmond M. Smith, *Emigration and Immigration* (New York: Scribners, 1892), chapter 7, "Competition with American Labor," and Gerd Korman, *Industrialization, Immigrants and Americanizers, the View from Milwaukee, 1866 - 1921* (Madison, State Historical Society, 1967).

Chapter Eight

1. Frederick C. Luebke, "German Immigrants and Churches in Nebraska, 1889 - 1915," *Mid-America: An Historical Review* 50 (1968), 116 - 30, and idem, "The Political Behavior of an Immigrant Group: The Germans of Nebraska, 1880 - 1900" (unpubl. Ph.D. dissertation, Lincoln: University of Nebraska, 1966). For additional reading on German-American religious life, see Tolzmann, *German-Americana: A Bibliography*, pp. 187 - 239

2. See Henry Metzner, *A Brief History of the American Turnerbund*, p. 54. "In matters of religion and conscience we demand freedom in the broadest sense. We strive for the dissemination of a philosophy based on knowledge of natural forces and their effects. . . ."

3. In the nineteenth century, the learned ecclesiastics of Europe heard with consternation about the fantastic proliferation of religious sects in America. For further reading see Philip Schaff, *America, A Sketch of its Political, Social, and Religious Character*, ed. Perry Miller (Cambridge, Mass.: Harvard University Press, 1961).

4. See in general Matthew A. Pekari, "The German Catholics in the United States of America," pp. 305 - 58, and Emmet H. Rothan, *The German Catholic Immigrant in the United States, 1830 - 1860* (Washington, D.C.: Catholic University Press, 1946). Before the revolutionary war there were at most 18,000 Catholics in the colonies, the majority of whom were French Canadian immigrants.

5. See Rudolf Cronau, *Drei Jahrhunderte deutschen Lebens in Amerika* (Berlin: Dietrich Reimer, 1909), pp. 46 - 96.

6. O'Connor, *The German-Americans*, p. 349.

7. Much has been written about the society. The best sources are Karl J. R. Arndt, *George Rapp's Harmony Society 1785 - 1847* (Philadelphia: University of Pennsylvania Press, 1965) and idem, "The Indiana Decade of George Rapp's Harmony Society: 1814 - 1824," *Proceedings of the American Antiquarian Society* 80, pt. 2 (1970), 299 - 323. See also H. K. Polt, "The Rappists and New Harmony, Indiana," *American-German Review* 10 (October, 1943), 17 - 20.

8. Arndt, *George Rapp's Harmony Society*, p. 208.

9. Ibid., p. 581.

10. Geroge B. Landis, "The Society of Separatists of Zoar, Ohio." *Annual Report of the American Historical Association for 1898* (Washington, D.C.: Government Printing, 1899), pp. 165 - 220.

11. Ibid., p. 179. See also H. K. Polt, "Zoar," *American-German Review* 7 (June, 1941), 16 - 21.

12. Bertha M. H. Shambaugh, *Amana, The Community of True Inspiration* (Iowa City: State Historical Society, 1909) and Barbara S. Yambura with Eunice W. Bodine, *A Change and a Parting, the Story of Amana* (Ames, Iowa: Iowa State University Press, 1960).

13. Shambaugh, pp. 88 - 89.

14. John A. Hostetler, *Amish Society*, rev. ed. (Baltimore: The Johns Hopkins Press, 1968) and William I. Schreiber, *Our Amish Neighbors* (Chicago: University of Chicago Press, 1962).

15. *Saturday Review*, January 15, 1972, pp. 52 ff.

16. C. Henry Smith, *The Story of the Mennonites*, rev. ed. (Scottdale, Pa.: Harald Press, 1945, and J. C. Wenger, *The Mennonite Church in America*, vol. II (Scottdale, Pa.: Harald Press, 1966). See also Harold S. Bender and C. Henry Smith, *The Mennonite Encyclopedia*, 4 vols. (Scottdale, Pa.: Mennonite·Publishing House, 1955 - 1959).

17. Wenger, *Mennonite History*, p. 167.

18. The best source of information on the Hutterites is John A. Hostetler, *Hutterite Society* (Baltimore: The Johns Hopkins University Press, 1974). Of comparable quality is Victor Peters, *All Things Common: The Hutterian Way of Life* (Minneapolis: University of Minnesota Press, 1965). See also A. J. F. Ziegelschmid, "The Hutterians on the American Continent," *American-German Review* 8 (February, 1942), 20 - 24; and John A. Hostetler and Gertrude Enders Huntington, *The Hutterites in North America* (New York: Holt Rinehart and Winston, 1967).

19. Peters, p. 45. See p. 52 for a map of all the North American colonies. See Hostetler, *Hutterite Society*, appendix fifteen for a complete list of Hutterite colonies in North America. See also Karl J. R. Arndt, "The Harmonists and the Hutterians," *American-German Review* 10 (August, 1944), 24 ff. for an interesting case of mutual aid betwen the Pennsylvania Harmonists and the Hutterians of Bon Homme County, South Dakota, and John W. Bennett, *Northern Plainsmen* (Chicago: Aldine Publishing, 1969), pp. 246 - 75.

20. Marvin P. Riley, "South Dakota's Hutterite Colonies 1874 - 1969," *South Dakota Agricultural Experiment Station, Bulletin* 565 (1970), pp. 5 - 37, and William Albert Allard, "The Hutterites, Plain People of the West," *National Geographic* 138 (July, 1970), 98 - 125.

21. Riley, p. 22 and Peters, pp. 128 - 50. See also Norman Thomas, "The Hutterian Brethren," *South Dakota Historical Collections* 25 (1951), 265 - 99.

22. Georg von Bosse, *Das deutsche Element in den Vereinigten Staaten*, pp. 448 - 71.

23. See Edward Langton, *History of the Moravian Church: The Story of the First International Protestant Church* (London: Allen & Unwin, 1956), and Rowe Findley, "Old Salem, Morning Star of Moravian Faith," *National Geographic* 138 (December, 1970), 818 - 37.

24. Carl E. Schneider, *The German Church on the American Frontier* (St. Louis: Eden Publishing House, 1939), pp. 11 ff. and pp. 69 - 82. See also George J. Eisenach, *A History of the German Congregational Church in the United States* (Yankton: The Pioneer Press, 1938).

25. Schneider, *The German Church*, especially chapter 3, "Founding of the Kirchenverein des Westens," pp. 98 - 132. See also Eve Bock, "Contribution of the German Reformed Church to American Culture," *German-American Studies* 6 (1973), 57 - 67.

26. Carl Wittke, *Willilam Nast* (Detroit: Wayne State University Press, 1959).

27. J. F. Köstering, *Auswanderung der sächsischen Lutheraner im Jahre 1838, ihre Niederlassung in Perry Co., Mo., und damit zusammenhängende interessante Nachrichten* (St. Louis: Wiebusch, 1867), Walter O. Forster, *Zion on the Misssissippi: The Settlement of the Saxon Lutherans in Missouri 1839 - 1841* (St. Louis: Concordia, 1953), and P. E. Kretzmann, "The Saxon Immigration to Missouri 1838 - 1839," *American-German Review*, 6 (October, 1939), 28 - 31.

28. Walter A. Baepler, *A Century of Grace: A History of the Missouri Synod 1847 - 1947* (St. Louis: Concordia Publishing House, 1947), pp. 97 ff. See also W. H. T. Dau, ed., *Ebenezer, Reviews of the Work of the Missouri Synod During Three Quarters of a Century* (St. Louis: Concordia Publishing House, 1922).

29. See the flow charts in E. Clifford Nelson, *Lutheranism in North America, 1914 - 1970* (Minneapolis: Augsburg Publishing House, 1972), inside covers and pp. 138 - 39. See also Edwin Scott Gaustad, *Historical Atlas of Religion in America* (New York: Harper and Row, 1962).

30. Frederick Nohl, "The Lutheran Church - Missouri Synod Reacts to United States Anti-Germanism during World War I," *Concordia Historical Institute Quarterly* 35 (1962), 49 - 66, Frederick C. Luebke, "Superpatriotism in World War I: The Experience of a Lutheran Pastor," ibid. 41 (1968), 3 - 11, and Frederick C. Luebke, "The Immigrant Condition as a Factor Contributing to the Conservatism of the Lutheran Church — Missouri Synod," *Concordia Historical Institute Quarterly* 38 (1968), 19 - 28.

31. Baepler, p. 189. See also Robert M. Toepper, "Rationale for Preservation of the German Language in the Missouri Synod of the Nineteenth Century," *Concordia Historical Institute Quarterly* 41 (1965), 156 - 67.

32. Nelson, p. 7. See also Everette Meier and Herbert T. Mayer, "The Process of Americanization," in Carl S. Meyer, ed., *Moving Frontiers* (St.

Louis: Concordia Publishing House, 1964), pp. 344, 355 - 62, 374 - 76, and 380.

33. Emmet H. Rothan, *The German Catholic Immigrant*, and Colman Barry, "The German Catholic Immigrant," in Thomas McAvoy, ed., *Roman Catholicism and the American Way*, (Notre Dame, Ind.: Univ. of Notre Dame Press, 1960), pp. 188 - 203.

34. Quoted in O'Connor, p. 349.

35. Philip Taylor, *The Distant Magnet*, p. 238.

36. Colman Barry, *The Catholic Church and the German Americans*, p. 46. See also Benjamin J. Blied, "John Martin Henni," *American-German Review* 11 (June, 1945), 24 - 27.

37. Barry, pp. 51 ff.

38. Written by Bishop William McCloskey of Louisville to Abbot Vernard Smith, O.S.B., who was his Roman agent. See Barry, p. 59.

39. Barry, p. 60.

40. Barry, p. 67.

41. Barry, footnote 45, p. 58.

42. John Gmeiner, *The Church and the Various Nationalities in the United States. Are Germans Fairly Treated?* (Milwaukee, 1887). See also Barry, p. 77.

43. Barry, p. 82. See also Benjamin J. Blied, "In Henni's Footsteps," *American-German Review* 12 (December, 1945), 29.

44. Barry, p. 84.

45. Barry, p. 118.

46. Barry, p. 136. See also John Meng, "Cahenslyism: the First Stage, 1883 - 1891," *Catholic Historical Review* 31 (1946), 389 - 413 and John Meng, "Cahenslyism: the Second Chapter, 1891 - 1910," *Catholic Historical Review* 32 (1946), 302 - 40.

47. James Cardinal Gibbons, *A Retrospect of Fifty Years* (New York: John Murphy Co., 1916), II, pp. 148 - 55.

48. Barry, p. 180.

49. Barry, p. 252.

50. James P. Shannon, *Catholic Colonization on the Western Frontier* (New Haven: Yale University Press, 1957), Harold E. Briggs, "The Great Dakota Boom, 1879 - 1886," *North Dakota Historical Quarterly* 4 (1929 - 1930), 87 - 90. See also Cpl. Gerhard G. Spieler, "The Germans of Colorado," *American-German Review* 10 (August 1944), 20 - 23.

51. The story of the *Central-Verein* has been told by Philip Gleason, *The Conservative Reformers: German-American Catholics and the Social Order* (Notre Dame: University of Notre Dame Press, 1968).

52. Philip Gleason, "The Early Years of Frederick P. Kenkel: The Background of an American Catholic Social Reformer," *American Catholic Historical Society of Philadelphia Records* 74 (1963), 195 - 203.

Chapter Nine

1. Elmer Schultz Gerhard, "The History of Schwenkfelder Schools and Education," *Schwenkfeldiana* 1 (1943), 5 - 21, Heinrich Maurer, "The Lutheran Community and American Society: A Study in Religion as a Condition of Social Accommodation," *American Journal of Sociology* 34 (1928), 282 - 95, Clyde S. Stine, "The Pennsylvania Germans and the School," in Ralph Wood, ed., *The Pennsylvania Germans*, pp. 105 - 27, and James A. Burns, "A History of the Catholic Parochial Schools in the United States," *The Catholic University Bulletin* 12 (1906), 434 ff. For additional reading, see Tolzmann, *Bibliography*, pp. 240 - 51.

2. Quoted in William Beidelman, *The Story of the Pennsylvania Germans*, pp. 85 - 87.

3. Faust, II, p. 207.

4. Andreas Dorpalen, "The Political Influence of the German Element in Colonial America," 151.

5. Noel Iverson, *Germania, U. S. A., Social Change in New Ulm, Minnesota* (Minneapolis: University of Minnesota Press, 1966).

6. Augustus J. Prahl, "The Beginning of the Gymnastic Movement in America," *American-German Review* 14 (June, 1948), 13, and idem, "The Turner," in Zucker, ed., *The Forty-Eighters*, pp. 79 - 110.

7. La Vern J. Rippley, *Of German Ways* (Minneapolis: Dillon, 1970), p. 224.

8. Wittke, *We Who Built America*, pp. 227 - 28.

9. Faust, II, p. 225. See also Charlotte Gillard, "German Influence in American Education," unpubl. manuscript (New York: Service Bureau for Intercultural Education, 1937), and John A. Walz, *German Influence in American Education and Culture* (Philadelphia: Carl Schurz Foundation, 1936).

10. Faust, II, p. 230, Markus F. Motsch, "H. L. Mencken and German Kultur," *German-American Studies* 6 (1973), 21 - 42 and the pamphlet, "Guide to the German Educational Exhibition in St. Louis, 1904" (Berlin: W. Büxenstein, 1904), 33 pages.

11. Elizabeth Jenkins, "How the Kindergarten Found its Way to America," *Wisconsin Magazine of History* 14 (September, 1930), 48 - 62, idem, "Froebel's Disciples in America," *American-German Review* 3 (March, 1937), 17.

12. Rippley, "The Columbus Germans," 26 and Edward W. Hocker, "The First Kindergarten Teacher," *American-German Review* 8 (February, 1942), 9 ff.

13. *Eleventh Annual Report of the Board of Directors of the Saint Louis Public Schools for the Year Ending August 1, 1865* (St. Louis, 1865), pp. 6, 26. *Twelfth Annual Report of the Board of Directors of the St. Louis Public Schools for the Year Ending August 1, 1866* (St. Louis, 1866), p. 38. For a statistical overview of state laws permitting German instruction see Heinz Kloss, *Das Nationalitätanrecht der Vereinigten Staaten von Amerika* (Vienna: Braumüller, 1963), pp. 95 ff.

242   THE GERMAN-AMERICANS

14. Audrey L. Olson, "St. Louis Germans . . . ," pp. 94 - 114. A streak of
nativism hastened the demise of German instruction, for, whenever the
budget was strained, German-language teaching was called into question.
15. Louise Phelps Kellogg, "The Bennett Law in Wisconsin," *Wisconsin
Magazine of History* 2 (Sept., 1918), 3 - 25, William F. Whyte, "The Bennett
Law Campaign in Wisconsin," *Wisconsin Magazine of History* 10 (June,
1927), 363 - 90 and Walter H. Beck, *Lutheran Elementary Schools in the
United States* (St. Louis: Concordia Publishing House, 1939), chapter 11,
pp. 225 ff.
16. Barry, *The Catholic Church and German Americans*, p. 186.
17. Roger E. Wyman, "Wisconsin Ethnic Groups and the Election of
1890," *Wisconsin Magazine of History* 51 (Summer, 1968), 269 - 93, Daniel
W. Kucera, O. S. B., *Church-State Relations in Education in Illinois*
(Washington, D. C.: Catholic University Press, 1955), pp. 111 ff. and "A
Historical Pronouncement: Wisconsin Bishops Protest the Bennett Law,"
Social Justice Review 31 (December, 1940 - January, 1941), 282 - 84,
318 - 20.
18. Gustav Koerner, *Das deutsche Element in den Vereinigten Staaten von
Nordamerika, 1818 - 1848* (Cincinnati: A. E. Wilde, 1880), p. 198.
19. Heinz Kloss, "Die deutschamerikanische Schule," *Jahrbuch für
Amerikastudien* 7 (1962), 147.
20. Ernest J. Becker, "History of the English-German Schools in
Baltimore," *The Report*, SHGM, 25 (1942), 13 - 17.
21. F. D. McKenzie, "The Neighborhood: A Study of Local Life in the
City of Columbus, Ohio," *The American Journal of Sociology* 27 (1921), 156,
164.
22. Louis Viereck, "German Instruction in American Schools," chapter 19,
Educational Report 1900 - 1901 of the Commissioner of Education
(Washington, D. C., Government Printing, 1902), pp. 648 - 49, Dr. Julius
Goebel, *Der Kampf um das Deutschtum: Das Deutschtum in den
Vereinigten Staaten von Nord-Amerika* (Munich: Lehman, 1904), pp. 64 ff.,
and Edwin H. Zeydel, "The Teaching of German in Cincinnati: An
Historical Survey," *The Bulletin of the Historical and Philosophical Society
of Ohio* 20 (1962), 34.
23. Max Heinrici, ed., *Das Buch der Deutschen in Amerika* (Philadelphia:
National German-American Alliance, 1909), pp. 783 - 84.
24. Quoted in Gustavus Ohlinger, *The German Conspiracy in American
Education* (New York: George H. Doran, 1919), p. 56, and idem, "Prussianiz-
ing American Schools," *Bookman* 48 (December, 1918), 415 - 22.
25. Frederick C. Luebke, "The German-American Alliance in Nebraska,
1910 - 1917," pp. 165 - 85.
26. Quoted in Jack W. Rodgers, "The Foreign Language Issue in
Nebraska, 1918 - 1923," *Nebraska History* 39 (March, 1958), 8.
27. Anonymous, "Recent Legislation Forbidding Teaching of Foreign

Languages in Public Schools," *Minnesota Law Review* 4 (May, 1920), 449 - 51, and Wallace H. Moore, "The Conflict Concerning the German Language and German Propaganda in the Public Secondary Schools of the United States, 1917 - 1919," (unpublished Ph.D. diss., Stanford University, 1937).

28. Harry Rider, "Americanization," *The American Political Science Review* 14 (February, 1920), 110 - 15.

29. Senate File 24, Senate Journal, 1919, p. 72, quoted in Rodgers, p. 12. See also William Beck, *Lutheran Elementary Schools*, pp. 330 ff.

30. Omaha Morning *World-Herald*, February 25, 1919, quoted in Rodgers, p. 13.

31. Meyer vs. State, *Reports of Cases in the Nebraska Supreme Court* 107 (1922), 657, quoted in Rodgers, p. 17.

32. Meyer vs. Nebraska, *U. S. Supreme Court Reports*, 262 U.S. 390, 399 (1923), Kloss, "Die deutschamerikanische Schule," p. 166, Paul Murphy, *The Constitution in Crisis Times* (New York: Harper & Row, 1972), 83 - 84, and William Beck, pp. 333 ff. See also Kenneth B. O'Brien, Jr., "Education, Americanization and the Supreme Court: The 1920's," *American Quarterly* 13 (1961), 161 - 71.

33. Robert N. Manley, "Language, Loyalty and Liberty; The Nebraska State Council of Defense and the Lutheran Churches, 1917 - 1918," *Concordia Historical Institute Quarterly* 37 (1964), 1 - 16, esp. 9 - 10.

34. *Dakota Freie Presse* (New Ulm, Minnesota) February 1, 1921.

35. Kloss, "Die deutschamerikanische Schule," p. 167. See also John E. Hofman, "The Language Transition in Some Lutheran Denominations," in *Readings in the Sociology of Language* (The Hague: Mouton, 1970), pp. 620 - 37.

36. John E. Hofman, "Mother Tongue Retentiveness in Ethnic Parishes," in Joshua A. Fishman, *Language Loyalty in the United States* (The Hague: Mouton, 1966), pp. 127 - 55. See also Wolfgang Fleischhauer, "German Communities in Northwesten Ohio: Canal Fever and Prosperity," *The Report* SHGM, 34 (1970), 23 - 34, especially 33.

37. Heinz Kloss, "German-American Language Maintenance Efforts," in Fishman, ibid., pp. 206 - 52.

38. The bilingual provisions are part of Public Law 90 - 247, 90th Congress. See Glenn G. Gilbert, ed., *The German Language in America, A Symposium* (Austin: University of Texas, 1971), p. 167.

39. "Supreme Court Rules in Lau vs. Nichols Case," *The Linguistic Reporter* 16 (March, 1974), 6 ff.

Chapter Ten

1. Hermann E. Rothfuss, "The Beginnings of the German-American Stage," *The German Quarterly* 24 (1951), 93 - 101.

2. Fritz A. H. Leuchs, *The Early German Theater in New York* (New York: AMS Press, 1966), pp. 3, 20.

3. Andrew Jacke Townsend, "The Germans of Chicago," *Deutsch-Amerikanische Geschichtsblätter* 32 (1932), 125 - 26 and Esther M. Olson, "The German Theater in Chicago," *Deutsch-Amerikanische Geschichtsblätter* 38 (1937), 71 - 124.

4. Ralph Wood, "Geschichte des deutschen Theaters von Cincinnati," *Deutsch-Amerikanische Geschichtsblätter* 32 (1932), 424 ff.

5. See Robert Heuck, "Show Business Over-the-Rhine," *Bulletin of the Historical and Philosophical Society of Ohio* 16 (1858), 121 - 42.

6. La Vern J. Rippley, "German Theater in Columbus, Ohio," *German-American Studies* 1 (1970), 81.

7. See Heinrich Börnstein, *Fünfundzwanzig Jahre in der Alten und Neuen Welt* (Leipzig. 1881).

8. C. Grant Loomis, *The German Theater in San Francisco, 1861 - 1864*, University of California Publications in Modern Philology, 36 (Berkeley: University of California Press, 1952), pp. 193 - 242.

9. Henrich Herbatschek, "Die Anfänge des deutschen Theaters in Milwaukee," *American-German Review* 13 (February, 1947), 17 - 18.

10. Oscar H. Rudnick, *Das Deutschtum St. Pauls in Word und Bild* (St. Paul: no publisher, 1924), pp. 69 - 107. See also La Vern J. Rippley, "Notes about the German Press in the Minnesota River Valley," *The Report*, SHGM 35 (1972), 42.

11. See Dieter Cunz, "Egg Harbor City: New Germany in New Jersey," *The Report* SHGM 29 (1956), 17, Rothfuss, "The Beginnings . . . ," p. 99 and Theodore Schreiber, "Berthold Kraus, Prairie Actor and Writer," *American-German Review* 19 (June - July, 1953), 14.

12. Hermann Rothfuss, "The Early German Theater in Minnesota," *Minnesota History* 32 (1951), 173.

13. Harold Jantz, "William Tell and the American Revolution," in *Schiller Symposium*, ed. A. Leslie Willson (Austin, Texas: University of Texas Press, 1960), pp. 65 - 81, and Audrey L. Olson, C. S. J., "St. Louis Germans, 1850 - 1920: The Nature of an Immigrant Community and its Relation to the Assimilation Process," p. 155.

14. Paul Nettl, "Immigration and American Music," *American-German Review* 9 (December, 1942), 6 ff.

15. Faust, II, p. 272.

16. William W. Forster, "The Liederkranz of New York," *American-German Review* 10 (1944), 10 - 13.

17. Martha and Earl W. Fornell, "A Century of German Song in Texas," *American-German Review* 24 (October-November, 1957), 29 - 31.

18. Stanley Mathews, "Aftermath of a Golden Jubilee," *The Bulletin of the Historical and Philosophical Society of Ohio* 16 (1958), 143 - 50.

19. See E. Irenaeus Stevenson, "The Saengerfest at Philadelphia," *Harper's Weekly* 41 (1897), 667.

20. Some respected Yankee American critics seem to agree. For example, Arthur Farwell wrote in his introduction to *Music in America:* "The one great

original influence acknowledged by the nation, in its musically creative life, is the mighty German tradition of the epoch of Beethoven." Another, Marion Bauer, asserts that from the birth of Bach to 1914, "not only the United States, but England, France, and even Russia were propagating music sired by German traditions and characteristics." Quoted in William I. Schreiber, "Karl Merz: A Chapter in German-American Music," *American-German Review* 7 (June, 1941), 24.

21. Faust, II, p. 261.

22. Theodore Thomas, *A Musical Autobiography*, ed. George P. Upton (Chicago: A. C. McClurg, 1905), and Hattie C. Fleck, "Theodore Thomas," *American-German Review* 9 (February, 1943), 22 ff.

23. Walter Damrosch, *My Musical Life* (New York: Scribners, 1937), and Ruth Berges, "The Damrosch Family," *American-German Review* 27 (February - March, 1961), 28 - 30.

24. Damrosch, pp. 187 ff.

25. Reprinted in Damrosch, p. 223.

26. Oscar Thompson, ed., *The International Cyclopedia of Music and Musicians*, 9th ed. (New York: Dodd & Mead, 1964), p. 1896.

27. Irving Kolodin, "The German Influence on the Metropolitan Opera," *American-German Review* 2 (March, 1936), 4 - 8.

28. See Irving Kolodin, *The Metropolitan Opera* (New York: Knopf, 1967), pp. 161 ff., and Montrose J. Moses, *Life of Heinrich Conried* (New York: Crowell, 1916).

29. John F. Cone, *Oscar Hammerstein's Manhattan Opera Company* (Norman: University of Oklahoma Press, 1964), pp. 4 - 5.

30. Moses, *Life of Conried*, p. 17.

31. Mary Lawton, *Schumann-Heink, the Last of the Titans* (New York: Macmillan, 1928). See also Henry and Dana Lee Thomas, *Living Biographies of Famous Women* (Garden City: Doubleday, 1942).

32. Schreiber, "Karl Merz," p. 27.

33. For this material I rely largely on the *International Cyclopedia of Music and Musicians*.

34. George Rochbert, "Schönberg's American Period," *International Cyclopedia*, p. 1915.

35. Ibid., p. 1922.

36. Bruno Walter, *Themes and Variations*, trans. James A. Galston (New York: Knopf, 1959), p. 248. See also Ruth Berges, "Bruno Walter: Striver for Perfection," *American-German Review* 27 (October - November, 1960), 7 - 9.

37. Walter, *Themes*, pp. 242 - 43.

38. Walter, *Themes*, p. 341.

39. Maria Augusta Trapp, *The Story of the Trapp Family Singers* (New York: Lippincott, 1949), *Time*, Dec. 19, 1938, p. 37 and *Time* July 18, 1949, p. 46.

40. Maria Augusta Trapp with Ruth T. Murdoch, *A Family on Wheels* (New York: Lippincott, 1959), pp. 71, 75 - 76.

Chapter Eleven

1. Faust, II, pp. 294 ff., and David F. Bowers, ed., *Foreign Influences in American Life* (Princeton: Princeton University Press, 1966). For further reading, see Tolzmann, *Bibliography*, pp. 252 - 91.

2. Emma Maria Di Lauro, "The Triumph of the Cross: A Painting by Emmanuel Leutze," and Cpl. Gerhard G. Spieler, "A Noted Artist in Early Colorado: The Story of Albert Bierstadt," *American-German Review* 11, no. 1 (1944 - 1945), 33 and no. 5, pp. 13 - 17.

3. John Francis McDermott, ed., "Minnesota 100 Years Ago," *Minnesota History* 33 (1952), 112 - 25.

4. Justus Bier, "Carl C. Brenner, A German American Landscapist," *American-German Review* 17 (April, 1951), 20 - 25.

5. Erwin Gustav Gudde, "Carl Nahl, California's Pioneer of Painting," *American-German Review* 7 (October, 1940), 18 - 20.

6. Michel Benisovich, "Peter Rindisbacher, Swiss Artist, *Minnesota History* 33 (1951), 155 - 62.

7. "Sketches from Northwestern America and Canada: A Portfolio of Water Colors by Franz Hölzlhuber," *American Heritage* 16 (June, 1965), 49 - 64.

8. Henry Lewis, *The Valley of the Mississippi Illustrated*, ed. Bertha L. Heilbron, tr. A. Hermina Poatgieter (St. Paul: Minnesota Historical Society, 1967).

9. Harold Donaldson Eberlein and Cortlandt Van Dyke Hubbard, "Household Furniture of the Pennsylvania Germans," *American-German Review* 4 (September, 1937), 4 - 8 and Preston and Eleanor Barba, "Lewis Miller: Pennsylvania German Folk Artist — Chronicler of York, Pennsylvania," ibid. (March, 1938), 32 - 38.

10. Oswald Villard, "Carl Bitter, Sculptor," *Common Ground* 5 (1945), 40 - 44.

11. See "Thomas Nast" in Dieter Cunz, *They Came From Germany* (New York: Dodd & Mead, 1966), pp. 106 - 20.

12. Faust, II, Appendix, pp. 685 ff.

13. Donald P. Kent, *The Refugee Intellectual: The Americanization of the Immigrants of 1933 - 1941* (New York: Columbia University Press, 1953), Laura Fermi, *Illustrious Immigrants: The Intellectual Migration From Europe 1930 - 1941* (Chicago: University of Chicago Press, 1968) and Donald Fleming and Bernard Bailyn, eds., *The Intellectual Migration, Europe and America, 1930 - 1960* (Cambridge: Harvard University Press, 1969). See also Robert Boyers, ed., *The Legacy of the German Refugee Intellectuals* (New York: Schocken, 1972).

14. Kent, p. 12.

15. Kent, p. 15.

16. Martin Duberman, *Black Mountain: An Exploration in Community* (New York: E. P. Dutton & Co., 1972).

17. Laura Fermi, pp. 97 - 99.

18. Quoted in Siegfried Giedion, *Walter Gropius: Work and Teamwork* (New York: Reinhold, 1954) on the introductory page of what is the single most comprehensive publication about the Bauhaus, Hans M. Wingler, *The Bauhaus: Weimar, Dessau, Berlin, Chicago*, tr. Wolfgang Jabs and Basil Gilbert (Cambridge, Mass.: M.I.T. Press, 1969).

19. William H. Jordy, "The Aftermath of the Bauhaus in America: Gropius, Mies, and Breuer," in Fleming and Bailyn, p. 489.

20. Wingler, pp. 65 - 66.

21. Wingler, pp. 93, 139, 167.

22. Wingler, p. 554. See Charles L. Kuhn, "America and the Bauhaus," *American-German Review* 15 (December, 1948), 16 - 22.

23. Wingler, p. 581. See also Eckhard Neumann, ed., *Bauhaus and Bauhaus People* (New York: Van Nostrand Reinhold, 1970).

24. Wingler, pp. 609 ff.

25. *Time*, December 4, 1972, pp. 97 - 98.

26. "An Architect Speaks His Mind: Mingling Work and Living," *House and Garden*, February, 1970, pp. 12 - 16.

27. *Time*, August 29, 1969, pp. 46 - 48, Werner Blaser, *Mies van der Rohe* (New York: Praeger, 1972) and Philip Johnson, *Mies van der Rohe* (New York: Museum of Modern Art, 1953).

28. Dirk Lohan in *Time*, October 29, 1973.

29. *Time*, October 29, 1973, p. 108.

30. *Time*, May 31, 1971, pp. 68 ff.

31. Siegfried Giedion, *Walter Gropius: Work and Teamwork*, *Time*, July 18, 1969, pp. 49 - 50 and Walter Gropius, *Town Plan for the Development of Selb* (Cambridge, Mass.: M .I. T. Press, 1969).

32. Frederick S. Wicht, "Lyonel Feininger," *American-German Review* 20 (August-September, 1954), 18 - 19.

33. Hans Hess, *Lyonel Feininger* (New York: Harry N. Abrams, 1955), p. 166.

34. Quoted in Hess, p. 170.

35. George Grosz, *A Little Yes and a Big No: The Autobiography of George Grosz*, tr. Lola Sachs Dorin (New York: Dial, 1946).

36. Ibid., p. 264.

37. Quoted in Hess, p. 147.

38. Quoted in Hildegard Binder Johnson, "Carl Schurz and Conservation," *American-German Review* 23 (February - March, 1957), 4 - 8.

39. David McCullough, *The Great Bridge* (New York: Simon and Shuster, 1972) and "Johann August Roebling," in Cecyle S. Neidle, *Great Immigrants*, pp. 23 - 42.

40. See "Ottmar Mergenthaler," in Cunz, *They Came From Germany*, p. 133 and Edmund C. Arnold, "The Mergenthaler Story," *American-German Review* 21 (December - January, 1954 - 1955), 16 - 18.

41. See "Abraham Jacobi 1830 - 1919," in Cecyle S. Neidle, *Great Im-*

migrants, pp. 67 - 87 and Joyce Cushmore, "Abraham Jacobi: Father of American Pediatrics," *American-German Review* 25 (August - September, 1959), 29 - 31.

42. Charles Weiner, "A New Site for the Seminar: The Refugees and American Physics in the Thirties," in Donald Fleming and Bernard Bailyn, eds., *The Intellectual Migration*, p. 191.

43. See "European-Born Atomic Scientists," in Laura Fermi, pp. 174 - 214 and Albert Rosenfeld, "This was Leo Szilard, Remembrance of a Genius," *Life*, June 12, 1964, p. 31.

44. Philip M. Stern, *The Oppenheimer Case: Security on Trial* (New York: Harper & Row, 1969), p. 455.

45. Robert Coughlan, "The Equivocal Hero of Science, Robert Oppenheimer," *Life*, March 3, 1967, pp. 34 ff., Thomas W. Wilson, Jr. *The Great Weapons Heresy* (Boston: Houghton Mifflin, 1970), and Henry Hewes, "The Submissive Society," *Saturday Review*, March 22, 1969, p. 72.

46. Donald Fleming, "Emigré Physicists and the Biological Revolution," in Fleming and Bailyn, pp. 152 - 89.

47. Dieter Cunz, "Wernher von Braun," pp. 139 ff.

48. *Newsweek*, June 5, 1972, p. 71.

49. David Landau, *Kissinger: The Uses of Power* (Boston: Houghton Mifflin, 1972), and Marvin and Bernard Kalb, *Kissinger* (Boston: Little, Brown, 1974).

Chapter Twelve

1. Carl Wittke, *The German-Language Press in America* (Lexington: University of Kentucky Press, 1957) and Karl J. R. Arndt and May E. Olson, *German-American Newspapers and Periodicals 1732 - 1955* (Heidelberg, Quelle & Meyer, 1961), and idem, *The German Language Press of the Americas 1732 - 1968* (Pullach: Verlag Dokumentation, 1973).

2. Henry A. Pochmann, *German Culture in America: Philosophical and Literary Influences 1600 - 1900* (Madison: University of Wisconsin Press, 1957), Paul C. Weber, *America in Imaginative German Literature in the First Half of the Nineteenth Century* (New York: Columbia University Press, 1926 — reprinted by AMS Press, 1966), George E. Condoyannis, "German American Prose Fiction, From 1850 - 1914" (unpubl. Ph.D. diss., Columbia University, 1953), Robert E. Ward, ed., *Deutsche Lyrik aus Amerika* (New York: Literary Society Foundation, 1969), and Robert E. Cazden, *German Exile Literature in America 1933 - 1950: A History of the Free German Press and Book Trade* (Chicago: American Library Association, 1970). See also Tolzmann, *Bibliography*, pp. 103 - 86.

3. Wittke, *German-Language Press*, p. 7.

4. Wittke, *We Who Built America*, p. 193 and A. E. Zucker, *Political Refugees*, p. 270.

5. See Wittke, *German-Language Press*, p. 77.

6. Wittke, *German-Language Press*, pp. 206 ff.

7. Wittke, *German-Language Press*, p. 264. See also Carl Wittke, *German-Americans and the World War With Special Emphasis on Ohio's German-Language Press* (Columbus: Ohio State Archaeological and Historical Society, 1936), pp. 128 ff.

8. *Ayer Directory of Publications*, 1974.

9. Albert B. Faust, "Non-English Writings — German," in *Cambridge History of American Literature*, (New York: Putnam's Sons, 1921), IV 572 - 90.

10. E. L. Jordan, ed. and trans., *America: Glorious and Chaotic Land, Charles Sealsfield Discovers the Young United States* (Englewood Cliffs, N. J.: Prentice-Hall, 1969) and Charles Sealsfield, *The United States of North America as They Are*, Karl J. R. Arndt, ed. (Hildesheim: Loms, 1972).

11. Hugo Schmidt, *Nikolaus Lenau* (New York: Twayne Publishers, 1971), p. 18 and Homer D. Blanchard, "Lenau's Ohio Venture," *Ohio History* 78 (1969), 237 - 51.

12. Arno Schmidt, *Sitara und der Weg dorthin, eine Studie über Wesen, Werk und Wirkung Karl Mays* (Frankfurt: Fischer, 1969).

13. George H. R. O'Donnell, "Gerstäcker in America, 1837 - 1843," *Publications of the Modern Language Association*, 42 (1927), 1036 - 43.

14. Carl Wittke, "The America Theme in European Literature," *Mississippi Valley Historical Review* 28 (1941), 14. See also Halvdan Koht, *The American Spirit in Europe* (Philadelphia: University of Pennsylvania Press, 1949).

15. Condoyannis, p. 61.

16. Heinz Kloss, "Deutsch-amerikanisches Schrifttum in USA," *Dichtung und Volkstum* 35 (1934), 399 - 403.

17. Condoyannis, p. 314.

18. Ward, *Deutsche Lyrik aus Amerika*. The journal, *German-American Studies* (Cleveland) and several German newspapers accept German poetry and fiction on a limited basis. Books have also appeared in recent years. See also Alfred Gong, ed., *Interview mit Amerika — 50 deutschsprachige Autoren in der neuen Welt* (Munich: Nymphenburger, 1962).

19. H. L. Mencken, "Die Deutschamerikaner," *Die Neue Rundschau* 39 (1928), 486 - 95.

Chapter Thirteen

1. Karl Stumpp, *The German-Russians: Two Centuries of Pioneering*, tr. Joseph S. Height (Bonn: Atlantic Forum, 1971). See also the publications of the *Landsmannschaft der Deutschen aus Russland* (Stuttgart), the *Heimat-Kalender der Bessarabiendeutschen* (Hanover), the *Jahrbücher der Dobrudscha-Deutschen* (Heilbronn), the American Historical Society of Germans From Russia (Lincoln, Neb.), and the North Dakota Historical Society of Germans From Russia (Bismarck).

2. Karl J. R. Arndt, "World War II and the Russian Co-Religionists of the Harmonists," *American-German Review* 15 (February, 1949), 10 - 11, Bennion, "Flight From the Reich . . . and Marschalk, *Deutsche. Uberseewanderung,* p. 33.

3. George J. Eisenach, *Pietism and the Russian Germans in the United States* (Berne, Ind.: Berne Publishers, 1946), p. 22.

4. Quoted in Stumpp, *The German-Russians,* p. 11.

5. William G. Bek, "Some Facts Concerning the Germans in North Dakota," *University of North Dakota Quarterly Journal* 5 (1915), 332 - 35 and John Pfeiffer, "The German-Russians and Their Immigration to South Dakota," *South Dakota Department of History Report and Historical Collections* 31 (1970), 304 - 21.

6. Stumpp, *The German-Russians,* p. 31.

7. For the complete story of the Russian-Germans, see Richard Sallet, *The Russian-German Settlements in the United States,* trans. La Vern J. Rippley and Armand Bauer (Fargo Institute for Regional Studies, 1974).

8. J. Neale Carman, "Germans in Kansas," *American-German Review* 27 (April - May, 1961), 4 - 8, and Norman E. Saul, "The Migration of Russian-Germans to Kansas," *Kansas Historical Quarterly* 40 (1974), 38 - 62.

9. George Rath, "Emigration from Germany Through Poland and Russia to the U. S. A.," *American Historical Society of Germans from Russia,* Work Paper 5 (February, 1971), p. 30 and George Eisenach, "The Volga Germans," *American-German Review* 10 (1944), pt. 1, 4 - 5 and pt. 2, 24 - 26.

10. Albert J. Petersen, Jr., "German-Russian Catholic Colonization in Western Kansas: A Settlement Geography" (unpubl. Ph.D. diss., Louisiana State University and Agricultural-Mechanical College, 1970).

11. Cornelius Krahn, "From the Steppes to the Prairies," *American-German Review* 11 (October and December, 1944), pt. 1 and pt. 2, 10 ff. and 30 ff., Frederick Simpich, "Speaking of Kansas," *National Geographic* 72 (August, 1937), 137, and Raymond F. Wiebe, "Commemorative Stamp Recognizes Hard Red Winter Wheat," *American Historical Society of Germans from Russia,* Workpaper 14 (April, 1974) 32 - 37.

12. Hattie Plum Williams, *A Social Study of the Russian German,* University Series XVI (Lincoln: University of Nebraska Press, 1916), Georg Rath, "Die Russlanddeutschen in den Vereinigten Staaten von Nord-Amerika: Vorbereitung zur Auswanderung," *Heimatbuch der Deutschen aus Russland* (Stuttgart: Landsmannschaft der Deutschen aus Russland, 1963), pp. 22 - 55, and C. Henry Smith, *The Coming of the Russian Mennonites* (Berne, Ind.: Mennonite Book Concern, 1927).

13. *Life Magazine,* August 2, 1937, pp. 15 - 23. See also Doris Isaak Seibert, "German-Russian Immigrants: Pioneers on the Dakota Frontier" (unpubl. M.A. thesis, Reed College, 1964).

14. *Fourteenth Census of the United States,* 1920, III (Washington, D. C.: Government Printing Office, 1923). See Adolph Schock, *In Quest of Free*

Land (San Jose State College, California, 1964), pp. 107, 116, 118, and William C. Sherman, "The Germans from Russia," *Sociologia Internationalis* 6 (1968), 224 - 34.

15. J. Neale Carman, *Foreign-Language Units of Kansas*, Historical Atlas and Statistics (Lawrence: University of Kansas Press, 1962), I, pp. 46, 188 - 95. See William Frank Zornow, *Kansas: A History of the Jayhawk State* (Norman: University of Oklahoma Press, 1957), pp. 181 ff.

16. Carman, *Foreign-Language Units*, pp. 88 - 91, 132, 260 - 63. See Rev. Francis S. Laing, O. M. Cap., "German-Russian Settlements in Ellis County, Kansas," *Kansas Historical Collections*, 11 (1909 - 1910), 489 - 528 and Jacob C. Ruppenthal, "The German Element in Central Kansas," *Kansas Historical Collections*, 13 (1913 - 1914), 513 - 34.

17. See photographs in Albert Petersen, "A Settlement Geography." See also Sister Mary Eloise Johannes, *A Study of the Russian-German Settlements in Ellis County, Kansas* (Washington, D. C.: Catholic University Press, 1946), pp. 27 - 52, and Jerome Blum, "The European Village as Community: Origins and Functions," *Agricultural History* 45 (July, 1971), 157 - 78.

18. Studies on settlements in a few states are available. Noel Fordsham, "A Study of the Russian-Germans in Fresno County, California" (unpubl. M.A. thesis, University of Redlands, California, 1949), James Ruben Griess, *The German-Russians: Those Who Came to Sutton* (Hastings, Neb.: privately printed, 1968), Aina Sirks, "A Study of a Nebraska German Dialect" (unpubl. M.A. thesis, University of Nebraska, 1956), and Alton D. Hill, Jr., "Volga German Occupance in the Windsor Area, Colorado" (unpubl. M.A. thesis, University of Colorado, 1959).

19. Eugene V. Smalley, "The Isolation of Life on Prairie Farms," *Atlantic Monthly* 72 (1893), 378 - 82.

20. Houses still stand near Tripp and Freeman, South Dakota, Glen Ullin and New Leipzig, North Dakota and near Hillsboro and Buhler, Kansas. See Cornelius Krahn, "Gnadenau in Kansas," *American-German Review* 10 (February, 1944), 18 - 19 and C. B. Schmidt, "Kansas Mennonite Settlements, 1877," tr. Cornelius Krahn, *Mennonite Life* 25 (April, 1970), 51 - 58, illustrations, 65 - 79. See also William C. Sherman, "Prarie Architecture," in Sallet, *Russian-German Settlements*, pp. 185 - 98.

21. William C. Sherman, "Assimilation in a North Dakota German-Russian Community" (unpubl. M.A. thesis, University of North Dakota, 1965).

22. Sallet, *Russian-German Settlements*, p. 84. For pictures of the churches, see Laing, pp. 499, 501, 509.

23. Phyllis A. Dinkel, "Old Marriage Customs in Herzog (Victoria), Kansas," *Western Folklore* 19 (1960), 99 - 105 and Father John B. Terbovich, O. F. M. Cap., "Religious Folklore Among the German-Russians in Ellis County Kansas," *Western Folklore* 22 (April, 1963), 79 - 88. See also Timothy J. Kloberdanz, "The Volga German Catholic Life Cycle: An Ethnographic Reconstruction" (unpubl. M.A. thesis, Colorado State University, 1974), and

Lawrence A. Weigel, "The History of the Germans from Russia Expressed in Song," *American Historical Society of Germans from Russia*, Workpaper 18 (Sept., 1975), 21 - 26.

24. Sallet, p. 88. See also William Urbach, "Our Parents Were Russian Germans," *Nebraska History* 48 (1967), 20 - 23.

25. La Vern J. Rippley, "The Dakota Freie Presse," *Heritage Review* (Bismarck) 7 (1973), 7 - 17. See also, idem, "The Dakota Freie Presse: Its Brightest and Its Darkest Hour," *Heritage Review* 9 (1974), 15 - 20.

26. William Sherman, "The Germans From Russia" in *Symposium on the Great Plains of North America*, ed. Carle C. Zimmerman and Seth Russel (Fargo: Institute for Regional Studies, 1965), p. 60.

27. See *Der Spiegel*, no. 50 (1972), 122 - 29 and several articles on the Volga Republic in *American Historical Society of Germans From Russia*, Workpaper 11 (April, 1973).

Chapter Fourteen

1. Hawgood, *The Tragedy of German-America*, pp. 290 - 91. The best study of the German-American experience during World War I is Frederick C. Luebke, *Bonds of Loyalty: German-Americans and World War I* (DeKalb: Northern Illinois University Press, 1974).

2. Max Heinrici, ed., *Das Buch der Deutschen in Amerika* (Philadelphia: Walther's Buchdruckerei, 1909), pp. 781 ff.

3. Clifton J. Child, *The German-Americans in Politics 1914 - 1917* (Madison: University of Wisconsin Press, 1939), p. 4.

4. Child, p. 12.

5. Child, p. 19. See also Richard W. Leopold, "The Mississippi Valley and American Foreign Policy, 1890 - 1941: An assessment and an Appeal," *Mississippi Valley Historical Review* 37 (1950 - 1951), 625 - 42.

6. Clifton J. Child, "German-American Attempts to Prevent the Exportation of Munitions of War, 1914 - 1915," *The Mississippi Valley Historical Review* 24 (1938 - 1939), 351 - 68. See also Guido A. Dobbert, "German-Americans Between New and Old Fatherland, 1870 - 1914," *The American Quarterly* 19 (1967), 663 - 80.

7. Luebke, *Bonds of Loyalty*, p. 94.

8. Felice A. Bonadio, "The Failure of German Propaganda in the United States, 1914 - 1917," *Mid-America* 41 (1959), 40 - 57. See also H. C. Peterson, *Propaganda For War: The Campaign Against American Neutrality, 1914 - 1917* (Port Washington, N. Y.: Kennikat, 1968), pp. 134 ff.

9. Child, *German-Americans in Politics*, p. 145.

10. Quoted in Louis L. Gerson, *The Hyphenate in Recent American Politics and Diplomacy* (Lawrence: University of Kansas, 1964), p. 65.

11. Dean R. Esslinger, "American-German and Irish Attitudes Toward Neutrality, 1914 - 1917, a Study of Catholic Minorities," *Catholic Historical*

Review 53 (1967), 194 - 216. See also Luebke, *Bonds of Loyalty*, pp. 166 ff.

12. *New York Times*, September 3, 1916.

13. Thomas J. Kerr IV, "German-Americans and Neutrality in the 1916 Election," *Mid-America* 43 (1961), 95 - 105.

14. *The Fatherland*, 5 (August 9, 1916), 10.

15. R. A. Burchell, "Did the Irish and German Voters Desert the Democrats in 1920? A Tentative Statistical Answer," *Journal of American Studies*, 6 (1972), 155. See also Edgar E. Robinson, *The Presidential Vote, 1896 - 1932* (Stanford: Stanford University Press, 1947), and Luebke, *Bonds of Loyalty*, pp. 190 ff.

16. Frederick C. Luebke, "The German-American Alliance in Nebraska, 1910 - 1917," *Nebraska History* 49 (1968), 183.

17. Robert Maxwell, ed., *La Follette* (Englewood Cliffs, New Jersey: Prentice-Hall, 1969), pp. 51 ff. and H. C. Peterson and Gilbert C. Fite, *Opponents of War 1917 - 1918* (Madison: University of Wisconsin Press, 1957), pp. 5 ff.

18. Carl Wittke, *German-Americans and the World War With Special Emphasis on Ohio's German-language Press* (Columbus, Ohio: State Archaeological and Historical Society, 1936), pp. 123, 140.

19. Joan M. Jensen, *The Price of Vigilance* (Chicago: Rand McNally, 1968), p. 30.

20. Joel Andrew Watne, "Public Opinion Toward Non-Conformists and Aliens During 1917, As Shown by the *Fargo Forum*," *North Dakota History* 34 (1967), 15, and Luebke, *Bonds of Loyalty*, pp. 3 ff.

21. Harry Rider, "Americanization," *American Political Science Review* 14 (February, 1920), 110. See also Merle Curti, *The Roots of American Loyalty* (New York: Columbia University Press, 1946) and Peterson and Fite, chapters 10, "A Lesson for the Teachers" and 11, "Disciplining the Clergy."

22. Luebke, *Bonds of Loyalty*, p. 252.

23. Franklin F. Holbrook and Livia Appel, *Minnesota in the War With Germany* (St. Paul: Minnesota Historical Society, 1928), p. 15.

24. Neil M. Johnson, "The Patriotism and Anti-Prussianism of the Lutheran Church — Missouri Synod, 1914 - 1918," *Concordia Historical Institute Quarterly* 39 (October, 1966), 101.

25. Wittke, *German-Americans . . .* , p. 151.

26. Ibid., p. 154. See also George Creel, "Beware the Superpatriots," *American Mercury* 51 (Sept., 1940), 33 - 41.

27. Neil M. Johnson, "Patriotism . . . ," p. 102.

28. Quoted in Cunz, *The Maryland Germans*, p. 395.

29. James J. Hudson, *Hostile Skies: A Combat History of the American Air Service in World War I* (Syracuse, N. Y.: Syracuse University Press, 1968), pp. 183 - 84, 279 - 80.

30. More than half of all conscientious objectors in World War I were German Mennonites. See J. S. Hartzler, *Mennonites in the World War:*

Nonresistance under Test, 2nd ed. (Scottsdale, Pa.: Mennonite Publishing House, 1922), Arlyn John Parish, *Kansas Mennonites during World War I* (Fort Hays, Kansas, History Series, May, 1968), and Luebke, *Bonds of Loyalty*, pp. 258 - 59.

31. Peters, *All Things Common*, pp. 43 - 50 and Allen Teichroew, "World War I and the Mennonite Migration to Canada to Avoid the Draft," *Mennonite Quarterly Review* 45 (July, 1971), 219 - 49.

32. *New Ulm Review* and *Brown County Journal*, April through August, 1917. See also Holbrook and Appel, *Minnesota in the War . . .* , II, 40 ff.

33. Johnson, "Patriotism and Anti-Prussianism of the Luthern Church," pp. 112 - 13. See also La Vern J. Rippley, "Xenophobia and the Russian-German Experience," *American Historical Society of Germans from Russia* Workpaper 18 (Sept., 1975), 6 - 11.

34. Clifford L. Nelson, *German-American Political Behavior in Nebraska and Wisconsin, 1916 - 1920* (Lincoln: University of Nebraska Publications 217, 1972), pp. 49 - 51.

35. Robert P. Wilkins, "The Nonpartisal League and Upper Midwest Isolation," *Agricultural History* 39 (April, 1965), 102 - 9.

36. Luebke, "The German-American Alliance in Nebraska," p. 184.

37. Quoted in Child, *The German-Americans in Politics*, p. 171.

38. Walter V. Woehlke, "The German-American: Confessions of a Hyphenate," *Century Magazine*, April, 1917, p. 933.

39. Gerd Korman, *Industrialization, Immigrants and Americanizers*, pp. 187 and 202.

40. Luebke, *Bonds of Loyalty*, p. 321 and Faust, II, Appendix, pp. 668 ff.

41. Roderick Nash, "Victor L. Berger: Making Marx Respectable," and Edward J. Muzik, "Viktor L. Berger: Congress and the Red Scare," *Wisconsin Magazine of History* 47 (Summer, 1964), 301 - 8 and 309 - 18.

42. James K. Mercer, *Ohio Legislative History*, III (Columbus, 1920), 71 - 74. See also John B. Duff, "German-Americans and the Peace, 1918 - 1920," *American-Jewish Historical Quarterly* 59 (1970), 438, John M. Allswang, *A House for all Peoples: Ethnic Politics in Chicago 1890 - 1936* (Lexington: University of Kentucky Press, 1971), pp. 37 ff. and Luebke, *Bonds of Loyalty*, p. 326.

43. Charles E. Strickland, "American Aid to Germany, 1919 - 1921," *Wisconsin Magazine of History* 45 (Summer, 1962), 257.

44. Richard Sallet, *Russian-German Settlements*, p. 104.

45. La Vern J. Rippley, "Gift Cows For Germany," *North Dakota History* 40 (Summer, 1973), 4 - 16.

46. Strickland, "American Aid to Germany," p. 266.

Chapter Fifteen

1. Ralph H. Smuckler, "The Region of Isolationism," *American Political Science Review* 17 (June, 1953), 386 - 401.

2. See Samuel Lubell, "Who Votes Isolationist and Why," *Harper's* 202 (April, 1951), 29 - 36, and Samuel Lubell, *The Future of American Politics*, 3rd edition (New York: Harper & Row, 1965), pp. 134 ff.

3. *Reports of the Immigration Commission*, presented by Senator William P. Dillingham, Chairman (Washington, D.C., Government Printing Office, 1911).

4. See Oscar Handlin, *A Pictorial History of Immigration* (New York: Crown, 1972), p. 284, and Max L. Franzen, "The Door of Immigration," *American-German Review* 14 (December, 1947), 12 - 14.

5. For pronouncements by Hitler and Third Reich officials with respect to German peoples living outside the borders of Germany, see *The German Reich and Americans of German Origin* (New York: Oxford University Press, 1938). The book contains facsimile German statements and English translations.

6. See Hawgood, *The Tragedy . . .*, p. 302.

7. Four books deal with the Nazi penetration of the United States, Sander A. Diamond, *The Nazi Movement in the United States 1924 - 1941* (Ithaca: Cornell University Press, 1974), Arthur L. Smith, Jr., *The Deutschtum of Nazi Germany and the United States* (The Hague: Martinus Nijhoff, 1965), Alton Frye, *Nazi Germany and the American Hemisphere 1933 - 1941* (New Haven: Yale University Press, 1967), and Klaus Kipphan, *Deutsche Propaganda in den Vereinigten Staaten 1933 - 1941* (Heidelberg: Universitätsverlag, 1971). See Frye, pp. 32 - 33.

8. Frye, p. 43. See also Hawgood, p. 304, and Handlin, *A Pictorial History*, p. 289.

9. Smith, *Das Deutschtum*, p. 4.

10. *Trial of the Major War Criminals Before the International Military Tribunal* (Nuremberg, Germany: The United States Government, 1948), X, 49. See Diamond, pp. 48 ff.

11. Ralph F. Bischoff, *Nazi Conquest Through German Culture* (Cambridge: Harvard University Press, 1942), p. 107.

12. Smith, *Das Deutschtum*, pp. 6 - 9 and Frye, pp. 42 ff.

13. See Oetje John Rogge, *The Official German Report: Nazi Penetration 1924 - 1942* (New York: Thomas Yoseloff, 1961), p. 98, and pp. 130 - 72. Rogge served as the chief prosecutor of Viereck and others in the sedition case brought against him and the German American Bund in January, 1943.

14. John W. Osborne, "Highlights of British and German Propaganda in the United States 1939 - 1941," *Journal of the Rutgers University Library* 24 (1960), 20. See also Kipphan, pp. 146 - 48.

15. Quoted in Neil M. Johnson, *George Sylvester Viereck: German-American Propagandist* (Chicago: University of Illinois Press, 1972), p. 234. See also Phyllis Keller, "George Sylvester Viereck: The Psychology of a German-American Militant," *Journal of Interdisciplinary History* 2 (1971), 59 - 108, esp. 102 ff.

16. Kipphan, pp. 78 ff. and Diamond, pp. 179 ff.

17. William B. Seabrook, *These Foreigners* (New York: Harcourt, Brace, 1938), pp. 224 ff.

18. See Joseph F. Dinneen, "An American Führer Organizes an Army," *American Magazine* 124 (August 1937), 14 ff.

19. O'Connor, p. 442.

20. Frye, pp. 82 and 88. See also Leland V. Bell, "The Failure of Nazism in America: The German American Bund, 1936 - 1941," *Political Science Quarterly* 85 (December, 1970), 585 - 99. See also Diamond, pp. 251 ff., esp., p. 266.

21. See, for example, William Seabrook, "Try to Make Nazis Out of Us!" *Current History* 50 (June, 1939), 22 - 23, and Harold Lavine, *Fifth-Column in America* (New York: Doubleday, Doran and Co., 1940), pp. 77 - 78.

22. *Newsweek*, August 22, 1938, p. 12. See also Martin Dies, "The Real Issue is Plain," *Vital Speeches* 4 (Sept. 15, 1938), 731 - 34 and Martin Dies, *The Trojan Horse in America* (New York: Dodd, Mead and Co., 1940).

23. Frye, p. 86, Kipphan, p. 82, Smith, p. 104, and Rogge, pp. 113 ff.

24. Rogge, p. 124.

25. *New York Times*, Feb. 9, 18, 20, 21, 1939; and *Newsweek*, March 6, 1939, pp. 14 - 15.

26. Rogge, 128. *New York Times*, August 17, 19, 21, 22, 23, 1939.

27. *New York Times*, July 1, 1943.

28. Joachim Remak, " 'Friends of the New Germany': The Bund and German-American Relations," *Journal of Modern History* 29 (1957), 38 - 41.

29. Kipphan, p. 98.

30. Alfred Hart, "Manhattan Heil," *American Magazine* 132 (July, 1941), 39 ff.

31. *Fortune*, September, 1942, pp. 72 ff.

32. See "The War of Nerves: U. S. Front," concerning Nazi agents in the United States in *Fortune*, October, 1940, pp. 47 ff. and continued in *Fortune*, November, 1940, pp. 85 ff. See also Lavine, *Fifth-Column*.

33. Louis De Jong, *The German Fifth-Column in the Second World War* (Chicago: University of Chicago Press, 1956), p. 216.

34. See Arthur L. Smith, Jr., *The Deutschtum*, p. 113, footnote 61.

35. Arthur L. Smith, Jr., "The Kameradschaft USA," *Journal of Modern History* 34 (1962), 402.

36. Arthur Smith, *The Deutschtum*, p. 117.

37. Arthur Smith, "The Kameradschaft," 406.

38. Arthur Smith, *The Deutschtum*, p. 151.

39. Frye, p. 56. See also Diamond, pp. 169 - 71.

40. Alfred McClung Lee, "Subversive Individuals of Minority Status," *The Annals of the American Academy of Political and Social Science* 223 (September, 1942), 170.

41. See "Wisconsin Federation of German-Americans Fight Against Pro-Nazi Groups in Milwaukee," *New York Times*, April 23, 1939, sect. IV, p. 7.

42. Virginia Brainard Kunz, *The Germans in America* (Minneapolis: Lerner, 1966), pp. 60 ff.

43. See Ingeborg Kayko, "On Being a German-American," *Atlantic Monthly* 171 (May, 1943), 97 - 98.

44. Samuel Lubell, *The Future of American Politics*, p. 133.

45. Howard W. Allen, "Studies of Political Loyalties of Two Nationality Groups," *Journal of the Illinois State Historical Society* 57 (1964), 146.

46. Samuel Lubell, "Who Really Elected Truman?" *The Saturday Evening Post*, January 22, 1949, pp. 15 ff.

47. La Vern J. Rippley, "Siege Without Shelling," *The Cresset* (Valparaiso, Indiana) 32 (May, 1969), 12.

Chapter Sixteen

1. Louis L. Gerson, *The Hyphenate*, p. 187.

2. Julius Epstein, *Operation Keelhaul* (Old Greenwich, Conn.: Devin-Adair Co., 1973).

3. See tables in Gerson, pp. 263 ff.

4. Gerard H. Wilk, "Yorkville, Twenty Years After. The Brownshirts Are Gone — and Much Else," *Commentary* 17 (January, 1954), 41. See also Hilde Walter, "Die Deutschamerikaner, Betrachtungen über das Schicksal einer Volksgruppe," *Der Monat* 4 (August, 1952), 478 - 82.

5. U. S. Census of Population: 1960, vol. I, *Characteristics of the Population*, p. 203 and U. S. Census of the Population: 1970, vol. I, Characteristics of the Population, p. 382.

6. Alfred Vagts, *Deutsch-Amerikanische Rückwanderung* (Heidelberg: Carl Winter, 1960), pp. 14 ff. and Betty Boyd Caroli, *Italian Repatriation From the United States 1900 - 1914* (New York: Center for Migration Studies, 1974).

7. Alfred Vagts, "The Ebb-Tide of Immigration. Germans Returning From America," *American-German Review* 21 (October - November, 1954), 30 - 33. See also Walter F. Wilcox, ed., *International Migrations*, vols. I & II (New York: Gordon and Breach, 1969).

8. Vagts, "The Ebb-Tide," p. 32.

9. See the appendix in Alberta Eiseman, *From Many Lands* (New York: Atheneum, 1970).

10. Information available from DANK, 4740 North Western Avenue, Chicago, Illinois, 60625.

Selected Bibliography

This bibliography is limited to entries the author feels are absolutely essential for a rudimentary knowledge of the Germans in America. Many more books and articles were used in preparation of the book as can be seen from a perusal of the notes to each chapter.

ARNDT, KARL J. R. *George Rapp's Harmony Society 1785 - 1847.* Philadelphia: Univ. of Pennsylvania Press, 1965.

ARNDT, KARL J. R. and OLSON, MAY E., *German-American Newspapers and Periodicals 1732 - 1955.* Heidelberg: Quelle & Meyer, 1961.

ARNDT, KARL J. R. and OLSON, MAY E., *The German Language Press of the Americas 1732 - 1968.* Pullach: Verlag Dokumentation, 1973.

BAEPLER, WALTER A. *A Century of Grace: A History of the Missouri Synod 1847 - 1947.* St. Louis: Concordia Publishing House, 1947.

BARRY, COLMAN. *The Catholic Church and the German Americans.* Milwaukee: Bruce, 1953.

BILLIGMEIER, ROBERT HENRY. *Americans From Germany: A Study in Cultural Diversity.* Belmont, Calif.: Wadsworth Publishing, 1974.

BITTINGER, LUCY F. *The Germans in Colonial Times.* New York: Russell & Russell, 1901, reissued 1968.

BOYERS, ROBERT, ed. *The Legacy of the German Refugee Intellectuals.* New York: Schocken, 1972.

BRUNCKEN, ERNEST. "German Political Refugees in the United States During the Period from 1815 - 1860." *Deutsch-Amerikanische Geschichtsblätter* 3 (1903), 33 - 59.

———. "The Political Activity of Wisconsin Germans, 1854 - 60." *Wisconsin State Historical Society Proceedings* 69 (1901), 190 - 211.

CARMAN, J. NEALE. *Foreign-Language Units of Kansas.* 1, Historical Atlas and Statistics. Lawrence: Univ. of Kansas Press, 1962.

CAZDEN, ROBERT E. *German Exile Literature in America 1933 - 1950: A History of the Free German Press and Book Trade.* Chicago: American Library Association, 1970.

CHILD, CLIFTON J. *The German-Americans in Politics 1914 - 1917.* Madison: University of Wisconsin Press, 1939.

259

CONDOYANNIS, GEORGE E. "German American Prose Fiction, From 1850 - 1914." Unpubl. Ph. D. diss. Columbia University, 1953.

CRONAU, RUDOLF. *Drei Jahrhunderte deutschen Lebens in Amerika.* Berlin: Dietrich Reimer, 1909.

CUNZ, DIETER. *The Maryland Germans.* Princeton: Princeton Univ. Press, 1948.

DIAMOND, SANDER A. *The Nazi Movement in the United States 1924 - 1941.* Ithaca: Cornell University Press, 1974.

EVEREST, KATE ASAPHINE. "How Wisconsin Came By its Large German Element." *Collections of the State Historical Society of Wisconsin* 12 (1892), 302 - 11.

FAUST, ALBERT B. *The German Element in the United States.* 2 vol. New York: Steuben Society, 1927.

FERMI, LAURA. *Illustrious Immigrants: The Intellectual Migration from Europe 1930 - 1941.* Chicago: Univ. of Chicago Press, 1968.

FISHMAN, JOSHUA A., ed. *Language Loyalty in the United States.* The Hague: Mouton, 1966.

FLEMING, DONALD and BERNARD BAILYN, eds. *The Intellectual Migration, Europe and America, 1930 - 1960.* Cambridge: Harvard Univ. Press, 1969.

FRYE, ALTON. *Nazi Germany and the American Hemisphere 1933 - 1941.* New Haven: Yale Univ. Press, 1967.

GERSON, LOUIS L. *The Hyphenate in Recent American Politics and Diplomacy.* Lawrence: Univ. of Kansas, 1964.

GILBERT, GLENN G., ed. *The German Language in America, A Symposium.* Austin: Univ. of Texas, 1971.

GLEASON, PHILIP. *The Conservative Reformers: German-American Catholics and the Social Order.* Notre Dame: Univ. of Notre Dame Press, 1968.

HANNEMANN, MAX. *Das Deutschtum in den Vereinigten Staaten, Seine Verbreitung und Entwicklung seit der Mitte des 19. Jahrhunderts* in *Petermanns Mitteilungen.* Gotha: Justus Perthus, 1936.

HANSEN, MARCUS LEE. *The Immigrant in American History.* Cambridge: Harvard Univ. Press, 1940.

HANSEN, MARCUS L. "The Revolution of 1848 and German Emigration." *Journal of Economic and Business History,* 2 (Aug. 1930), 630 - 658.

HAWGOOD, JOHN A. *The Tragedy of German-America.* New York: Arno Press, 1970.

HEINRICI, MAX., ed. *Das Buch der Deutschen in Amerika.* Philadelphia: National German-American Alliance, 1909.

HOSTETLER, JOHN A. *Hutterite Society.* Baltimore: The Johns Hopkins Univ. Press, 1974.

IVERSON, NOEL. *Germania, U. S. A. Social Change in New Ulm, Minnesota.* Minneapolis: University of Minnesota Press, 1966.

JOHNSON, HILDEGARD BINDER. "The Location of German Immigrants in the Middle West." *Annals of American Geographers* 41 (1951), 1 - 41.

———. "Intermarriages Between German Pioneers and Other Nationalities in Minnesota in 1860 and 1870." *The American Journal of Sociology* 51 (Jan., 1946), 299 - 304.

————. "German Forty-eighters in Davenport." *Iowa Journal of History and Politics* 44 (Jan., 1946), 3 - 60.

JOHNSON, NEIL M. *George Sylvester Viereck: German-American Propagandist.* Chicago, Univ. of Illinois Press, 1972.

JORDAN, TERRY G. *German Seed in Texas Soil: Immigrant Farmers in Nineteenth-Century Texas.* Austin: Univ. of Texas Press, 1966.

KAPP, FRIEDRICH. *Aus und Über Amerika: Thatsachen und Erlebnisse,* vol. I & II. Berlin: Julius Springer, 1876.

KAUFMANN, WILHELM. *Die Deutschen im amerikanischen Bürgerkriege.* Munich: R. Oldenbourg, 1911.

KENT, DONALD P. *The Refugee Intellectual: The Americanization of the Immigrants of 1933 - 1941.* New York: Columbia Univ. Press, 1953.

KIPPHAN, KLAUS. *Deutsche Propaganda in den Vereinigten Staaten 1933 - 1941.* Heidelberg: Universitätsverlag, 1971.

KLOSS, HEINZ, *Atlas of German-American Settlements.* Marburg: N. G. Elwert, 1974.

————. "Die deutschamerikanische Schule." *Jahrbuch für Amerikastudien* 7 (1962), 141 - 75.

————. "Deutsch-amerikanisches Schrifttum in USA." *Dichtung und Volkstum* 35 (1934), 399 - 403.

————. "Über die mittelbare kartographische Erfassung der jüngeren Volksinseln in der Vereinigten Staaten," *Deutsches Archiv für Landes-und Volksforschung* 3 (July, 1969), 453 - 74.

————. *Um die Einigung des Deutschamerikanertums.* Berlin: Volk und Reich Verlag, 1937.

LAING, FRANCIS S., O. M. Cap. "German-Russian Settlements in Ellis County, Kansas." *Kansas Historical Collections* 11 (1909 - 1910), 489 - 528.

LEVI, KATE EVEREST. "Geographical Origin of German Immigration to Wisconsin." *Collections of the State Historical Society of Wisconsin* 14 (1898), 341 - 93.

LUEBKE, FREDERICK C., ed. *Ethnic Voters and the Election of Lincoln.* Lincoln: Univ. of Nebraska Press, 1971.

LUEBKE, FREDERICK C. *Bonds of Loyalty: German Americans and World War I.* DeKalb: Univ. of Northern Illinois, 1974.

————. "The German-American Alliance in Nebraska 1910 - 1917." *Nebraska History* 49 (1968), 165 - 85.

————. "German Immigrants and Churches in Nebraska, 1889 - 1915." *Mid-America: An Historical Review* 50 (1968), 116 - 30.

————. "The Immigrant Condition as a Factor Contributing to the Conservatism of the Lutheran Church — Missouri Synod." *Concordia Historical Institute Quarterly* 38 (1968), 19 - 28.

————. *Immigrants and Politics: The Germans of Nebraska, 1880 - 1900.* Lincoln: Univ. of Nebraska Press, 1969.

MANLEY, ROBERT N. "Language, Loyalty and Liberty: The Nebraska State

Council of Defense and the Lutheran Churches, 1917 - 1918." *Concordia Historical Institute Quarterly* 37 (1964), 1 - 16.

MARSCHALCK, PETER. *Deutsche Überseewanderung im 19. Jahrhundert: Ein Beitrag zur soziologischen Theorie der Bevölkerung, Industrielle Welt.* Stuttgart: Klett, 1973.

MAURER, HEINRICH H. "The Earlier German Nationalism in America." *American Journal of Sociology* 22 (1917), 519 - 43.

MENG, JOHN. "Cahenslyism: the First Stage, 1883 - 1891." *Catholic Historical Review* 31 (1946), 389 - 413.

————. "Cahenslyism: the Second Chapter 1891 - 1910." *Catholic Historical Review* 32 (1946), 302 - 40.

O'CONNOR, RICHARD. *The German-Americans.* New York: Little, Brown and Co., 1968.

PEKARI, MATTHEW ANTHONY, REV. "The German Catholics in the United States of America." *Records of the American Catholic Historical Society* 36 (Dec. 1925), pp. 305 - 58.

PETERS, VICTOR. *All Things Common: The Hutterian Way of Life.* Minneapolis: Univ. of Minnesota Press, 1965.

PETERSEN, ALBERT J., JR. "German-Russian Catholic Colonization in Western Kansas: A Settlement Geography." Unpubl. Ph. D. Diss. Louisiana State University and Agricultural-Mechanical College, 1970.

————. "The German-Russian Settlement Pattern in Ellis County, Kansas," *Rocky Mountain Social Science Journal* 5 (1968), 52 - 62.

RIPPLEY, LAVERN J. "The Chillicothe Germans." *Ohio History* 75 (1966), 212 - 25.

————. "The Columbus Germans." *A Journal of German-American History, SHGM Report* 33 (1968), 1 - 45.

————. "The Dakota Frei Presse." *Heritage Review* 7 (1973), 7 - 17.

————. "German Theater in Columbus, Ohio." *German-American Studies* 1 (1970), 78 - 101.

————. "Gifts Cows for Germany." *North Dakota History* 40 (Summer, 1973), 4 - 16.

————. "Notes About the German Press in Minnesota River Valley." *Society for the History of Germans in Maryland*, Report 35 (1972), pp. 37 - 45.

————. *Of German Ways*, Minneapolis: Dillon, 1970.

RODGERS, JACK W. "The Foreign Language Issue in Nebraska, 1918 - 1923." *Nebraska History* 39 (March 1958), 1 - 22.

ROTHAN, EMMET. *The German Catholic Immigrant in the United States, 1830 - 1860.* Washington, D.C.: Catholic Univ. Press, 1946.

RUPPENTHAL, JACOB C. "The German Element in Central Kansas." *Kansas Historical Collections* 13, (1913 - 1914), 513 - 34.

SALLET, RICHARD. *The Russian-German Settlements in the United States.* Trans. La Vern J. Rippley and Armand Bauer. Fargo: Institute for Regional Studies, 1974.

SAUL, NORMAN E. "The Migration of the Russian-Germans to Kansas." *Kansas Historical Quarterly* 40 (1974), 38 - 62.

SCHAFER, JOSEPH. "The Yankee and the Teuton in Wisconsin." *The Wisconsin Magazine of History* 6 (Dec., 1922), 125 - 145.

SCHMIDT, CARL. "Kansas Mennonite Settlements, 1877." Trans. Connelius Krahn *Mennonite Life*, 25 (April, 1970), pp. 51 - 58.

SCHMIDT, CARL B. "Reminiscences of Foreign Immigration Work for Kansas." *Transactions and Collections of the Kansas State Historical Society* 9 (1905 - 1906), pp. 485 - 97.

SCHNEIDER, CARL. E. *The German Church on the American Frontier*. St. Louis: Eden Publishing House, 1939.

SMITH, ARTHUR L., JR. *The Deutschtum of Nazi Germany and the United States*. The Hague: Martinus Nijhoff, 1965.

———. "The Kameradschaft USA." *Journal of Modern History* 34 (Dec., 1962), 398 - 408.

SMITH, C. HENRY. *The Coming of the Russian Mennonites*. Berne, Ind.: Mennonite Book Concern, 1927.

TOLZMANN, DON HEINRICH. *German Americana: A Bibliography*. Metuchen, N.J.: Scarecrow Press, 1975.

TOWNSEND, ANDREW J. "The Germans of Chicago." *Deutsch-Amerikakanische Geschichtsblätter* 32 (1932), 1 - 153.

VAGTS, ALFRED. *Deutsch-Amerikanische Rückwanderung*. Heidelberg: Carl Winter, 1960.

VON PHILOPPOVICH, EUGEN, ed. *Auswanderung und Auswanderungspolitik*. Leipzig: Duncker & Humblot, 1892.

WALKER, MACK. *Germany and the Emigration 1816 - 1885*. Cambridge: Harvard Univ. Press, 1964.

WILCOX, WALTER F., ed. *International Migrations*. 2 vol. New York: Gordon and Breach, 1969.

WINGLER, HANS. M. *The Bauhaus: Weimar, Dessau, Berlin, Chicago*. Trans. Wolfgang Jabs and Basil Gilbert. Cambridge: M.I.T. Press, 1969.

WITTKE, CARL. "The America Theme in European Literature." *Mississippi Valley Historical Review* 28 (1941), 3 - 26.

———. *German-Americans and the World War With Special Emphasis on Ohio's German-Language Press*. Columbus: Ohio State Archaeological and Historical Society, 1936.

———. *The German-Language Press in America*. Lexington: University of Kentucky Press, 1957.

———. *Refugees of Revolution: The German Forty-Eighters in America*. Philadelphia: Univ. of Pennsylvania Press, 1952.

———. *We Who Built America: The Saga of the Immigrant*. Cleveland: Case Western Reserve Univ. Press, 1964.

WOOD, RALPH, ed. *The Pennsylvania Germans*. Princeton: Princeton Univ. Press, 1942.

WUST, KLAUS. *The Virginia Germans*. Charlottesville: University of Virginia Press, 1969.

ZUCKER, A. E., ed. *The Forty-eighters: Political Refugees of the German Revolution of 1848*. New York: Columbia Univ. Press, 1950.

Index

265

Thi

W
C

AU